PROFESSIONAL REPORT WRITING

C

For
Justin

PROFESSIONAL REPORT WRITING

SIMON MORT

Gower

First published in hardback 1992 by Gower Publishing. Reprinted 1997.

Paperback edition published 1995 by
Gower Publishing
Gower House
Croft Road
Aldershot
Hants GU11 3HR
England

Gower
Old Post Road
Brookfield
Vermont 05036
USA

Reprinted 1997

British Library Cataloguing in Publication Data
Mort, Simon
  Professional report writing.
  1. Reports. Composition (Arts)
  I. Title
  808.066651

ISBN 0–566–02712–7 (Hbk)
      0–566–07669–1 (Pbk)

Typeset in 10pt Cheltenham by Poole Typesetting (Wessex) Ltd, Bournemouth
Printed and bound in Great Britain by
Biddles Ltd, Guildford and King's Lynn

Contents

Preface

The favourable reception of *How to Write a Successful Report* in 1983 focused on the breadth of examples and the fact that these examples included numerous recent reports. Encouraged to keep the book updated, I have extensively revised the text and produced many new examples. These not only bring the illustrations into line with the 1990s but demonstrate the points better.

I have retained a number of examples which, although they originated in reports of the early 1980s or the 1970s, still seem to provide the best examples of the points being made. They add a historical dimension to the book which I believe is valuable.

The book is equal in length to its predecessor, but the emphasis has been changed to reflect areas which have been of particular interest to people attending my company's courses. Much of the historical information has been reduced and some of the specialized sections have been eliminated or incorporated into other chapters.

Special attention has been given to structure and the nebulous question of style. Summaries have been given increased treatment. Too often they are the subject of misunderstanding and are produced as a matter of routine – frequently at disproportionate length – and serving no useful purpose. Some comments on desktop publishing appear at various points in the book. Too often, however, the equipment is allowed to dictate not just the form but also the content of the report.

As before, thanks are due to many people, and in particular to the following for permission to reproduce various items from their reports:

John Leach (American Airlines)
John Howell (American Underwriters International)
Chris Gebbie (Argos Distributors Limited)
S. A. Anfield (Bank of America)
R. H. Sellers (British Vita plc)
Elizabeth Bryant (Centre for British Teachers Ltd)
John Norton, Torres Carlos, Pat de Jager, Raymond Langmead, Cephas Nyambauro and Peter Pritchard (Citibank NA)

Mark Alder (Clarity)
Maurice Tull (Coca-Cola Southern Bottlers Limited)
Brian Maclean (The Colt Car Company)
Dr David Yardley (Commission for Local Administration in England)
Stephen Connell (Communication Studies and Planning Ltd in Respect of a
    report produced in conjunction with the Equal Opportunities Commission)
A. R. Young and S. J. Dickenson (Currys Ltd)
C. Tomkins (Esso Petroleum Company Ltd)
David Gambles and John Joyce (General Council of British Shipping)
Peter Luscombe (Hacker Young)
David Pipe (The Jockey Club)
John Hawkins (Johnson Matthey Chemicals Ltd)
D. F. Drakes (National Nuclear Corporation Ltd)
N. Crawford (North British Properties plc)
Michael Moynihan (Organization for Economic Co-operation and Development)
John Hope (Oxford City Council)
Paul Masters and Mike Phillips (Price Waterhouse)
Phil Gibson for a private example
Dennis Roper (The Prudential Assurance Company Ltd)
Mike Bishop (QANTAS Airways Limited)
Graham Rudge (Rank Xerox)
Philippe Schiever (Schering Corporation USA; Sentipharm AG)
Felicity Beech (Shannon Free Airport Development Company Ltd)
Martin Harris (Sidleys)
K. Cornish (The Sports Council)
Norman Le Cheminant (States of Guernsey)
Gordon Fawcett and Janine Le Pivert (States of Jersey)
F. D. Claridge (Trustee Savings Bank Central Executive)
K. Leigh (Trustee Savings Bank Group Computer Services Ltd)
Philip Hare (UAC Ltd)
Ron Foley (Warner-Lambert)
Trevor Freeguard (Watson Services Ltd)

Peter Bassett, Vice Chairman of the Queen's English Society, carried on a helpful and – since our views are widely divergent – generously amicable correspondence. My thanks go to him for his comments and permission to reproduce parts of our exchanges.

I am very grateful to Margaret Ferré of the Publications Division of Her Majesty's Stationery Office, for her helpful and energetic pursuit of requests for reproduction of various illustrations from Command papers, and from the County Nat West Investigation report. These are all reproduced by kind permission of the Controller of HMSO.

My thanks are due to Oxford University Press for their permission to reproduce Figure 20.

Desmond Fennell, Chairman of the King's Cross inquiry, was generous with his time and wisdom. His report is possibly pre-eminent amongst the investigation reports of the 1980s in its readability, logic, fluency and presentation. It may serve as a model for authors of all inquiries, whatever the length or subject matter.

I am also indebted to Mr Fennell for pointing out how the report of the inquiry into the Challenger disaster played a part in his own investigation. To a great extent, he modelled his own work on it and I too make numerous references to it in these pages. It is a formidable achievement representing a sensitive and thorough coverage of a subject of great national and international concern within a very tight timeframe.

The first version of this book was much illuminated by the experience and good sense of Lord Bullock. His comments shone through many of the original chapters and, although *A Language for Life* and *Industrial Democracy* are 16 and 14 years old respectively, his observations seem still as valid as ever. I am delighted to repeat my acknowledgements for his advice.

Glen P. Haney, Director of the Office of Information Resources Management in the United States Department of Agriculture, generously provided me with copious literature used in the quality control of his department's written output.

Whilst many debts are owed to my editor, Malcolm Stern, I am particularly obliged to him for pointing out that my attitude to sexist writing was simplistic and my judgements sweeping. This debt also extends to Judith Byrne Whyte of the Equal Opportunities Commission who put me right in respect of my approach to this topic.

Since the publication of *How to Write a Successful Report*, one major dictionary has joined the Concise Oxford, Chambers Twentieth Century and Collins. I am grateful to Brian O'Kill, a prolific author and a wise and sensible lexicographer, for his guidance on the *Longmans Dictionary of the English Language*. Brian is not only a congenial companion but displays endless patience and good manners in dealing with those lay people who feel that they can invade the technical labyrinth of his professional field with impertinence.

While new words immediately attract interest due to their novelty, more subtle changes have also taken place during the 1980s; for example in punctuation, idioms and layout. These are covered in this edition. In the main, they represent greater tolerance of what would have been widely regarded as unacceptable solecisims at the beginning of the decade. In layout there has been a rapidly increasing emphasis on presentation. Desktop publishing equipment has made this both possible and convenient. The facilities have been matched by preference for such things as bullet-pointed sub-paragraphs, variety – sometimes excessive – of heading styles and fonts, as well as occasionally over-elaborate visual illustrations.

Research into the range of desktop publishing equipment was carried out by Janice Coventry, my company's Administration Manager (as if she had not got enough to do). Janice has also added the typing of several revisions of the book to her seemingly Herculean duties running the whole administration of my company. More important – she has done so with a good grace. For this patience and understanding I am extremely grateful.

Finally, Victoria has crowned 25 years of marriage with allowing me to complete the book in peace and isolation without a single word of complaint. There were plenty of expressions of surprise when I returned from numerous expeditions through three continents, each time with an uncompleted typescript; but never anything stronger.

Simon Mort

List of figures

1 Types and purposes of reports

Written communication calls for a more deliberate, economical approach than the spoken form. A report is not supported by the theatre of a meeting or an oral briefing. Its message may be read by the addressees at a time of their own choosing. They may be tired; they may be in a hurry; they may be impatient or irascible. The writer has no further control over how the readers assimilate this information: there can be no correction if they misinterpret a sentence or a diagram; they cannot ask questions at the end; there can be no dialogue to check that the message has sunk in or to eliminate ambiguity and no visual aids can be utilized if the original explanation is inadequate.

Therefore it is essential at the outset, to define the characteristics that distinguish written communication, such as report writing, from other forms of communication.

TYPES OF COMMUNICATION

Communication can be divided into three basic categories:

1. Written.
2. Oral.
3. Non-verbal. (*Verbal* is here used in the first and original sense: 'of or concerned with words', as opposed to the newer secondary sense 'oral, not written').

DIFFERENCES BETWEEN WRITTEN COMMUNICATION AND THE OTHER FORMS

Compared with the other two forms, written communication:

1. Is more concise.
2. Should be more discreet.
3. Is often more accurate.

4. Is free from ambiguity.
5. Suffers from the disadvantage that response and feedback are less immediate.

Some languages have developed two separate forms: one oral and one written. This has not yet happened in English and probably enables the written word to be more natural and less stilted.

Conciseness

Written communications are usually more concise, but often require more concentration than spoken briefings. The writers must therefore be economical in their use of words.

Conversely, in oral communication, the recipient's attention may wander. There may be distractions. Certain points may be missed. The speaker is thus justified in stating complex concepts at length and repeating the most important points several times in a way that would be unacceptable in writing.

Furthermore because the written form is permanent, it can afford to be more concise. The reader can check detail which he has forgotten.

Accuracy

The permanence of the written form means that it must be more accurate.

Generalized or approximate figures which may be acceptable in meetings (even quite formal ones) are frequently too vague for recording in the written form. Readers naturally expect greater care to be taken in the preparation of a permanent written document.

Discretion

Caution must be exercised in the preparation of a written report as the author has no control over where the paper goes or who reads it. Jokes and flippant comments are more dangerous in writing than they are in speech, when audience reaction can be controlled to a degree. Additionally the law of defamation applies more severely to the written form.

Freedom from ambiguity

The physical detachment of the writer from the reader means that there is no control over how the information is interpreted. Therefore, double-meanings and misunderstandings which may be intercepted and avoided face-to-face, must be anticipated in writing.

With documents involving a high cost of failure, friends and colleagues may be invited to look over drafts and point out potential pitfalls. After about a fortnight the document should be foolproof. However, friends and colleagues do not always have the patience, the inclination or the time to dedicate to this kind of help. Coming back to a document after an hour or so, after lunch or – ideally – the next day, will frequently reveal horrifying misjudgements in expression which were missed at the first reading.

Use of tools and raw materials

Formal sentence structure is frequently disregarded in speech. Yet, in writing, every sentence may be expected to have a finite verb and a subject and to be of reasonable length. Punctuation scarcely exists in speech and, where it does, takes the form of pauses in delivery: in writing, greater precision is demanded, and is available through the range of marks in the canon of punctuation. In speech, frivolous expressions can be used which would, even for the same audience, be unsuitable in writing.

TONE SUGGESTED BY PURPOSE

It is of course the purpose of a report that will suggest the appropriate tone.

A report may be an opinion, such as an analysis of an accident, recommending ways to avoid recurrence. It may be a suggestion, such as an unsolicited paper recommending organizational changes, or a Government Green Paper. It may be fact, e.g. a banker's analysis of a company's robustness. Or it might equally take the form of an explanation: a sales manager accounting for the unhappy performance of his sales force.

A report may make recommendations or it may not. Sometimes the terms of reference will require recommendations to be made. A routine monthly or weekly report may contain recommendations, suggesting possible improvements. On other occasions, however, this is totally inappropriate, for example, if the report is just descriptive, such as an archaeologist's report.

The tone of the recommendations themselves will vary. They may be insistent for example, in a report on nuclear safety. They may be monitory, as in a surveyor's report. Or they may be advisory as in a broker's suggestion.

Very often just a few words will convey the change of tone. Here are some examples.

Descriptive

The tone of Amnesty International's annual report is brilliantly descriptive and neutral:

> Critics and opponents of the government were detained without trial, most of them for short periods, and some were reportedly tortured or ill-treated.[1]

Then in specific detail when describing political occurrences:

> On 25 February President Eris Arturo Delvalle was dismissed from office by the Panamanian National Assembly, hours after he had unsuccessfully tried to remove General Manuel Noriega as head of the Defence Forces. President Delvalle went into hiding in Panama and Education Minister Manual Solis Palma was appointed Acting President on 26 February.

and elsewhere:

> Among those imprisoned in 1988 for attempting to leave the country illegally were Marin Istoc and his cousin Mihai Bogonas, both from Resita. They and their families

had applied to the authorities for permission to emigrate in order to join relatives in Canada but were repeatedly refused. According to reports they were eventually told that they would be arrested if they continued to apply for permission. The two men and their families attempted to cross the border into Yugoslavia without permission on 18 April and were arrested. The women and children were allowed to go free but Marin Istoc and Mihai Bogonas were sentenced in May to 10 months' imprisonment and to pay a monthly fine for the duration of the sentence.[2]

This clinical tone is achieved by almost total absence of adverbs and adjectives other than those adding legal or temporal factual information such as 'unsuccessfully', 'illegally' and 'repeatedly'.

Instructive

With a report such as an internal audit report in which a definite recommendation is made, the tone will be instructive:

Personal Accident claim cheques must be recorded, when issued, and be used in numerical sequence . . . Cheque numbers should not be repeated within, at a minimum, a two-year period.

Monitory

Surveyors have to give warnings and advice. Some professional advisers make suggestions which are too equivocal in tone. Despite the 'probably', the vague 'considerable value' and euphemistic 'considerable modernisation', the following passage shows a tone and precision which will be helpful to the prospective purchaser:

The house quite obviously needs considerable modernisation most of it in the field of services and of course there are some necessary repairs needed to the main structure as described. Such improvements as central heating, insulation of the roof areas and proper redecoration could add considerable value to the property. Given these items are probably going to be carried out we can see no substantial reason for not proceeding in the purchase.

Selling

In the following paragraph, just a handful of adjectives, 'major', 'stronger', and 'competitive', express the appropriate hype of a selling report.

There was a major increase in home and export deliveries in 1987–88, reflecting stronger UK and world demand, although the market remained very competitive. Furthermore British Steel increased its market share in the UK and in the European Community as a whole despite the constraints imposed by the application of the Community's quota system.

Many non-commercial annual reports also have a discreet selling role and an appropriately bubbly tone. This is achieved by inserting the adverbs and adjectives which antiseptic reports such as the earlier Amnesty International document omitted.

In this seemingly simple paragraph from the C Division (North Devon) section of the Devon and Cornwall Constabulary, the writer's choice of words has added a spirited optimism to the passage. Note the impact of 'significant', 'well', 'considerable' and 'rapidly' on the short passage.

> North Devon is witnessing significant changes brought about by the progress of the new link road. Commercial and residential development is well underway and alteration to the traffic Systems, particularly in Barnstaple, has involved considerable police time. The area is rapidly changing, bringing opportunities for commerce and opportunities for crime.[3]

THE RANGE OF REPORTS

These principles of report writing apply to the whole gamut. The following fourteen examples of report types will serve to show the numerous ways in which reports may vary in length and tone.

This cannot be a comprehensive catalogue of report types. Neither is it intended to be one, but it does indicate the range of uses to which reports can be put.

The chapters examine in detail specific aspects of report writing. These examples give overviews of various reports as complete individual entities, describing their purpose, their problems and – in general terms – their layout.

Shift reports

Shift reports are almost non-reports or reports by exception. They are reports where only the most simple variables need to be recorded and the routine of the shift – using that term in the loosest sense – can be presumed to have been in order and to have passed uneventfully.

If such a simple form of reporting is not appropriate, but the areas of interest are likely to be the same every week, a proforma is likely to be a good idea. More room will be provided for comments on unusual occurrences. (The weekly changeover report of the supervisor of information services in a retailer illustrates this (Figure 1). The comment space is somewhat compressed: the original report is spread over five sheets.)

Manufacturers' inspection and test reports

Two further examples of the use of forms will illustrate the value of this type of report. A motor car manufacturer relies on a great deal of documentation to keep control of his product. To this end a dealer report form, which will be consistently and regularly used throughout the distribution network, will be helpful. The Colt Car Company's report is shown in Figure 2. This has the following advantages:

1. It ensures consistent and similar reporting throughout the network.
2. It ensures that all points are covered.
3. It keeps the replies simple and ensures that the report does not ramble into unnecessary detail.

Conversely, it is important that the space 'General Comments' should be large enough for any observation likely to be helpful. In the design of such forms there is sometimes an inclination for the size of this box to be dictated by the paper size.

WEEKLY CHANGEOVER REPORT

DATE:

TO:

FROM:

NOTE: (i) Any additional information should be put on a separate sheet of paper and attached to this report.

       (ii) Other areas to be consulted:
Incident reports
Network incident reports
Program amendment binders
Fails/faults log

HARDWARE (Central Site)
Problem areas and machinery currently 'down'

People/manufacturers who need contacting, and for what reason

Pre-arranged maintenance/repair

SYSTEMS, SOFTWARE, LIBRARY
Problem areas

People with whom to liaise

Amendments done

Note: Please consult 'INCIDENT REPORTS' binder and 'PROG AMENDS' binder

---

COMPUTER ROOM ADMINISTRATION AND QUALITY
Problem areas, i.e. ribbon usage, print quality, etc.

Problem areas currently being monitored

Unfinished reports, etc.

NETWORK CONTROL (including remote site hardware)
Problem areas

People/offices who need contacting, and for what reason

Areas requiring further attention

Note: Consult 'NETWORK INCIDENT LOG' binder

Figure 1   Weekly changeover report

COLT CAR COMPANY LTD.

DEALER REPORT FORM

No. 0333

To:

Copy ....

....

COLT

Dealer

Address

Proposed/Number

Telephone No. ....

	Area Sq Ft.	Appearance and Condition
Workshop		
Workshop Office		
Reception		
Bodyshop		
Paintshop		
Service Parking		

External Condition of Building ....

Proposed Extension ....

Number of Work Bays	Body Bays ....
Lifts .... Type	Spray Bays/Booth
Pits	Preparation Bays ....
Wash Bay	....
Lubrication Bay	....

Sub-Contractor Bodywork ....

....

Job Card System	Wheel Alignment ....
Warranty Record Book	Engine Diagnostic ....
Recovery Service	C.O. Meter ....
M.O.T. Facility	Battery Charger ....
Part Binning	Wheel Balance ....
Micro Fische Reader	Stock Control System ....

Service Manager	Skilled Mechanics	Training Courses ....
Workshop Foreman	Semi-Skilled Mechanics	Name .... Date .... Course
Parts Manager	Apprentices	....
Warranty Clerk	Partsmen	....

General Comments

Signature ....   Date ....

Parts and Service Area Manager

Figure 2   Dealer report form

Bank reports

Many routine bank reports are set out on forms. Reproduced below are two extensively used forms employed by a merchant bank.

The first (Figure 3) is a straightforward two-sided Basic Information Report (known as BIR). The details covering all aspects of a customer's operations are available for reference by the bank's officers at any time. It should be noted that provision is made (bottom right-hand corner foot of front side) for recording updating of the particulars. The report is both useless and dangerous unless frequently updated. It is also important that the revision and its date should be recorded.

More difficult, if only due to pressure of time, is the Call Report (Figure 4). Such a report must be completed after every meeting between an officer of the bank and his customer. With several calls throughout the day and associated travelling, it demands strict self-discipline to write up a detailed analysis of the day's business on return to the bank in the evening. Yet this must be done. What might seem crystal clear on coming out of the customer's office will be shrouded in confusion by the time the next call comes around in three months' time, if a full record is not made. Furthermore, the call report helps to maintain a complete record of the bank's dealings with the customer, in case the account officer should have the misfortune to fall under the proverbial bus or the good fortune to have a holiday.

The layout of the call report is important. The call will yield three kinds of information:

1. The objectives (which will, of course, be known when the officer sets out on his visit).
2. The results of the call, which must reflect all the objectives (however unsuccessful) and may throw up more information.
3. The follow-up action. There is bound to be further action, even if it is just another visit in six months' time.

Visit report

Closely related to the bank report is the more widely used visit report. Such reports will often be compiled from copious, perhaps rambling, verbatim notes made at the time of the visit. Different visit reports will demand different treatments, but the following points should be addressed regardless of the type of visit made:

1. How can the report best be divided and structured?
2. Is a chronological approach the most suitable or will that be laborious and uneconomical?
3. Is it helpful to explain the personalities and perhaps, company structures, at the beginning?
4. What background information will interest the next visitor when the next visit comes along?
5. What headings will help subsequent readers select the information that they want?

BASIC INFORMATION REPORT

526A

BRANCH/DISTRICT		
DATE	LINE OF BUSINESS	DATE ACCOUNT OPENED
NAME		HOW OBTAINED
ADDRESS		

OWNERSHIP

OPERATIONS

Products

Administrative And Manufacturing Facilities

Where Applicable Distribution And Selling Terms – Domestic And Export

MANAGEMENT AND DIRECTORS

AFFILIATED COMPANIES AND RELATED BUSINESS

SUBSIDIARIES	owned %	Account with FNCB HO. Br. NO	AFFILIATES	owned %	Account with FNCB HO. Br. NO

HISTORY OF THE BORROWER AND ITS RELATIONSHIP WITH FNCB

BANKING AND OTHER FINANCIAL (LIST LINES OF CREDIT WHERE KNOWN)

DIR INFORMATION REVISED

.... 19
.... 19
.... 19
.... 19

OTHER COMMENTS:-

Figure 3 Bank basic information report

9

TBP 166   **CALL PLAN AND REPORT**

LOCAL COMPANY	BRANCH OR PRODUCT OFFICE	DATE
	CALLING OFFICER	

CALLING ON

1) OBJECTIVES. 2) RESULTS OF CALL. 3) FOLLOW-UP

Figure 4   Bank call plan and report

6. Are the objectives of the visits – many reports will cover more than one – clearly identified and prominently placed?
7. Is it helpful to itemize action points?

New business reports

New business reports, whether conceptual or formal proposals, are increasingly important in a competitive marketplace. They are particularly significant for insurance brokers and chartered accountants, although the relevant disciplines apply to anyone selling a service:

1. The writer must fit into the reader's/potential client's shoes. Nothing should seem to be standard.
2. Benefits should be itemized prominently and early.
3. A layperson's summary, perhaps including the benefits, is often a good idea. The decision will often be made by a director who is not conversant with the terminology and nuances of the product which is being sold.
4. Data of a complex tabulated kind should be relegated to appendices.
5. Use a suitable style: in particular shorter sentences than usual and optimistic selling words.

Appraisal reports

Appraisal reports, which also make extensive use of proformas, are a very special responsibility. They represent, in an absurdly small number of words and symbols, an employee's performance over (usually) an entire year.

The appraisal report system will usually be closely involved with much wider aspects of an organization's personnel policy: training, promotion and the whole pattern of appointment.

The lapse into generalization is almost inescapable in appraisal. However, each one will lay the writer open to a request to substantiate the generalized comment. Such a request may come from above as in the case of the use of words such as 'adequate' or 'satisfactory'. It may come from the subject of the report as in 'unpunctual' or 'on one or two occasions', which immediately invite the enquiry from the appraised: 'What were the occasions?' It must be possible to justify every word and every phrase. This, of course, is true of all reports, but particularly so in the highly poignant phrasing of appraisal reports. To this end, a notebook of significant points about each employee may have to be kept. Although entirely personal to the writer, it will ensure that he/she produces a balanced account of the whole period. Otherwise, it is easy for the events which have taken place in the last three or four months to achieve a disproportionate significance.

It is a good way to ensure fair, consistent and accurate appraisal. The very good and, conversely, the dreadful employees are fairly easy to deal with, as their performances will be remembered in some detail for their excellence or their awfulness. It is with those whose achievements are routine and unmemorable that the writer will grasp at unfair generalizations if he has no such pocket record to assist his thinking. The nebulous person in the middle will therefore benefit from this type of record.

Because of the shortage of space on a report, direct style of writing is necessary. In particular:

1. Avoid euphemism. In military reports the expression 'a good mess member' was once fashionable to describe a species of time-serving senior non-commissioned officer who spent most of his time in the bar. This is evasive writing which relies on the reader interpreting the arcane code correctly.
2. Understatement is generally unhelpful. Terms such as 'not unindustrious' can cover the whole range from 'just avoids being bone idle' to the superlatives of hard work.

There are three clear but interrelated purposes of appraisal:

1. To improve performance.
2. To highlight training needs.
3. To identify promotion potential.

The second and third will result from the first. As with any other report, the design must reflect these objectives.

American management has for much of this century adopted a more structured approach to management appraisal than has been fashionable in Europe. British practice has followed American techniques rather slowly. The feeling that there is something slightly improper about describing an employee's performance in anything except the most general platitudes has hindered developments in this field. Three phases can be detected which represent refinements of the techniques which bring the design of reports nearer to the objectives they set out to satisfy. These are:

1. Personality reporting.
2. Performance criteria.
3. Job objectives.

Companies have introduced the stages at varying paces. Some may have good reason for a more cautious approach. Others, such as the Civil Service, have always been in the vanguard of progress.

Accident reports

The significance of this type of report cannot be overstated. The safety of equipment and the lives of those who handle it depend not only on the perception of the inspectors and the completeness of their investigation, but also on the lucidity of their recommendations.

In internal investigations these recommendations will usually be completed on a form which will ensure that various critical questions are answered. These outlines will be supported by a number of statements: from the relevant line, production or traffic managers, from the drivers or operators, and from the inspectors both before and after the accidents.

An accident (or incident) report is, by its nature, remedial. It must, of course, describe the event for future reference. It must apportion responsibility and, above all, stop similar accidents occurring in the future.

All accident sketch-maps, whether part of a proforma or on a separate sheet, must be drawn at the scene of the event. If circumstances, such as foul weather or the lack of suitable materials, prevent a reasonable copy being made, the fair copy must be produced as soon as possible afterwards. Rough notes lose their meaning, and abbreviations that seemed clear at the time become indecipherable. They should be as near to scale as possible and a fine grid on the paper may help to achieve this.

Listed below are just some of the very wide range of facts likely to be required in an accident report involving vehicles or equipment on a public highway. Of the routine reports considered here, this is likely to be the most complex. Other reports such as accidents to individuals caused by working parts of static machinery are simplifications of this.

The list represents a progression from the permanent (starting with the natural permanent then moving on to the man-made permanent) to the impermanent (first the natural impermanent such as the weather and then the artificial impermanent).

Statements, whether from witnesses or those involved, must be taken as quickly as possible after the incident. Whatever the type of report, the statements should be taken formally:

1. Surnames and initials should be used. The fashion in some companies to use first names or nick-names is not appropriate. Disciplinary or legal proceedings may follow compilation of the report.
2. Colloquialisms should be eliminated.
3. Fact should be distinguished from opinion. If expert opinion is included, the expert's status and qualifications must be mentioned.
4. Hearsay must not be included.

The statements must be prefaced by

1. The witness/participant's name.
2. Address.
3. Occupation.
4. Position in the company (if appropriate).

The statement should start with the witness's position at the time of the accident. It is usually advisable to record this sort of evidence in chronological order giving some indication of the passage of time, where possible.

All statements must be typed. They should then be signed and dated (with the date of signature).

Scientific and technical reports

This broad heading covers all types of report that rely heavily on technical content. The following three examples all show different approaches:

A Department of the Environment/National Water Council paper, *Copper in*

Potable Waters by Atomic Absorption Spectrophotometry[4] is a glossy-covered ten-page report. It is one of a series describing methods for determining water quality aimed at bodies responsible for handling water and sewage. The method, hazards, reagents, apparatus and sampling are described and the analytical procedure is spelled out in 14 detailed steps. The paper ends with checking procedures and sources of error. It is entirely self-contained, which would be unusual in more complex technical reports. Most technical layouts would provide for extensive tables and figures. The layout of National Nuclear Corporation reports is demonstrated by the specimen structure of a hazard assessment in Figure 5. The logical development of the discussion through the chronology from the contingency to the evaluation is easy to see from the list of sections.

An interesting example of a semi-technical report is Dame Mary Warnock's *Report into Human Fertilisation and Embryology*[5]. This steers a meticulously careful path through a moral, medical and legal minefield. In it, Dame Mary avoids using more than a few technical terms and these are clearly defined at the outset. Thus she keeps up the pace of discussion without losing non-medical or non-legal readers.

The Royal Astronomical Society's *Report on the Scientific Priorities for UK Astronomical Research for the Period* 1990–2000[6] solves the problem of technical language by producing excellent summaries at the front of each chapter which are written in layperson's terminology. Acronyms and abbreviations are clearly explained on the last two pages.

The Black report[7] wrestles with sensitive medical and nuclear issues in examining the incidence of cancer cases in the village of Seascale near Sellafield. It has a full glossary but nevertheless remains a scientist's report. The technology of the subject-matter means that this is inevitable. The report remains extremely readable, however, through helpful paragraphing (not always a feature of scientific reports), helpful tables and illustrations, and valuable headings set in a generous margin.

Strategy documents

Strategies for the forthcoming years are frequently set out in the form of a report. A significant Chemical and Allied Products ITB report laid out its strategy centred on three interconnected aims:

1. Improved organizations.
2. Better use of manpower.
3. More effective training practices which it was hoped would follow from the first two.

The report opened with a summary in suitably encouraging language. The nine key areas, which were described as 'missions' in the summary, were then explained in detail, such as:

> To secure an improvement in Health and Safety by ensuring that all managers, safety representatives and safety advisers are trained in the hazards likely to be encountered and that all firms have adequate training arrangements to meet the requirements of Health/Safety legislation for all employees.[8]

The assessment of the radiological hazards at Hartlepool/ Heysham I Power Stations that could result from a dropped fuel stringer accident during on-load refuelling

Contents

Figure 5   Hazard assessment

They were then plotted on a matrix as functions of the chemical firms' needs and the ITB's specific commitments.

Structure plans

Local government authorities, subject to increasing financial and political pressure, produce elaborate plans – frequently running into several volumes – covering developments over the next quarter of a century. The text is normally economically produced, while frequently supplemented by highly coloured elaborate maps to show the complex inter-relationship of such things as historic settlements, tourism pressure areas, areas of outstanding natural beauty, district council boundaries, arterial routes, proposed transport developments, etc.

Such plans are often structured around specific policies which are usually numbered. These can be usefully highlighted by capitalization as in this example from a Cornwall County Council Plan (significantly sub-titled 'Cornwall into the 21st Century'):

POLICY H3
THE PROVISION OF A WIDE RANGE OF DWELLING TYPES AND SIZES OF HIGH QUALITY DESIGN STANDARDS WILL BE ENCOURAGED, IN PARTICULAR TO MEET THE DEMAND ARISING FROM SMALLER HOUSEHOLDS. WHERE PRACTICABLE, A SUITABLE PROPORTION OF THE NEW DWELLINGS SHOULD BE OF A TYPE AND DENSITY SUITABLE FOR THOSE PEOPLE NOT ABLE TO COMPETE EASILY IN THE EXISTING HOUSING MARKET.

The policy items are helpfully lettered to indicate the subject-matter so that H denotes Housing policy, S denotes Shopping policy and so on[9].

Financial forecasts

Budgets and financial forecasts may be put into report form. Certainly the comparison of performance against budget will be presented in this way and may be analysed in financial and percentage terms. The headings will, of course, vary according to the industry. The outline shown in Figure 6 is taken from such a report by a water treatment consultancy and illustrates a helpful sequence.

Professional advisers' reports

Amongst the longer types of unpublished reports are chartered accountants' and management consultants' reports. These are of particular significance as they embody the whole of the professional advisers' work. The accountants' and consultants' reputations stand or fall by the advice contained in their reports. It is thus essential that they should be carefully structured.

The system of layout employed by Price Waterhouse's British firm is an excellent example of the sort of discipline required in reports with this degree of complexity. Their reports will begin with a covering letter of up to a dozen paragraphs explaining:

1. The reason for carrying out the investigation. The letter instructing them to do so may well be attached as an appendix.

Introduction

Selling expenses

Net operating profit

Selling expense/Gross margin ratio

Manpower

On-site availability, % sale time in hours
actual sales hours spent on site

Sales hours spent per new client gained

Number of new clients gained

Average EAV (estimated annual value) per new client

Total EAV of new clients gained

Percentage EAV invoiced of new business in 1980

New business invoiced

Service hours

GP (gross profit) per service hour

Figure 6   Budget and financial forecast

2. The use of any particular techniques or methods during the investigation (such as statistical sampling).
3. Any records or audits to which reference is made. This enables the reader to have the documents to hand and highlights the authorship of such supporting papers.

After the covering letter the report will move on to a number of 'Parts'. The outline of these Parts depends on the particular company or topic being examined, but the first Part is likely to be a summary of the salient points to emerge from the investigation. An outline of an examination of a company for a flotation or acquisition might be:

Part I   Salient features
Part II   History and actIvities
Part III   Trading results
Part IV   Net assets
Part V   Future prospects
Acknowledgement

Either the report or the covering letter will always end with an acknowledgement of assistance. The exact form of words would depend on the extent and type of assistance given.

The reports are extremely detailed and the paragraphs of minutiae will be compiled in accordance with the laudably strict systems of layout the partnership lay down, thus ensuring uniformity of presentation and consistency of layout throughout the practice. Where there are general lessons to be learnt from these conventions, allusion is made to them in ensuing chapters of this book.

Because their coverage is so detailed, these reports rely extensively on appendices, which will include voluminous tabulations of financial details and may include some graphs, bar charts, and so on, to indicate changing patterns. There will also probably be some appendices in prose describing products, remuneration policies and so on. It will not be uncommon for about half the pages of such a report to consist of appendices. It is important, however, in such cases where lavish appendices are customary, to avoid including every available piece of information. Relevance must be carefully assessed.

It is interesting to note that some of the more rigid layouts prescribed by the firm in the 1970s are now less rigid. Documents such as internal control reports, whereby the housekeeping of a client company is examined, must now reflect a format and style appropriate to the size and business of the client. This is rightly considered more important than strict adherence to any traditional format.

Another field closely involving the accountancy profession is the preparation of annual reports. Strangely, there is very little statutory guidance as to the requirements for an annual report except that set out in the various Companies Acts. Most of the post-war legislation was consolidated into the Companies Act 1985 and further – largely EEC related aspects – have been added in the Companies Act 1989.

Companies are required to file accounts within six or nine months of the year end. Certain details have to be shown, such as the names of directors, details of their appointments and resignations, and nature of trade. Various excellent guides to such provisions exist. Principal among these are Roy Warren's *How to Understand and Use Company Accounts*[10] and Geoffrey Holmes and Alan Sugden's *Interpreting Company Reports and Accounts*[11]. The Institute of Chartered Accountants in England and Wales produce an interesting and instructive annual analysis of the year's financial reports. It appears around February or March each year[12].

Nationalized industries are subject to special requirements, such as the Coal Industry Nationalisation Act 1946 in the case of British Coal. The Civil Service College has produced a useful booklet *The Reports and Accounts of Nationalised Industries*, which helps the reader to interpret the reports of nationalized industries.

Reports in the private sector are astonishingly varied. In size alone there is a great range. For example the Burton Group 1987 report was produced on unfashionable A3 paper. Land Securities 1989 report was prepared on the more conventional A4 sheets but printed in landscape, rather than profile.

Coloured photographs of the products in context or action shots have now generally replaced the more traditional and prosaic boardroom illustrations. Indeed in some reports, such as Severn Trent Water 1988–89 report and Lynton plc 1989 report, the area occupied by photographs greatly exceeds that taken up by prose and tabulated numerical detail.

Thumb-indexing or sections with graded page sizes sometimes makes the sections easier to find quickly. The Burton Group 1988 report does this successfully with its six sections.

Great efforts were made throughout the 1980s to ensure that just because reports are prepared to meet a statutory requirement, they do not have to be boring. The Devon and Cornwall Constabulary Chief Constable's Annual Report is a good example of such a report, covering serious subjects but still readable and lively.

Government Green and White Papers

Government policy is frequently expressed in Green Papers and White Papers. The former indicate proposed policy and the latter specific intentions. The difference is well demonstrated by the conclusion paragraph from a Green Paper on *The European Monetary System*:

> The Government cannot yet reach their own conclusions on whether it would be in the best interests of the UK to join the exchange rate regime of the EMS as it finally emerges from the negotiations. However, the Government's basic objectives will remain unchanged whatever decision is taken. The Government will vigorously pursue the policies which are necessary for improving growth and reducing unemployment. The foundation for these policies must be an improvement in our industrial performance and victory in the battle against inflation. Only these can provide a lasting basis for the stability of the exchange rate.

Green Papers will usually invite comment. The Green Paper *Supervision and Punishment in the Community: A Framework for Action*[13] circulated in February 1990 tackled problems anticipated for the probation service as a result of new sentencing policies. It assessed the need for organizational change, working methods, functions, training and raised particularly sensitive areas regarding the interface with the voluntary and private sectors. The Conclusion ends with this invitation.

> The Government would therefore welcome comments, both on the specific points raised at the end of Chapters 5 to 10, and more generally. The issues raised in Chapter 10 are dealt with in more detail in a separate discussion paper, 'Partnership in Dealing with Offenders in the Community' to be published shortly. Comments on the Green Paper should be sent by 30 June 1990 to:
> Home Office
> Criminal Justice and Constitutional Department
> Room 440
> 50 Queen Anne's Gate
> London SW1H 9AT

The role of a White Paper in declaring specific intentions is demonstrated by the annual Defence White Paper. This is presented to Parliament by the Secretary of State for Defence, generally every spring[14]. It covers, in considerable detail, the Government's defence priorities, its interpretation of the threat, the specifics of its deployment of the three services and its allocation of the budget.

The European Commission also produces White Papers. The Commissioner, Lord Cockfield's celebrated plan for completing the internal market was produced as a White Paper *Completing the Internal Market*[15].

Reports of committees of inquiry

Committees of inquiry are easily the most complex type of report considered here. Involving large numbers of contributors (of deliberately different persuasions) and even larger numbers of witnesses, they are required to examine, often in an almost impossibly tight time-frame, a subject that inevitably has wide-ranging philosophical and moral implications. Frequently their terms of reference are so general that the chairman has to spend some time restricting the vast area of his investigation.

Two reports with the same chairman will serve to demonstrate these problems. In 1972 Sir Alan (later Lord) Bullock was appointed by the then Secretary of State for Education and Science (Margaret Thatcher) to investigate the teaching in schools of reader and other uses of English. At the end of 1975 he was invited (by Peter Shore) to advise on the matter of extending representation on boards in the private sector in the interest of industrial democracy. Both reports, *A Language for Life*[16] and *Industrial Democracy*[17], have been known by the nickname 'the Bullock Report' which is logical yet confusing.

One of the most substantial inquiry reports of the 1980s was that emanating from the Sizewell B Public Inquiry[18]. This detailed work produced nine volumes. The first covered an introduction and a Summary of Conclusions and Recommendations. The eighth housed appendices, index, glossary and list of acronyms. The ninth gave Conclusions and Recommendations in more detail. The inquiry sat from January 1983 to March 1985 and the report was presented in December 1986.

At the other end of the scale, such bodies as local authorities may carry out inquiries and produce suitable reports. The Chief Education Officer of Buckinghamshire County Council produced a report based on the visit to Cornwall by Stoke Poges County Middle School[19], during which four boys were drowned. The report was less lavishly presented and briefer than the aforementioned, but was nevertheless full and sensitive. It drew lessons and made 22 appropriate recommendations.

READERSHIP

Whatever the purpose, the needs of the readership are the most important consideration. In principle the reader to whom the report will be geared is the principal addressee. Sometimes, however, a hidden readership is more important. The Fennell report on the King's Cross disaster is addressed to Paul Channon, who was Secretary of State for Transport[20]. However, asked if he was writing to the public or to the Minister, Desmond Fennell replied that it never occurred to him as regards style, tone or content that he was writing to Channon. He said that he saw himself as preparing the report for an interested public. Accordingly he assumed nothing and wrote in what he called 'direct, plain and simple English'.

Likewise the findings must be easy to identify. *The Falkland Islands Review*[21] (or Franks report) was criticized for its somewhat obscure and evasive presentation. Writing in *The Spectator* Colin Welch said 'Its strictures were like an Argentine minefield – difficult to locate, map and lift'[22].

SUMMARY

This chapter has described the range of uses to which reports can be put.

The examples have been discussed in varying amounts of detail since the problems they represent differ so greatly. At one end of the spectrum are the moral and political wrestlings that faced Lord Bullock and Dame Mary Warnock. At the other end are the note form reports on motor vehicles testing or on a bank's customers. All are reports.

All must respect the principles of written communication: discretion, accuracy and conciseness. Yet each will do so in a different way. Every type of report calls for slightly different treatment. Each must be as concise as possible whilst enabling the writer to do justice to the problem.

2   Structure: introduction and body

If you want something that's genuinely unstructured you have to plan it carefully.

There is more than a grain of truth in Howard Kirk's apparently fatuous observation in *The History Man*[1]. For a report to read fluently and not appear stilted or brittle it must be planned diligently.

Most reports fall, like Gaul, into three parts. There will be an Introduction. Following this will be the main body of the report, sometimes called the discussion section, or the argument (although it should not be given any of these general labels). Finally there will be Conclusions, to which Recommendations may be added (Figure 7).

TITLE

Every report must have a title. It must be set out in a way that makes it stand out clearly from the rest of the report and should be in a script which is at least as pronounced as any subordinate headings within it (Figure 8). A title typed in lower-case letters, when subsequent headings appear in block capitals, is unlikely to stand out sufficiently.

Many organizations require reports to be enclosed in a cover. In this case, the title will appear on the front of it in whatever format suits the company's practices and the distribution of the paper. The subject of report presentation is treated in detail in Chapter 12.

The wording of a report title requires a balance between brevity and clarity. A regular routine report may have a title such as:

FOOD DIVISION MONTHLY REPORT MARCH 1990

or as in this Esso Petroleum example:

SIGNATURE VERIFICATION: POSITION PAPER

Extraordinary reports which do not follow an expected pattern may have to be more wordy. The Engineering Industry Training Board produced a title:

```
┌─────────────────────────────────────────┐
│                                           │
│          INTRODUCTION                     │
│                                           │
└─────────────────────────────────────────┘
                      │
┌─────────────────────────────────────────┐
│                                           │
│                                           │
│            MAIN BODY                      │
│                                           │
│                                           │
└─────────────────────────────────────────┘
                      │
┌─────────────────────────────────────────┐
│                                           │
│           CONCLUSIONS                     │
│                                           │
└─────────────────────────────────────────┘
                      │
┌ ─ ─ ─ ─ ─ ─ ─ ─ ─ ─ ─ ─ ─ ─ ─ ─ ─ ─ ─ ─ ┐
│                                           │
│        RECOMMENDATIONS                    │
│                                           │
└ ─ ─ ─ ─ ─ ─ ─ ─ ─ ─ ─ ─ ─ ─ ─ ─ ─ ─ ─ ─ ┘
```

Figure 7   Basic sequence of a report

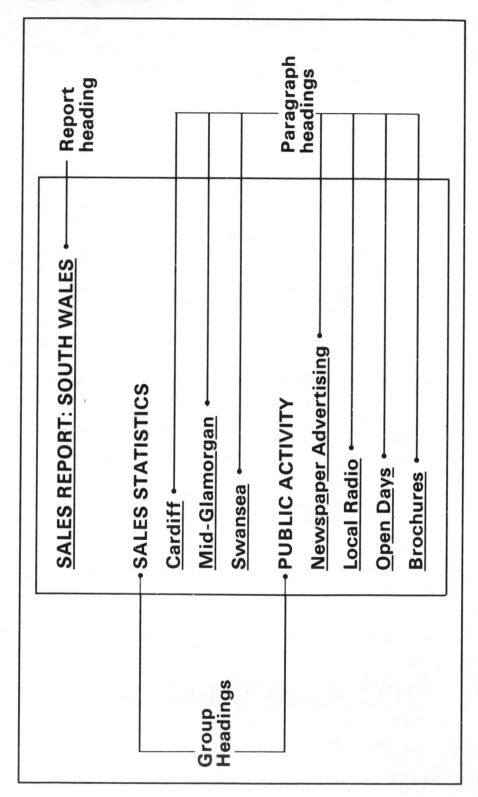

Figure 8   Specimen sequence of headings and sub-headings

EMPLOYMENT AND TRAINING IN THE TELECOMMUNICATIONS
EQUIPMENT MANUFACTURING INDUSTRY

In an academic or contemplative report a more cryptic title can be used, provided that it is clarified by a sub-title[2]

FAITH IN THE CITY:
A CALL FOR ACTION BY CHURCH AND NATION

or perhaps[3]

NOT JUST FOR THE POOR:
CHRISTIAN PERSPECTIVES ON THE WELFARE STATE

If there is the temptation to use more than about ten or a dozen words as in the example below, some of the points must be eliminated from the title and relegated to the introduction.

REPORT ON STAFFING LEVELS IN ALL DEPARTMENTS LESS
MARKETING AND RESEARCH AND DEVELOPMENT EXCLUDING SITES IN
SCOTLAND AND NORTH-EAST BUT INCLUDING BELGIAN BRANCHES

The inquiry into the affair of Commander Trestrail has an enormous title. This seems unnecessarily ponderous and it is difficult to pick out the subject at a glance.

> Report of an inquiry by the right honourable Lord Bridge of Harwich into the appointment as The Queen's Police Officer, and the activities, of Commander Trestrail; to determine whether security was breached or put at risk, and advise whether in consequence any change in security arrangements is necessary or desirable.

The need for microscopic precision in choosing words in titles and various sorts of headings will be discussed later. Such precision is needed because in a title every word is significant, whereas in a paragraph of the report an ill-chosen word can be corrected by other words in that paragraph.

The expression *Re* to introduce a heading is a foolish encumbrance which should be avoided. It adds nothing to a title which should be adequately pronounced if it is in block capitals or underlined. In any case, the Re does not stand for Regarding, as many of its users believe, but *In Rem* (Latin meaning 'in the matter of')[4].

INTRODUCTION

If the introduction of a report is poorly drafted, the writer will have difficulty in maintaining the reader's attention, understanding or sympathy. In an oral briefing, a gimmicky introduction, a poorly told joke or a joke which is already well-known can destroy any rapport with the audience. If the speaker fails to state his objective or explain the rationale of his approach, he will lose his audience. It is exactly the same with a report. Even after a good introduction, the writer may still stand the chance of losing his reader, but after a bad introduction, he stands little hope of attracting him at all.

It is impossible to provide an all-purpose list of contents for an introduction. It should, however, include everything that the reader needs to know before he tackles the main argument of the report. It is highly likely that the following will feature:

Why the report is being written

Who told the writer to produce the paper? When did he do so?

In your memorandum dated 1 April 1992 you asked me to investigate ways of improving delivery times.

Perhaps it is just a monthly return, as in:

Set out below are sales figures for the month of May 1992.

On the other hand, the report may have been compiled on the writer's own initiative. He may have noticed some shortcoming. Perhaps there has been excessive turnover of staff or there is some significant safety hazard.

Occasionally a potted history of the relevant events is an obvious start point. The first page and a half of the Press Council report into the Sutcliffe case[5] give a superbly concise account of the relevant crimes, police activity and criminal prosecution which preceded the press activity under review.

Likewise the Introduction to the interim Hillsborough report gives such background in its first paragraph:

On 15 April 1989 a football match to decide a semi-final round of the FA Cup competition was to be played between the Liverpool and Nottingham Forest clubs. The neutral venue chosen was Hillsborough Football Stadium, Sheffield Wednesday's ground. Only six minutes into the game, play was stopped when it was realised that spectators on the terraces behind the Liverpool goal had been severely crushed. In the result 95 died and over 400 received hospital treatment.[6]

Background may be an important aspect of the reason for the report having been written, and it can be both important and complex. The Cleveland child abuse report[7] opens with a two and a half page section on 'Background' which is wide-ranging and instructive in its content. It follows the following sequence:

The statutory basis of the investigation
'On the 9th July 1987, the Secretary of State for Social Services ordered that a Statutory Inquiry should be established under section 84 of the National Health Service Act 1977 and Section 76 of the Child Care Act 1980 to look into the arrangements for dealing with suspected cases of Child Abuse in Cleveland from the 1st January 1987.'
The announcement of the inquiry
The terms of reference
Chronology of the beginning of the inquiry
The approach
Representation of interested parties
Assessors who helped Lord Justice Butler-Sloss
The timing and duration of the inquiry
Acknowledgements

The opening paragraph of the County NatWest investigation also demonstrates this with an admirable three-paragraph historical background:

> On 4 August 1987 Blue Arrow announced the launch of a cash tender offer for Manpower, a much larger company listed on the New York Stock Exchange. On 21 August 1987 a revised offer was announced, the acceptance of which was recommended by the Board of Manpower.

Opinion varies as to whether a report introduction should open with an Objective/Purpose or with Background. In principle it is usually more logical to start with the Objective unless it is necessary to read some Background to make sense of the Objective.

Sometimes it will be helpful to set out the scope of a report as a mini-table of contents as in this illustration from American International Underwriters.

AUDIT OBJECTIVES AND SCOPE
The objective of the audit was to review operational procedures, identify exposures and assess the level of control exercised at the Data Centre. The scope of the review and an index to the findings follows:
1. DATACENTRE CONTROLS
    1.1   Organisation Controls
    1.2   Access Controls
    1.3   Operation Controls
    1.4   Continuation Controls
2. APPLICATION CONTROLS
    2.1   System Development & Maintenance Controls
    2.2   Direct Entry Controls
    2.3   Processing Controls
    2.4   Output & Stored Data Controls

What terms of reference have been given?

Any particular approach to the problem to be taken by the report must be stated at the outset. This is likely to have been given by the authority for whom the report has been prepared:

> ... in the light of the proposed closure of the Birmingham offices ...

or

The last Chester report on the Football League quoted its exact terms of reference early in its text:

> Our terms of reference were
> 'to review the structure of the League's championships and cup competitions and to make recommendations as to future viability'.[8]

Terms of reference are particularly important where the findings may be sensitive or controversial. They remind or should remind the reader of the original purpose of the document. The Serpell report into the funding of the railways[9] caused much public exclamation and complaint. It was felt by many interested parties that swingeing reductions in the network were being proposed; in extreme cases the wholesale closure of branch lines. Nothing was further from the truth.

Sir David Serpell's terms of reference did not require him to make recommendations. He was required 'to examine the finances of the railway and associated operations, in the light of all relevant considerations, and to report on options for alternative policies, and their related objectives, designed to secure improved financial results in an efficiently run railway in Great Britain over the next 20 years'[10].

Describing options was precisely what he did.

Significantly the opposite was true of the Cleveland child abuse report. Here, as Lord Justice Butler-Sloss states early in the report:

> I was asked to chair the Inquiry, with the following Terms of Reference;
> 'To examine the arrangements for dealing with suspected cases of child abuse in Cleveland since 1st January 1987, including in particular cases of child abuse, and to make recommendations.'[11]

The report was not intended to investigate the extent of child abuse, nor the reasons for it (although inevitably these topics were discussed). It was restricted to looking at the arrangements for dealing with cases. There was also a time limit 'since 1st January 1987'. Nothing was to be considered before that time. The Franks report[12] also quotes a time limit in its terms of reference:

> To review the way in which the responsibilities of Government in relation to the Falkland Islands on 2 April 1982, taking account of all such factors in previous years as are relevant . . .

In this case, the limit excludes all events after the specified date, that is excepting the military operations.

The Mandate of the Challenger Commission[13] was to:

1. Review the circumstances surrounding the accident to establish the probable cause or causes of the accident, and
2. Develop recommendations for corrective or other action based upon the Commission's findings and determinations.

When the Department of Transport Lockerbie report[14] was published in September 1990 it was received with criticism, especially by spokesmen for the bereaved. It was suggested that the report covered only aircraft design with no comments on safety at Heathrow airport or elsewhere. It would have been proper to include an Introduction to clarify whether the inquiry was supposed to cover these wider aspects or not. The report lacks any such Introduction. However, the Department of Transport (Air Accidents Investigation Branch) and the Royal Aerospace Establishment have since (December 1990) confirmed that they will, in future, refer to their regulations in the Introduction to their accident reports.

What limitations may have been imposed on the treatment of the subject?

If the treatment of the subject as described in the title is subject to any restrictions, these must be shown in the Introduction. Not only should the limitations be given, but also the reasons:

> This report does not cover the current financial year, as figures are not yet available.

or

> . . . excluding our exports to Italy which are the subject of another report.

An ITB report explained a limitation on its treatment of its subject in these terms:

> The telecommunications equipment manufacturing industry is concerned particularly with the telephone system, including public and private switching equipment, transmission equipment and subscriber apparatus. It is important to note that this classification concerns the manufacture of telecommunications equipment and therefore does not include The Post Office itself or other aspects of telecommunication.

A more positive mode of expression is seen in the Cabinet Office's *Industrial Innovation*:

> In this report we have restricted ourselves essentially to an examination of the innovative process, and the manner in which it has operated in Britain compared to other countries.[15]

The Challenger report gave specific limitations:

> . . . the Commission did not construe its mandate to require a detailed investigation of all aspects of the Space Shuttle program; to review budgetary matters; or to interfere or supersede Congress in any way in the performance of its duties. Rather the Commission focused its attention on the safety aspects of future flights based on the lessons learned from the investigation of the objective being to return to safe flight.

The limitations complement the terms of reference (p. 27). Between them they will point out the approach taken by the report.

A simple schematic representation of these first three possible components of an introduction is given in Figure 9. Every report will have an objective or purpose. The terms of reference give its positive side and any limitations will balance it with a negative aspect.

What sources have been used?

It may be that the number of other reports and papers to which reference has been made are too numerous to describe in the Introduction. It will then be appropriate to list them in an attachment. On the other hand, if the report makes continual reference to two or three other papers, Acts of Parliament or sets of safety regulations, these should be mentioned:

> Comparisons are made with the report for 1987.

Perhaps the report has been prepared in accordance with the specifications of some other document:

> This is the annual report for 1988 of matters within the Insurance Companies Act 1982.[16]

29

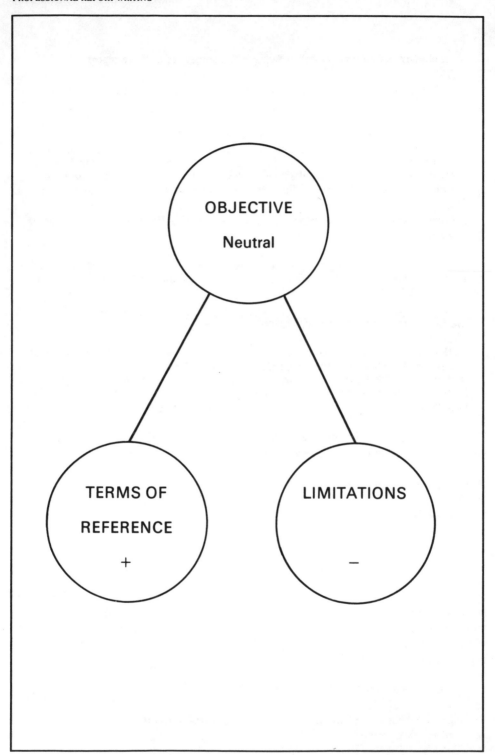

Figure 9   Schematic representation of the first three components of an Introduction

If any sampling has been done, this should be described as in the following report by the Communication Studies and Planning Ltd/Equal Opportunities Commission, called *Information Technology in the Office: the Impact on Women's Jobs*:

> To gain an impression of the attitudes and experience of operators of the new office technologies we distributed one hundred self-completion questionnaires through management, trade union and independent contacts to word processing operators and other workers who used office computer terminals, e.g. data entry clerks. We did not restrict the distribution to women workers since we felt that the views of male operators in similar jobs were just as relevant. The questionnaire is shown at Annex A. We received 51 completed replies. Characteristics of the respondents are shown in Annex B.[17]

The questionnaires themselves would then be shown in attachments, or,

> The report covers a sample of 1 in 20.

A particularly clear and helpful statement of sources occurs in the Trustee Savings Bank's *Economic Trends No. 4*:

> The forecasts used in compiling this section include Phillips & Drew, de Zoete & Bevan (Stockbrokers) and the Treasury. The National Institute Review has not been included because it was published prior to the budget and although the London Business School figures are included in the tables, they arrived too late to be incorporated in the commentary.

Method of working

In technical papers the method of working would be explained in a similar way. An outline of work done may suffice, with detailed work being laid out in an attachment.

In the Communication Studies and Planning Ltd/Equal Opportunities Commission report just quoted there is a sub-paragraph to the Introduction:

1.4 Method
The source material for this report was gathered by means of:
- a literature review plus interviews with specialists in the electronic office field
- self-completion questionnaires from 51 users of word processing and office computer terminals
- case studies of ten organizations using new technology[18]

The Challenger report remarks on:

a. Importance placed on open disclosure.
b. NASA's attitude.
c. Congress's emphasis on the need to have a single investigation.

Overview of structure

The County NatWest investigation[19] report which is divided into 18 chapters starts each chapter with an Introduction which leads into the various topics (Contingency Plans, the various meetings and phases of the story, and so on).

MAIN BODY OF THE REPORT

The main body, or meat, of the report will, of course, be divided into easily digestible chunks. It is neither necessary nor helpful to surmount it by a heading 'Discussion' or 'Argument'. Like the Introduction it needs to follow a sequence of points.

In a QANTAS report justifying the hiring of six extra summer staff the manager developed his/her argument in several short logically sequenced paragraphs (Piccadilly and Strand were QANTAS' principal points of sale in London):

HISTORY
PICCADILLY
STRAND
AGENCY-SERVING
WORKLOAD
TICKETS ISSUED
PASSENGERS SEEN
RETURNING PASSENGER SERVICING
TOTAL TRAVELLED
WEEKLY REPORTS
OTHER FACTORS
TRAVELLED REVENUE
ELIMINATION OR COMBINATION OF WORK
OVERTIME
ANALYSIS OF NEED
PENALTIES
ALTERNATIVES
PRODUCTIVITY IMPROVEMENTS
COSTS

Sometimes instead of just paragraphs, the report's main body can take the form of a number of formally numbered sections. For instance, a report on warehousing by an Argos supervisor has four sections:

Section No	Description
3	Remote Terminal Operations
4	The Office
5	Proposed Site
6	The Cost

The precise layout will be dictated by the subject. In a simple internal report dealing with stock adjustment, a very basic layout of the discussion such as that shown in Figure 10 from Warner-Lambert may suffice. In more substantial reports the sections may be dignified by the title of 'Chapter' as in Lord Bullock's *Industrial Democracy*[20]:

Chapter 1: Introduction
Chapter 2: Size and shape of the private sector
Chapter 3: Socio-Economic characteristics of inward migrants.

There may be a need for further sub-division: *Industrial Democracy* is broken down as shown in Figure 11. Of course the need for such sub-divisions may not be uniform. Some sections of the report may call for sub-division, while with others it is not necessary.

1. PRESENT SITUATION AND BACKGROUND: BULK TABLETS
   (Problem is described in nine introductory lines)

   Alternative 1
   Comments
   Alternative 2
   Comments
   Alternative 3
   Comments

2. PRESENT SITUATION AND BACKGROUND: BULK BACKGROUND:
   PART-FINISHED STOCK
   (Problem and two solutions are described in six introductory lines)

   Solution 2
   Comments

Figure 10   Layout of discussion of objectives from an internal Warner-Lambert report

Contents of the Main Report

Figure 11   Table of Contents for Industrial Democracy

A slight flaw in the otherwise outstanding Health and Safety Bentley Colliery report[21] is the choice of headings in the body of the document. The report itself is entitled:

The Accident at Bentley Colliery, South Yorkshire, 21 November 1978.

It is therefore surprising to find a heading within the report labelled 'The Accident'. Nevertheless this can probably be justified: the previous section deals with 'Description' and the following one 'The Investigation'. On the other hand it is not sensible for the section heading 'The Accident' to be repeated as a sub-section covering 6 of its 20 paragraphs as in Figure 12.

The Flixborough report[22] also provides a model of sound accurate reporting but falls down towards the end with half a dozen unspecific headings (along with an optimistic little heading 'Miscellaneous'):

Description
General
The Manriding Installation

The Accident
Events leading to the accident
The accident
The recovery

The Investigation
Inspection of the site
No 18 locomotive
The carriages
The couplings
The Godwin Warren Arrestor
Surface testing

Matters arising out of the Investigation

Figure 12   Sub-sections of the report of the Accident at Bentley Colliery

Lessons to be learned
Specific lessons
General lessons
Miscellaneous lessons

Vague and sensational headings should be avoided. The Denning report on the security aspects of the Profumo Affair in 1963 had some entertaining headings but they were perhaps too euphemistic for helpful signposts: 'The Borrowed Car', 'The Cup of Tea', 'The Man in the Mask', 'The Man without a Head'.

LAYOUT OF ROUTINE REPORTS

If a report is submitted regularly and the content is likely to follow a similar pattern on every occasion, a standard format should be evolved for the main body of the report. This will ensure uniformity and enable comparisons to be made as a check on progress.

Direct supervision of the routine work and administration of the Centre for British Teachers in Malaysia is the responsibility of Regional Project Directors, former Centre teachers with experience of the peninsula. Their areas may cover several hundreds of square miles. The body of the reports, which they submit monthly to their Director in Kuala Lumpur, is laid out under the heading of Duties, as a diary. The entries are of variable length. Days of travel are also included. Important, difficult or confidential visits are then supplemented by separate visit reports to which cross-reference is made in the main report.

I. <u>SALES REVIEW</u>

II. <u>CYCLE MEETING HIGHLIGHTS</u>
<u>Previous cycle</u>
<u>New cycle</u>

III. <u>MARKET INFORMATION</u>
always including a subordinate heading:
<u>New laws and regulations affecting business</u>

IV. <u>INSTITUTIONAL BUSINESS</u>

V. <u>HEALTH REGISTRATION</u>

VI. <u>OTHER COMMENTS</u>

Figure 13 Outline of Sentipharm AG cycle report

The Middle East Office of Sentipharm AG in Athens is responsible for promotion and sale of the group's pharmaceutical products throughout the East Mediterranean (Greece, Syria, Egypt, Saudi Arabia and elsewhere). The geographical diversity and size of the area makes consistency in reporting particularly important. The promotional cycles for their products are therefore reported under the headings shown in Figure 13.

The sequence laid down for the internal audit reports of American International Underwriters provides four somewhat generalized sections between the cover page and the appendices:

COVER PAGE
EXECUTIVE SUMMARY
INTRODUCTION & BACKGROUND
AUDIT OBJECTIVES & SCOPE
COMMENTS & FINDINGS
APPENDICES

SUMMARY

The Introduction must set the scene for the report and must outline the necessary points for the reader to be able to comprehend the body of the report. The reader should therefore have a precise idea of the purpose, direction, limitations and approach of the document.

This will also be broadly reflected in the structure. The structure of the body must be logical and readers must be guided through it by precise, accurate signposts.

3   Structure: conclusions and recommendations

The Introduction will have posed various questions. The reader must be able to find the answers to these problems in the Conclusions and, if relevant, the Recommendations. For the report to achieve its aim this must be the case even if the Conclusion is that further work must be undertaken to provide a fuller investigation.

CONCLUSIONS

The conclusions of a report should set out the answers to the questions posed by the report. Conclusions may, of course, be given a practical interpretation in Recommendations.

The difference between the two is an important one. Conclusions draw together the threads from the preceding argument. Recommendations suggest steps that should be taken to improve the situation. Any reader who does not completely understand this vital distinction should compare the examples given under this heading with those under 'Recommendations'.

In the main body of the report, the different facets of the problem will have been examined in isolation. In a report on area sales staffs, North-West, North-East, Wales, and so on, will all have been examined separately. No comparison will be made between one area and another, thus ensuring that the order in which the areas are treated does not prejudice the argument.

In the Conclusion it is appropriate to make the comparisons which have been avoided up to that point. For instance the report might reveal a staffing shortfall at Bradford (covered in the section on the North-East region) and a surplus at Warrington (covered under the North-West). In the Conclusion these two facts will be brought together.

Further good examples, in which even more diverse main bodies are drawn together into some comprehensive conclusions, were found in the Price Commission reports, for instance, the last on Whitbread and Company Ltd.[1] The sections cover company background, operational structure, management structure, tied houses, take-home sales and many other relevant aspects. Among the conclusions were:

> We examined the distribution of the company's products and the operation of its transport fleet and found that both were efficiently organised. Indeed, the company has been an innovator in efficient trailer design.

and

> The company's profitability increased substantially in 1978–79 and was planned to increase by a further significant amount in 1979–80.

It must he noted, of course, that the Conclusions are not an opportunity to restate how the writer has gone about his business. This temptation does arise and must be resisted. The first 15 words of the first Price Commission conclusion above, are just a helpful lead into the result of the investigation.

Readers will often look for a Conclusion to represent the physical balance of a report, sometimes erroneously. In his memoirs General Lord Ismay describes a report prepared for Churchill by the Joint Chiefs of Staff just before Dunkirk. The report was 13 paragraphs long. The body of 12 paragraphs showed that the Germans had the advantage in almost – but not quite – every sphere. The exception was more important as was demonstrated in the Conclusion:

> Our conclusion is that, *prima facie*, Germany has most of the cards; but the real test is whether the morale of our fighting personnel and civil population will counter-balance the numerical and material advantages which Germany enjoys. We believe it will.[2]

Ismay expressed surprise at such a conclusion when the bulk of the report pointed in a different direction. He found it 'somewhat inconsistent'. Subsequent events proved that the conclusion was justified.

It may be desirable to sub-divide the conclusions. Figure 14 shows those of a report by a retail chain entitled *Identification and Development of Potential Branch Management*. The views of all and sundry have been solicited on their experiences of a centre for the assessment of potential branch managers. In drawing the conclusions it is important to keep the points separate so that the originators can be identified.

The terms Conclusions and Recommendations are not the only ones used, although the principles will be the same. Sometimes the expression Options is used in place of Conclusions.

The Monopolies Commission report on the Government of Kuwait and BP[3] used the titling:

CONCLUSIONS
REMEDIES

Examples of the wording demonstrate the difference in content and style. For example under Conclusions

8.114. The size of the Government of Kuwait's shareholding is such that it could be

CONCLUSION

DISTRICT MANAGERS' VIEW

Where possible I have obtained views of the District Managers familiar with Assessment Centres. (see Appendix v).

The District Managers all acknowledge having benefited in terms of increased knowledge of trainees and an increased awareness of assessment methods.

TRAINEE MANAGERS' VIEW

The trainees have indicated they enjoy the experience and through exposure learn more about management.

PERSONNEL MANAGERS' VIEW

The Assessment Centres in operation have worked successfully. They provide an information system which up to now has not been available in reviewing a trainee's performance over a concentrated period of time rather than for short occasions over a period of several years.

Using these two processes Branches Control are now in a position to identify and train development areas at the very earliest opportunity.

Figure 14   Sub-division of conclusions

used to influence the policy of BP on many matters including research into and the development of substitute or alternative sources of energy or oil products, the exploration for oil or the development of new or marginal existing oilfields or acquisitions.

and

8.115. Furthermore, we believe that in future the perception in some third party countries, including the United States of America, of this influential shareholding by a member of OPEC is a factor which could have adverse effects on BP's activities.

The Remedies take the form and tone associated in other contexts with Recommendations:

8.123. In these circumstances we consider that the only effective remedy is for the shareholding to be reduced to a level at which it could be expected not to exert material influence. We consider that the maximum level of shareholding should be 9.9 per cent, i.e. just below the 10 per cent level at which it could requisition company meetings or call for a poll. We therefore recommend that the Government of Kuwait should be required to divest its holdings of BP shares to 9.9 per cent of the issued ordinary share capital of BP.

Only the last sentence is a genuine Recommendation. The rest of the paragraph has been pared down to information which is an essential lead-in to the final point.

The Jockey Club report on the 1989 St Leger meeting[4] helpfully subdivides its Conclusions according to responsible bodies and individuals:

CONCLUSIONS
8.1   *Relating to events on 13th, 14th and 15th September 1989*
8.2   *Relating to the role and conduct of persons involved in organising, administering or controlling the Doncaster September meeting.*
    8.2.1   *Doncaster Racecourse Meeting*
    8.2.2   *The General Manager*
    8.2.3   *Clerk to the Course*
    8.2.4   *Inspector of Courses*
    8.2.5   *Doncaster Stewards*
    8.2.6   *Stewards' Secretaries*

Usually the closing paragraphs of the best-written leading articles in broadsheet national newspapers will provide an informal conclusion. For example *The Times* produced some wide-ranging advice to John Major for his first Budget. After covering various options and lines of thinking, the First Leader concludes:

The Chancellor should frame his Budget on the sound principle that fiscal policy should support, not replace, monetary policy. What precisely that should mean for the size of the Budget surplus next year will be the product of many different influences. It is most unlikely to mean a net cut in taxation.[5]

RECOMMENDATIONS

It is sometimes suggested that conclusions are written in the past tense and Recommendations in the future. While this is dreadfully simplistic, it does provide a valuable touchstone. If any comment does not concern the future, then it has no place in a Recommendation.

Recommendations must follow directly and obviously from the conclusions. They should never surprise the reader. They should be brief and to the point. Frequently one or two lines will suffice.

It is sometimes a helpful expedient for the writer to discipline himself to start every recommendation 'It is recommended . . .' or 'We recommend . . .'. This has two important effects:

1. It gives the Recommendation directness and emphasis.
2. It ensures that the writer does not fill the Recommendation with woolly justification which should properly be placed in the Conclusions.

In the case of the staffing discrepancy between Bradford and Warrington described above (p. 38), the comparison between the two would be made in the Conclusions, and the Recommendation might read: 'It is recommended that six sales representatives be reallocated from Warrington to Bradford'.

Accident reports provide excellent examples of the clear watershed between Conclusions and Recommendations. The following excerpts from a railway accident report on a crash that occurred near Wembley Central Station in 1984[6] illustrate variations in content but also in tone.

Under Conclusions:

> I do not believe that it is possible to be fully certain as to the cause of the accident. I am satisfied that as the 17.54 Euston to Bletchley train approached Wembley Central the signals were set for the move of the Freightliner train from the Goods line onto the Down Slow line and that the signals on the Down Slow line protecting this move were showing the correct cautionary and stop aspects. I am further satisfied that the automatic warning system (AWS) associated with the signals and the corresponding equipment on the train was functioning correctly, and that adequate brake power was available to stop the train within the required braking distances.

Under Recommendations:

> . . . there is no reason why a driver should not continue to drive trains efficiently up to the age of 65.

Also in the Recommendations section was a requirement asking for the finding that the accident was the result of a transient medical condition. The report found that the risk of the same thing happening to other drivers was not great but recommended:

> Consideration must therefore be given to reducing even this risk.

The expression 'consideration must be given' is common in this kind of report as in the earlier Health and Safety Executive report *The Accident at Bentley Colliery*[7]:

> Consideration should be given to the more widespread use of locomotives such as the 'rack' and 'captive rail' types.

Using this formula a comment may be introduced which is outside the report's original remit but which has emerged in the investigation. In the Wembley Central example, the Recommendations will doubtless give rise to a further investigation on the medical feasibility of eliminating blood flow disorders in train drivers. In the Bentley Colliery case, there were doubtless engineering and geological factors which would need to be considered in a separate report.

Sometimes a writer might find it expedient to set out his Recommendations in a slightly different way. Bogdanor in his National Council for Educational Standards report, *Standards in Schools*[8], calls them 'Summary of Proposals':

1. Strengthen HM Inspectorate and re-institute cyclical inspections.
2. Secure a consensus between teachers, industrialists and government upon the skills with which schools should equip young people.
3. Establish standardised national tests for all children at the ages 9 and 13.
4. Require all local authorities to publish CSE, 'O' and 'A' level results . . .

Increasingly it is important to categorize recommendations. Rank Xerox internal audit reports do so in the form of a table (Figure 15).

Where responsibility is allocated as in public disasters, these can be categorized by time. The Herald of Free Enterprise report[9] divided them into:

IMMEDIATE ACTION
ACTION IN THE NEAR FUTURE
LONGER TERM RECOMMENDATIONS

The Recommendations in the Hillsborough interim report[10] are incorporated in its Chapter 24. There are 43 of them and about half are marked with an asterisk to denote that they should be carried out before the 1989/90 season, such as:

*7. All gates in radial or perimeter fences of pens or other self-contained areas should be painted in a different colour from the rest of the fence and marked 'Emergency Exit'.

Identification of Recommendations by a title with a number is used by the internal audit function of American International Underwriters. The text of these Recommendations is indented from both sides. The example also demonstrates a suitably forthright style for Recommendations.

RECOMMENDATION 1

The treatment of the operating expense recoveries needs to be adjusted. The recoveries should be used to reduce operating expenses and not be included as income.

Some house styles enclose such Recommendations in a box when they occur in the body of the text.

> *RECOMMENDATION E*
> It is recommended that . . .
> . . . .
> . . . .

Norman Le Cheminant, States Supervisor of the Guernsey Civil Service, has laid down a useful guideline for formulating Recommendations for Policy Letters.

Rec. No.	Recommendation	Description of Actions	Action Resp.	Completion Date
	Topic Heading 1			
1	XXXXXXXX XXXXXXXXXXX XXXXXXXX XXXXXXXXXXXXX XXXXX XXXXXXXXX XXXXXXXXX:- - XX XXXXXXXXX XXXXXXXX XXXXXXXX, - XXXXXXX XXXXXXXX XXXXXXXXXXX XXXXX - XXXXXXX XXXXXX, - XX XXXXXXXX XXXXXXXXXXX XXXXX XXXXXXX XXXXXXX.	1. XXXXX XXXXXXX XXXXX XXXXX XXXXXXXXXXXX XXXXX XXXXXXXX XXXX. 2. XXXXX XXXXXXX XXXXX XXXXX XXXXX XX XXXXXX XXX XX XXXXXXXX XXX. 3. XXXXX XXXXX XXX XXX XXXXXX XXXX XXXXX XX XXXXX XXX XX XXXXXXX XXX. 4. X XXX XXXXXX XXXXX XXXXXX XX XXXXXX XXX XX XXXXXXXXX XXX.	J Smith 	End Aug 99 End Sept 99 End Sept 99 End Oct 99
2	XXXXXXXX XXXXXXXXXX XXXXXXXXX XXXXXXXXXXX XXXXX XXXXXXXX XXXXXXXXX XXXXXXXXXXXXXXX XXXXX XXXXXXXXX XXXXX.	XXXXX XXXXXXX XXXXX XXXXX XXXXX XX XXXXX XXX XX XXXXXXXXX XXX.	J Smith	End June 99
3	XXXXXXXX XXXXXXXX XXXXXXXXXX XXXXX XXXXXXX XXXXXXXXXXX XXXXXXXX XXXXX XXXXXXXXX XXXXXXXXX XXXXXXXX XXXXX.	1. XXXXX XXXXX XXXXX XXXXX XX XXXXX XXX XX XXXXXXXXX XXX. 2. XXX XXXXX XXXXX XXXXX XX XXXXXX XXX XX XXXXXX XXXXX XXX XX XXXXXXXXX XXX.	J Smith A Miller	End July 99 End Oct 99
4	XXXXXXXX XXXXXXXXX XXXXXXXXXX XXXXX XXXXXXX XXXXXXXXXX XXXXX XXXXXXXXXX XXXXXXXXXX XXXXXXXX:- - XX XXXXX XXXXX XXXX XXX; - XXX XXXXX XXXX XXX; - XXXX XXXXX XXXX XXXX XXXXX XXXXX XXX; - XXXX XXXX XXX; - XX XXXX XXXX XXXXX XXXXX XXX.	1. X XX XXXXX XXX XX XXXXXXXXX XXX. 2. XXXXXX XXXXX XXXX XXXXXX XXXX XX XXXXXX XXX XX XXXXXXXXX XXX. 3. X XXXXX XX XXXXXX XXX XX XXXXXXXXX XXX.	J Smith 	End July 99 End Sept 99 End Oct 99

Figure 15 Format of Recommendations and Action Plan (Rank Xerox internal report)

These are a type of report presenting policy decisions for consideration and, it is hoped, agreement by the States.

Each policy letter should set out clearly the recommendations of the Committee on which a States decision is required.

It is good practice to formulate the recommendations so that, with appropriate minor alterations, they can form the proposition which is laid before the States by the Bailiff. The object of the recommendations must be to facilitate the taking of decisions. It is, therefore, for consideration in each case whether the decision can be encompassed in one Resolution or whether it might be better to break down the recommendations into smaller units so that different decisions can be taken on different aspects of the proposals without inviting amendments, which may cause difficulty later, or loss of the whole proposal.

There are two points in this which can be extrapolated to any report:

1. It is a good idea to formulate a recommendation so that it can provide the basis for action.
2. It is helpful to the reader to consider whether a recommendation will constitute the basis of one decision or whether it should be broken down into several recommendations.

SIGNATURE

All reports must bear some sort of signature. In many organizations initials will suffice for internal reports. The TSB report just discussed bears the initials and reference:

3160/12
KL

at the bottom left-hand corner of the cover sheet.

External documents produced by a professional firm will be signed by the name of the practice, indicating joint responsibility for the partnership:

Yours faithfully
PRICE WATERHOUSE

Precise authorship (for guidance within the issuing firm) will be denoted by the reference.

A document produced by a committee will frequently bear the names of the whole committee somewhere at the front, at the foot of the introductory section or possibly on a separate sheet. The report on the Challenger disaster carried the names of the Chairman and 12 members.

Typewritten documents carry a manuscript signature. In such cases it is important that the author's name, and usually appointment, should be typed underneath.

David Guard
Project Director

Some companies may have special signature requirements, such as the need for countersignature. Companies that are part of non-British groups may be subject to the laws or commercial law of other countries, for example German requires two signatures.

A few companies permit, or encourage, the issue of anonymous reports. There is little to be said for this mischievous and unhelpful practice.

DATE

A date must appear somewhere on the report. This serves two essential purposes:

1. It is a means (in addition to the reference) of distinguishing the document from others with a similar title.
2. It identifies the moment at which the report's comments are timed.

The time taken to prepare the report and the period it covers will suggest how precisely the date should be given. The great majority of reports will be timed to the day. Government Green and White Papers are usually dated to the month. A few documents, such as Civil Service College Occasional Papers, are dated to the year. On the other hand, shift reports, representing one of perhaps three shifts in a day, will be timed to the minute.

It would be dreary to catalogue all the different ways in which a date may be expressed. However, a word of caution is appropriate about all-figure dates such as:

5. 1. 1992

which would be interpreted as 5 January by a British reader and 1 May by an American. The month should be written in full even if only one copy is being sent to an American addressee.

With reports dated to the day there may be merit in inserting the date in ink. The month and year would be typed and the date inserted when the report is signed. This is a particularly good idea if there is a delay between typing and signature, as when:

1. The typing is done elsewhere.
2. The author's work is peripatetic so that he may be away from his office for some days.

What matters is the day on which the writer authorizes the document and associates himself formally with its contents. The date on which the typist chanced to type the date block is of little consequence and of no interest to the reader.

ACKNOWLEDGEMENTS

Many reports involve assistance from outside the originating organization. Acknowledgement must be made for this assistance. Sometimes it will appear as part of an Introduction. Often, if the assistance has come from many different sources, it will be necessary to put aside a separate section to do justice to this.

In other cases, such as the report of the Court of Inquiry into the Flixborough disaster[11], it appears at the end:

> We would finally like to acknowledge the assistance we received from a great number of people. It is not possible to list everybody but we would mention specially the following:
> 1. The parties represented before us together with their Counsel, Solicitors and expert advisers.
> 2. The witnesses both lay and expert.
> 3. Sir Frederick Warner, his staff and associates . . .

and so on for a list of 11 bodies, some described generally and some named specifically.

It is most important that the form of words should reflect in some measure the amount of help received. It should not become stereotyped and thus stale.

SUMMARY

The Conclusions and Recommendations are the end-product of the report-writing process. They should be brief but comprehensive. They must be derived from the body of the report and the Recommendations must follow directly and naturally from the Conclusions.

The difference between the Conclusions and Recommendations is one both of tone and of content. The Conclusions are descriptive and the Recommendations are suggestive. The reader should be able to look at each recommendation and decide whether to take action or not.

All reports should be dated. All should have a signature (or some other means of identifying authorship). Some will contain acknowledgements.

4 Appendices and other attachments

Attachments are a valuable way of removing detail from a report. The more common terms for describing them are: Attachments; Appendices; Annexes; Enclosures; Exhibits (in American-controlled companies). These expressions are roughly synonymous and choice of term is largely a matter of house style. Enclosures, however, are generally taken to be documents which are complete in themselves, such as other reports or a section of an Act of Parliament. Quite possibly the letter or memorandum setting out the terms of reference might be added in this way.

In the Worsley Report on the organization of the Institute of Chartered Accountants in England & Wales[1] the term Annex is used. In one case an annex has an attachment:

> Annex A shows the Membership and Terms of Reference of the Working Party.
>
> Annex B shows a joint statement of the Institute and CIPFA.
>   This is followed by an Attachment to Annex B, which sets out a Programme of Co-operation between the 2 bodies.

Some report writers must decide whether or not to include appendices or look for some alternative approach. Two questions should be asked:

1. *As to relevance*: does it add useful detail? If not, leave it out.
2. *As to extent*: does it endorse or helpfully expand some generalized claim? If it just repeats information that appears in the body of the report leave it out.

Some systems use appendices as sub-divisions of annexes. Figure 16 shows an example of this. Great care must be taken to ensure:

1. That such an elaborate system is justified before it is used.
2. That the appendices do stem from the annexes as is shown in this obvious geographical illustration.

Annex 1:   Staff strengths Scotland
        Appendix A: Glasgow staff by grade,
                       sex and age
        Appendix B: Aberdeen staff by grade,
                       sex and age
        Appendix C: Inverness staff by grade,
                       sex and age

Annex 2:   Staff strengths Midlands
        Appendix A: Leicester staff by grade,
                       sex and age
        Appendix B: Nottingham staff by grade,
                       sex and age
        Appendix C: Birmingham staff by grade,
                       sex and age
        Appendix D: Walsall staff by grade,
                       sex and age

Figure 16   The use of Appendices and sub-divisions of annexes

REQUIREMENTS FOR ALL ATTACHMENTS

With all attachments, however they may be described, four points must always be remembered;

Lettering or numbering

They must he allocated letters (as in the case of the Communication Studies and Planning Ltd/Equal Opportunities Commission Ltd report on women's employment discussed earlier[2]): Annex A, B, C, etc. Alternatively they may be given Arabic numbers as in the case of Health and Safety Executive reports. Some companies use Roman numerals.

Letters and Roman numerals have the advantage that they do not get muddled with paragraph numbers. Care should be taken with Roman numbering in reports with numerous attachments, as many junior clerical staff are not familiar with many Roman numerals.

The letters (or numbers) must be allotted in the order in which they are mentioned in the text as this will enable the reader to keep moving his book-mark or thumb down through the attachments as he reads. Spurious numbering of attachments is misleading and unhelpful.

A useful system of appendix numbering is used in the Kuwait/BP report as demonstrated in Figure 17. The first number in each case indicates the chapter in which reference is made. The second number does not indicate the sub-para-

Contents

Figure 17   Table of Contents with list of appendices

graph. Thus Appendix 3.4 is a cross-reference to Chapter 3 but not to sub-paragraph 3.4.

Mentioning

They must be mentioned in the report itself. They are supplementary to the main core of the report. They may, perhaps, deal with specialist or esoteric matters. Thus as they sit on the fringe of affairs, if the reader's attention is not drawn to them he may never see them.

A note in brackets may be used. A water-treatment consultancy report includes the sentence:

> The tests we made (see appendix 1) indicate that more data is required, for it could be that the system is picking up hardness, from previously deposited scale.

The Neill report on Lloyd's says

> These are set out in Schedule 7 to the Act (the text of which is quoted in Appendix 3)[3]

It is often more comfortable to integrate the cross-reference into the sentence as in this extract from the Clapham Junction report:

> As can be seen in Appendix K.2 there are only 4 signals which a train must pass on the Up Main Line from Earlsfield before coming to Clapham Junction station.[4]

It may be more precise, as in the Flixborough disaster report[5]:

> Many of the stainless steel pipes taken from the disaster site had suffered cracking due to a process of embrittlement caused by zinc. The zinc had come into contact with the steel whilst it was under stress and elevated temperature. The conditions under which such embrittlement can occur are described in Appendix II.

Sometimes the references can point specifically to a part of the Appendix, as in the Hillsborough Final report[6]

> (See also Recommendation 16 of the report of the Technical Working Party at Appendix 3.)

and

> Accordingly I consider that when perimeter fencing is used it should not exceed a prescribed maximum height and all spike arrangements and top sections angled inwards should go. This view is in accord with the recommendations of the Technical Working Party (Appendix 3 paragraph 20).

Listing

They must be listed in or immediately after the table of contents. Figure 18 shows the list from an Organization for Economic Co-operation and Development report on traffic control.[7]

If there is no list of contents they should be itemized at the foot of the report.

Figure 18   List of Appendices

Apart from being a guide to the reader, such a list acts as an instruction to the functionary who staples or binds the report. Some report writers find this a tedious or tiresome measure. On many occasions, when this has not been done, the wrong sections have been appended to the report. In the list the attachments should be described minutely and precisely in their titles. This will include date (and reference numbers) where one exists, as in the County NatWest report: Appendix 4. Agency agreement between NWIB and CNW dated 1 June 1987.[8]

It will also mention the scale and sheet title of a map or plan.

INDEPENDENCE OF THE REPORT

The report must be able to stand on its own without the attachments. Figure 19 demonstrates this important point graphically. Consider Figure 19 (a) as a schematic representation of the report and its attachments. It must be possible to start from the introduction, follow through the body, agree with the conclusions and accept the recommendations as in Figure 19 (b) without reading the attachments as in Figure 19 (c), unless the reader's whim or specialization takes him there. For this purpose, it may be necessary to produce short two- or three-sentence summaries of the contents of the attachments. These summaries can then be incorporated into the main report so that it will stand on its own.

As attachments are so commonly used to remove detail it will be helpful to look at the way some report producers have used them:

The Hillsborough interim report[9]

This demonstrates ideal use of appendices. In summary, Appendix 1 was a map giving an overview of the Sheffield Wednesday football ground at which the disaster had taken place and the surrounding streets. Appendix 4 was an extended and more detailed plan of the relevant West Terrace. Appendices 2 and 3 were general photographs of parts of the stadium and Appendix 5 was a photograph of a particular episode in the tragedy. Appendix 6 described specific episodes and individuals' accounts which gave exceptional views of the events or were of unusual poignancy.

In his final report[10] Lord Justice Taylor includes further photographs of both British and continental grounds. He also quotes from other reports in his appendices, including Mr Justice Popplewell's report on the events at the Bradford and Birmingham grounds.

The Scarman Report[11]

Lord Scarman uses five appendices:

1. A brief history of the inquiry, with particular reference to the visits to Brixton and other places and the hearings.
2. A detailed (13-page) description of Scarman's peregrinations around Brixton, Birmingham, Coventry, Liverpool and so on, and including the discussions which he had and the impressions made on him by social groups and individuals.

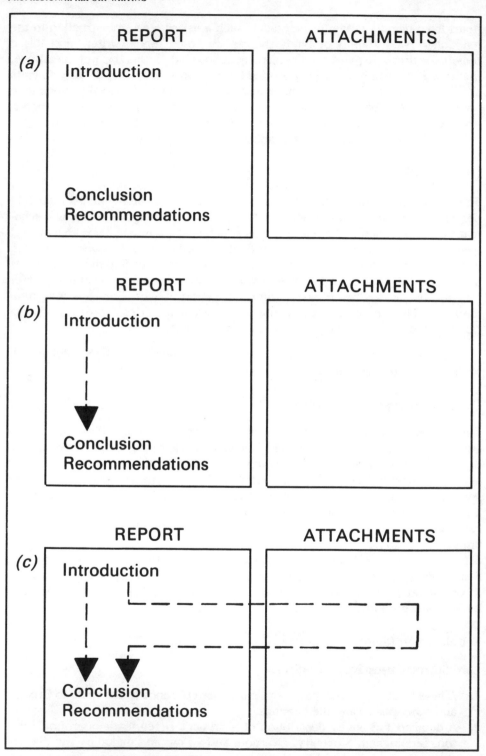

Figure 19   Schematic representation of the report and its appendices

3. A list of those giving evidence in various ways.
4. A bibliography.
5. A detailed fold-out street map of Brixton showing every house.

The Kingman Report

In the Kingman report on standards of English teaching[12] the terms of reference occupy the whole of appendix 1, with three numbered points:

1. To recommend a model of the English language, whether spoken or written, which . . .
2. To recommend the principles which should guide teachers on how far and in what ways the model should be made explicit to pupils to make them conscious of how language is used in a range of contexts.
3. To recommend what, in general terms, pupils need to know about how the language works and in consequence what they should have been taught, and be expected to understand, on this score, at ages 7, 11 and 16.

American International Underwriters

The internal audit section of the international group American International Underwriters make extensive use of Appendices. As the main reports are numerous and complex, it is important to keep them short as they have to be read in large numbers by senior readers. Their routine calls for

> Appendix I: Summary of Recommendations
> Appendix II: Prior Recommendations

after which a variety of other appendices may follow according to the subject matter.

The Prior Recommendations in each Appendix II are categorized as:

> Implemented
> Partially Implemented
> Not Implemented

The system is reminiscent of other audit systems. For example in the Internal Audit Reports prepared by Price Waterhouse on their clients' internal administration, the covering letter regularly states that Price Waterhouse: 'are delighted to note that Recommendations 1 to 9 in our last report have been implemented but are sorry to see that Recommendation 10 has been outstanding since 1987'.

The Peacock Report

This Home Office report on the financing of the BBC[13] uses an appendix for biographies of its Committee. A similar expedient is used in proposals and new business reports by consultancies and similar professions to outline the background and competence of their staff proposed for a new assignment.

AFTER NOTE

In exceptional cases information may have to be added as it arises. The Jockey Club report on the 1989 St Leger meeting[14] has a short addendum after the closing signatures. After this report had been agreed a written statement was received from Mr Cook in which he said, amongst other things:

> About two and half furlongs out, Madraco dropped in front and tried unsuccessfully to recover his footing. This happened in a split second. He lost his action in front, his off fore. He temporarily tried to recover but could not and went down. I did not hear a crack either before or after the accident.

In the light of the contents the Committee saw no reason to change its views.

It is significant that the Committee felt that it was appropriate to include this item from the jockey – who had earlier refrained from giving evidence for legal reasons – in the interests of completeness; even though it did not change their findings.

DETAILED FIELDWORK

In many cases detailed fieldwork will be set out as a series of attachments. The principal items will then be discussed in the main body of the report. The second of Lord Scarman's appendices is along these lines. The point assumes greater significance in scientific reports.

In some reports the results of the research will be considered too important for relegation to an attachment. It may be considered absolutely germane to the argument.

If there is any question of a series of reports, consistency is particularly important. Johnson Matthey Chemicals, the metallurgists, generally require all experimental work to appear in the main paper. They suggest the following material as suitable for appendices in this sort of work:

1. Results that are negative.
2. Unsatisfactory routes.
3. Side, or quasi-relevant, routes.
4. Associated relevant documents.
5. Duty specifications.

On the other hand, in non-scientific reports, a separate attachment explaining the method of working and sampling may be suitable. Such an example is the sole appendix, 'Method and tests of significance', to the 119-page Building Research Establishment report, *Bracknell and Its Migrants*[15].

BIBLIOGRAPHIES AND REFERENCE LISTS

References may well take the form of one of the attachments, as in the Scarman report. However, their particular form of presentation calls for special mention.

References will be quoted in a report for three reasons:

1. As a courtesy to the source author.
2. To guide the reader in further investigation.
3. To substantiate a questionable claim in the report.

The amount of direction the reader needs must be borne in mind when the layout of the detail is devised. It may take several forms.

1. A list of books and reports just showing author/originator, date and publisher (if published) to which general reference has been made, thus:

   ENVIRONMENTAL POLLUTION, ROYAL COMMISSION ON. Tenth report: Tackling Pollution – Experience and Prospects. Cmnd 9149 [Chairman: Sir Richard Southwood] viii + 130 pp; HMSO London, 1984 (ISBN 0 10 191490 3)

   The page references here are totals, i.e. II (xi) introductory pages and 233 proper pages.
   Reference numbers of the documents are important as in[16]:

   (1) Department of the Environment, *File* WS/646/56 Paper SCA/4.41
   (2) Hunt D T E, Filtration of Water Samples for Trace Metal Determinations, Water Research Centre *Technical Report* TR 104, 1979
   (3) Department of the Environment, *File* WS/646/56. Paper SCA/4.4/2
   (4) Standing Committee of Analysts, Atomic Absorption Spectrophotometry – an Essay Review, HMSO, London 1980[21]

   and from the controversial report *The Health Divide*[17]:

   90 Carstairs V, **Small area analysis and health service research** Community Med. *3*, 131–139, 1981
   91 Redfern P. **Profile of Our Cities** Population Trends *30*, 21–32, 1982
   92 Greater Glasgow Health Board **Ten Year Report** 1974–1983 Greater Glasgow Health Board 1984.

   Scarman[18] quoted 75 documents which had been 'available to the Inquiry', such as:

   ALDERSON, John 'Policing Freedom', McDonald and Evans, 1979.
   ANDERTON, Bill 'Police and Community: a review article' – in New Community, Vol. III, No 3, Summer 1974

2. A number of more detailed cross-references giving paragraph or even line[19]:

   Wright, P. Pointing the way to the ideal terminal. Computer Weekly, 20th September 1979, p. 24
   AUEW (TASS) and National Computing Centre. Computer Technology and Employment. Manchester, 1979 p. 105

3. Sometimes the referencing may be taken a stage further, with the reference list including back references to the main paper[20]:

   LAMBERT P (1976): Perinatal mortality: social and environmental trends *4* 4–8 (3.1.1)

   The 3.1.1 refers to the sub-sub-paragraph of the report alluding to the Lambert paper.

   There are two ways of including mention of the referenced document in the main report.

   (a) The name of the author and date is given in brackets in the text (the Harvard system), e.g.[21]:

> The test described here is essentially a modification of a technique described as applicable to the diagnosis of viral diseases (Bradstreet and Taylor 1962) and may be found particularly convenient in laboratories already undertaking viral complement fixation test.

The full title is then shown in the reference list:[22]

> Bradstreet & Taylor C.M.P. & Taylor CED (1962). Technique of complacent-fixation test applicable to the diagnosis of virus diseases. Monthly Bulletin of the Ministry of Health and the Public Health Laboratory *21*,96

(b) Alternatively just a number can be inserted in the text, e.g.[23]:

> In the Metropolitan Police District the statutory provision for accountability is different. Very briefly, the Secretary of State is the Police Authority and the Commissioner, who is appointd by the Sovereign, is the Chief Officer of Police(1).

The note (1) will be explained as a footnote:[24]

> 1 Section 62 and Schedule 8 of the 1964 Act and Sections 1, 4 and 5 of the Metropolitan Police Act 1829 (as later amended.)

or as a reference in a list at the end. The wider problems of footnotes are discussed later.

Provided the author's name (or, more difficult, authors' names or the name of a professional body) is reasonably short, the Harvard system is preferable. With such an arrangement it will often be unnecessary for the reader to turn to the bibliography. It is not used here because the references to source material are mixed with other note information.

The complementary list of references is best placed at the end of the whole document where it can be found easily and quickly. If there are only a few they may be placed at the foot of the relevant page. The reader can then see them without turning over. Preparation of a report in this way is time-consuming, as it calls for careful calculation by the wordprocessor operator during production. Some, such as the Challenger report, list the references at the end of each section or chapter. This compels the reader to use a bookmark in the relevant reference page.

In general, reference should not be made to documents which are not likely to be available to the readership either through the document being out of print or of restricted distribution through confidentiality.

The mechanics and specifics of both schemes are further explained (along with other useful points) in an admirable little booklet published by The Royal Society called *General Notes on the Preparation of Scientific Papers*[25].

It is desirable to distinguish between specific References and Further Reading. The latter is just a general bibliography. The Church of England's report *Not Just for the Poor* does this extremely well, carefully segregating the notes into chapters.

FOOTNOTES

The need to avoid distraction from the main drift of the report is particularly relevant to footnotes. Sometimes they will be inevitable:

1. To show a reference.
2. To clarify a term.
3. To amplify a point with detail which is insufficient to justify an appendix. The author should ask these questions:
   (a) Is the information necessary?
   (b) Could it be contained in the main script of the report?
   (c) Is it best placed at the foot of the page or on an attachment at the back?

Solution of the last problem is easier when a report is to be printed or produced on a desk top publishing system. The smaller print-sizes available enable the footnotes to take up less room and be less obtrusive. With typewritten documents a note of more than four or five lines intrudes into the script and disturbs the flow of reading, thus defeating the object of relegating the detail to a footnote. Some of the novels of Sir Walter Scott are particularly irritating in this way. The need for speed of reference must be balanced with the distraction of massive notes on the same page.

Dame Mary Warnock's report makes excellent and modest use of footnotes. There are never more than three on a page and most pages do not have them. A handful of definitions, items of a legal nature and a few references are helpfully placed in a small but legible typeface where the reader can find them without turning pages.

SUMMARY

The theme of this chapter has been the need to maintain the reader's interest in the subject. The more attachments, footnotes and other encumbrances there are, the greater the danger of distraction. Yet it must be acknowledged that people receiving copies of the report have different levels of interest. They will read at varying speeds and in varying detail.

Summaries and abstracts can ensure that the glancing reader picks up what is important. The writer can highlight the points that are important for him to take away. It is not left to chance that the reader might overlook important points.

Specialists and those who wish to work in detail must have the opportunity to pursue the topic in greater depth if they wish. The attachments and the signposts of the bibliography and footnotes will give them this opportunity, while leaving the main argument intact and comprehensible.

5   Choosing words

'Language is our most precious instrument' says Arnold Wesker[1]. He goes on to explain the wonderful and dreadful things that have been achieved by language. People can be encouraged, rebuked and seriously misled, either by accidental misuse or deliberate manipulation of the language.

In many societies competence in a particular language can lead to professional advancement. Lack of fluency can be disastrous[2]. Some cultures and religions place great importance on the minute accuracy of their holy works and guiding moral treatises. The Koran is the best example: Arabic as the language of God is the only vehicle for these divine pronouncements[3]. The precise wording of the Koran has, therefore, an importance unequalled in the holy texts of any other religion. However, the obstacles that were encountered by early translations of the Bible into vernacular languages illustrate similar problems[4]. As late as 1903 riots in Greece accompanied a new translation of the Bible[5].

It is impossible to pursue this study further without tackling the all-important and enthralling subject of words. This is not an optional sidetrack to the main theme of report writing but a vital component. Words are the raw material of a report. A report cannot exist without them. Even a report that consists largely of diagrams and tables must depend on words for its fluency. The illustrations must have headings. The axes must be marked. The variables must be labelled. All the illustrations must, indeed, be glued together with words. The Balance of Payments is a document of about 70 pages in length[6]. Of these, most are closely packed tables, yet words are needed to explain the numbers and to reconcile apparent anomalies and contradictions between tables.

It is words that elevate human communication above that of the animals[7]. Perhaps more important, it is words that limit human expression. There are many figures of speech which highlight this restriction: 'It defied description' or 'It was beyond words'. The third of Philip Howard's five volume set of semantic essays is aptly named *Words Fail Me*[8].

LANGUAGE AS A REFLECTION OF COMMUNICATORY NEEDS

Various languages show how their needs are reflected in language. Ewe (an African language of Togoland) and certain Amerindian languages satisfy themselves with the same word for 'yesterday' and 'tomorrow', i.e. not today[9]. The people of Lesu in the Pacific have at least 12 words for 'pig' indicating different aspects such as colour, sex and so on, as pigs are particularly important in their society[10]. The Yanomami, in common with most other Latin American peoples, lack sophisticated counting systems and acknowledge only 'one', 'two' and 'more-than-two'[11]. The kind of economic pressures which prevail in even simple European societies have no relevance in their culture.

To achieve the most accurate transmission of ideas, as rich a language and vocabulary as possible is desirable. English has the richest vocabulary of any language using the Roman alphabet[12].

THE DIFFERENCE OF EVERY WORD

English has some quarter of a million words in current use. (Half a million are shown in the new edition of the *Oxford English Dictionary* but they include many words which are defunct. Those which were once current now only feature as puzzling curiosities in the TV programme 'Call My Bluff' or Philip Howard's column on the back page of *The Times*.)

No two words mean exactly the same thing. Consider the difference between the following words:

The Chairman was {
sorry
appalled
outraged
ashamed
furious
vexed
upset
perturbed
surprised
astonished
} to hear of the results

Guides to managerial communication sometimes produce lists of words and phrases that are desirable and undesirable, sometimes even dividing these into such titles as 'English' and 'Businessese'[13]. This is to avoid the issue. Every word has its uses.

One such guide[14] produces two columns: 'Business English' and 'Good English'. It is suggested that 'letter' is to be preferred to 'communication', 'want' or 'wish' to 'desire', 'clear' to 'apparent'. There are undoubtedly many situations when this may be so. To suggest that they are interchangeable is surely misleading, however.

In principle there are no true synonyms in English. If they do exist for a short time, as a result of an inrush of foreign vocabulary or through careless or thoughtless use for a number of years, either their meanings are likely to diverge or one of them will fall into disuse.

THE VALUE OF EVERY WORD

If every word means something slightly different, then every word must count for something. Cyril Connolly has pointed out:

> The perfect use of language is that in which every word carries the meaning that it is intended to, no more and no less.[15]

Few managers treat their vocabulary – one of the most valuable assets available to an English-speaking executive – with the care that they would accord to their staff or their product. Report writing should not be a necessary evil to managers. It is an opportunity to express decisions, attitudes, values and priorities to colleagues, customers and others with whom they deal. Precision of words is required. Generalization and inaccuracy have no place in word choice for reports. Philip Howard writes of the 'common and deplorable pattern of blunting the precision of a word by firing it from a blunderbuss instead of a rifle in the hope of hitting everything in sight'[16].

'Verbally', derived from Latin 'verbum' (word), traditionally and etymologically means having to do with words. In recent years a secondary sense has developed, referring to the spoken as opposed to the written word. There can be no harm in this. It is a natural drift in the use of the language. The reader may have a problem, however, if faced with the following sentence in an auditor's report (from the Bank of America):

> No significant criticisms were noted during our review and minor items were verbally brought to the management's attention.

Were the items expressed by use of words (as in the first sense) – perhaps, in this context, as opposed to numbers – or specifically by the spoken word (as in the second and more restricted sense)?

A first-class example of the value and use of every word occurs in this passage from a Colt Car Company report comparing vehicles of various makes:

> The tallest Importer Representatives naturally, complained about accommodation, although they agreed that there was an improvement. I felt that in the search for space, the seating padding was marginal and *may* lead to complaints sagging.

The tallest representatives have been commenting adversely on the inside of the car. The word 'naturally', which may seem insignificant, is absolutely essential to a proper appreciation of this paragraph of the report. The single word makes it quite clear that their comments – while not invalid – were very much the result of their great height. Those of more conventional build would be unlikely to be inconvenienced.

THE DIRECTIONS OF MOVEMENT IN THE LANGUAGE

If a language, in which every word counts for so much, is to reflect the writer's needs so precisely, it must perforce develop and evolve to take account of things that he wants to describe. English, a magnificently dynamic and uninhibited language, develops in two directions, as shown in Figure 20.

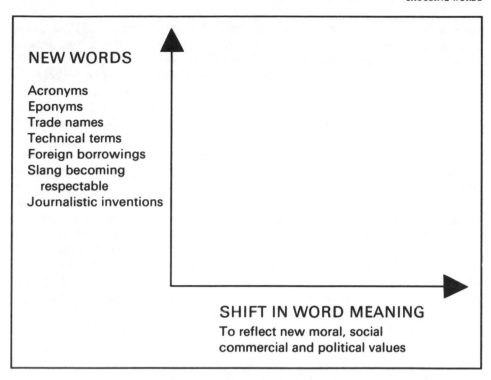

NEW WORDS

Acronyms
Eponyms
Trade names
Technical terms
Foreign borrowings
Slang becoming
    respectable
Journalistic inventions

SHIFT IN WORD MEANING
To reflect new moral, social
commercial and political values

Figure 20   Directions of development in the English language

Language is expanding all the time. Dr Robert Burchfield, former Chief Editor of the Oxford Dictionaries, estimates that English adds 460 words a year, more than one a day. Some new words are the work of manufacturers, through the currency of the market names of their products or through technical expressions achieving widespread use. 'Teleconferencing' is now a well accepted function of which much use was made in compiling the Challenger report. 'Contraflow' has been born of the need to carry out extensive maintenance on motorways now that they are into their third decade. 'Faction', a straightforward agglutination of 'fact' and 'fiction', describes an increasingly popular type of TV drama. The events, usually of a period of recent history, are amplified by fictional episodes and putative conversations of the protagonists. At Heathrow and other airports a 'travelator' is a welcome amenity for those with heavy luggage, or not much energy.

Analogy produces many useful new terms. The ending '-ise' (or '-ize') enabled report writers to describe the Thatcher Government's wish to 'privatize' extensive parts of nationalized industries. Similarly '-ism' gives 'entryism', a technique of covert political infiltration by extremists (who are, of course, engaged in 'extremism'). A local transport executive preparing reports on 'ridership' is following the pattern set by 'horsemanship', 'statesmanship', and so on. Some such formations are humorous and many are not intended to stay the course.

The formation of verbs and adjectives from nouns is well established. Sometimes imaginative wordsmiths coin other parts of speech from prepositions. The word 'outing', meaning the act of coming out and announcing homosexual preferences by public figures, has achieved currency during the summer of 1990[17]. After Watergate, the ending '-gate' produced a plethora of entertaining if ephemeral terms and has continued to do so. For example, the Westland saga of 1986 threw up both 'Brittangate' (a short-lived term after Sir Leon Brittan, then Secretary of State for Trade and Industry) and the more durable 'Westlandgate'. The enthusiasm for the word 'quango' when the Conservative party opened the quango-hunting season in the late 1970s gave rise to the more fanciful 'quangocrat', 'quangocracy' and 'quangology'.

The introduction of eponymous words, frequently by accident, has always been entertaining. A 'mae west' was named after a film actress who was built in a way which suggested she was wearing a life jacket. The verb to 'boycott' is derived from the wretched experiences of Captain Boycott, a land agent in Ireland, in 1880. His problems with the estate he managed were brief, but the impact was such that this unhappy term has survived and led a useful life. It is intriguing to reflect that among British political leaders (but *cf.* Bonapartism), Margaret Thatcher is the only one to have given her name to a political philosophy and thus to coin an eponymous noun, 'Thatcherism'. The formation of such adjectives is commonplace as 'Gaitskellite', 'Heathite', 'Wilsonian'. If these are used as a noun form, it is as an extended adjective as in a Heathite supporter.

Lewis Carroll's invention of the word 'chortle' as a fusion of 'chuckle' and 'snort' has had more recent imitators. For instance Anita Brookner in her 1984 Booker Prizewinning novel *Hotel du Lac* contrived the word 'puttered' somewhere between 'potter' and the onomatopoeic 'putt-putt' of an engine[18].

Trade names and proprietary words have made an important contribution to the precision of the language. Sometimes there is understandable opposition by manufacturers to general use of their specific terminologies. Burroughs Wellcome have defended their term 'tabloid' by legal process and Bernard Levin has described Ansafone's irritation with irregular use of that title in a *Times* feature entitled 'Gradual Acceptance of Answer Phones'[19].

New words are easy to detect, and often startle the reader by their informality. It is therefore easy for report writers to distance their work from new, trendy or excessively modish vocabulary. The shift in word meaning is, however, less obvious and therefore more dangerous. The subtle changes are not so evident as the introduction of new expressions or senses in media or in technology. A few examples will illustrate the point. A quarter of a century ago, the adjective 'imperial' was an epithet of splendour or magnificence. Even the word 'colonial' was functional and neutral. Now all writers will reflect carefully before choosing either word. 'Obscene' meant, in about 1960, sexually lewd or offensive to chastity. Since then it has become a popular term to describe attitudes that are widely different from the writer's. The term 'picket' has a traditional and legal meaning referring to someone who goes to a workplace and discourages people from going in. It now has a much wider implication of someone involved generally and even peripherally in an industrial dispute. The original meaning of 'censure' as being an opinion of any kind has tightened to mean an adverse (and now 'censorious') opinion[20]. 'Orchestrate' is slowly achieving a derogatory meaning, which means that it must be employed with care. Some time ago Peter Jenkins expressed fears that the hitherto innocent 'moderation' and 'pragmatism' were going the same way[21]. More recently, the adverb 'seriously' has adopted a wider colloquial meaning (as in 'seriously' rich). The erstwhile Chancellor of the Exchequer, Mr Nigel Lawson, may have irreparably stretched the word 'blip' when he used it at the 1988 Conservative Party Conference to describe a then apparently temporary movement in inflation and interest rates.

EEC regulations provide an interesting example. The zeal of the late 1970s and early 1980s call for member-nations to 'harmonize' their standards. The late 1980s produced more pragmatic 'approximate'.

Some interesting developments in this field are to be seen in the area of racial terms. A more cautious approach to the use of racial terms has been evident lately. This reflects the urgency of the need for more tolerant attitudes in a multi-racial society. In South Africa, the term 'kaffir' has become actionable in some areas[22].

It is desirable to keep track of new developments. This is possible through many books. The *Longman Guardian Original Selection of New Words* was intended to be the pilot of a series. In early January 1989 a second in the sequence appeared entitled the *Longman Register of New Words*. It has now settled with the timetable of appearing every three years. A comparable work was published in Australia in 1990: *The Macquarie Dictionary of New Words*.

Although these works make report writers aware of the changes, it is necessary to make a judgement on the acceptability of both new words and new meanings of old words. Clearly reports must no more be written in Victorian English than they would be written in the Middle English of Chaucer[23]. The report writer, however conservative, cautious or staid his approach to business, must keep abreast of developments. It is no more and no less than keeping up with fashion. Failing to do so will make the report – and thus the organization – appear dowdy, out-of-date and reactionary.

Most continental countries have academies which give prescriptive guidance on currency of word choice. This rather patronizing approach has had little appeal in the UK – despite a flirtation with the idea about 1712 – and the answer is the descriptive approach of the dictionary.

THE OXFORD ENGLISH DICTIONARY

The great watershed in the development of dictionaries was the production of the *New English Dictionary*, later renamed the *Oxford English Dictionary (OED)*. In its original form this monumental task was completed in 1928, having started in about 1857[24]. The precise starting point cannot be determined as the enterprise was beset by financial problems and disputes as to scope, before the Philological Society and Oxford University Press reached a firm business arrangement. The protagonists were Frederick Furnival, a brilliant man of eccentric habits and a lack of tact which frequently jeopardized the whole undertaking, and Dr (later Sir) James Murray, a Scotsman of enormous vision and dedication. Murray's puritan way of life and great industry enabled him to work long hours in his scriptorium, a large garden shed stuffed with citations from diverse sources. By 1879 he had assembled one and three quarter tons of material. By 1881 he had 800 readers, one of whom had submitted 100 000 quotations[25]. Murray's contribution to the use of words cannot be overstated. In particular he is responsible for the proper historical analysis of word meaning. His personal strength of character prevented the great dictionary being abbreviated into a shorter, less comprehensive work which would have been more convenient to the financiers of the Oxford University Press.

The length of time taken to prepare an entry was formidable. For instance, to prepare the entry on the suffix '-ing', Murray took three weeks of research and two weeks of writing.

The size and depth of the OED is unparalleled in lexicography. Professor Randolph Quirk says: 'no one can form an adequate impression of the great Oxford Dictionary from a mere description'[26]. The first edition of the dictionary comprises 12 volumes, and the fourth and final volume of the Supplement was published during the summer of 1986.

The dictionary was republished in March 1989. The Oxford lexicographers had to address the problem of where to go next once the last of the four volumes of the Supplement was completed. They contemplated keeping the Supplement separate and republishing it at periodic intervals, but this was rejected on the grounds that it was cumbersome for readers to have to consult two books each in alphabetical order to find a word or sense.

The new edition has been produced in a time-frame permitted by the computer, a new arrangement of the existing data with some additions. The Supplement's words are inserted into the main sequence. Some 5000 new words have been added. Important modifications have been made to presentation of pronunciation, spellings and some other aspects. It has been described as easier to read and more forthright in condemning words which are racially offensive.

New additions near the beginning of the dictionary include those such as 'alien' (in the sense of from another planet) and 'disinformation' (with its origins in 1932) which are older than the average age of the new additions at the end (such as 'toy boy' and 'yuppification'). The first volumes of the Supplement were published some time before the last (A–G in 1972 and H–N in 1976). So great is the current interest in words, word usage and word development that Oxford University Press has a hot line for enquiries on such topics. It is called OWLS, an acronym for Oxford English Dictionary Word and Language Service[27].

One of Murray's greatest contributions to an understanding of language is shown in Figure 21[28]. It shows a hard core of English beyond which lie the vocabularies of an infinite number of specialisms. Regionalisms can be broken down into English regionalisms, few of which will be suitable for reports, and Commonwealth regionalisms, many of which will be appropriate in certain documents. These can, of course, be further broken into South African English, Canadian English, Australian English, and so on. Yet again, different parts of, say, Australia will produce different standard words. The diversity of American English, for instance between New England and Georgia, is even more pronounced.

British users of the language are becoming increasingly aware of Australian usages. The word 'interstate' (as an adjective) clearly has a local application when referring travel or distribution throughout the various states of the big island. On the other hand 'simulcast', meaning simultaneous broadcasting on two or more channels at the same time, appears to be the creation of the Australian Broadcasting Corporation. Yet it may soon come to have a wider use. The Australian use of 'privatization' is wider than the British use. It covers the buying up of shares in a family company to the exclusion of outside investors.

One detailed dictionary of American slang[29] shows a diagram covering slang

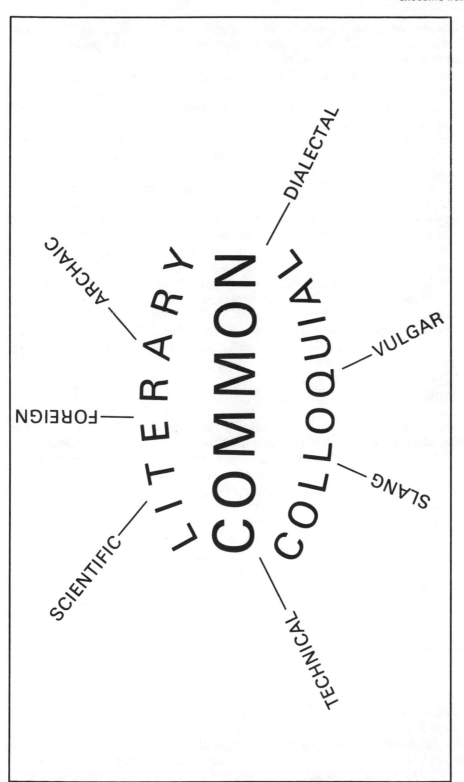

Figure 21   Murray's diagram of the scope of the English language

variations. The thirteen petals to the diagram cover such areas as the cant of narcotic addicts, hobos and tramps and also more respectable jargons such as those of soldiers and railway workers.

Many further extensions of Murray's diagram can be drawn for all the professions involved in report writing. Architects, bankers, chartered accountants, chemists, lawyers, nuclear physicists all have their own special argots. Further subdivisions of, for example, accountants into the specialist parlance of auditors, insolvency accountants, tax inspectors and so on can be devised. Likewise, there are constitutional lawyers, criminal lawyers and specialists in divorce and family law. Murray's diagram can be expanded as shown in Figure 22.

The need to deal carefully with these esoteric and sometimes arcane terms is covered in Chapter 6.

Dictionaries give a clear – and indeed the only – guide as to what vocabulary can reasonably be used in a layperson's report as at that dictionary's date of publication. There are four British dictionaries in the middle size category and the first rank of scholarship. The middle size is suggested since the larger dictionaries such as the *OED* and the *Shorter Oxford English Dictionary*[30] are too large for office use. They also cast the net too wide to provide accurate definitions of terms used in management reports. The very small dictionaries are admirable for checking spelling or rudimentary word differences. As they often have only room to define one word with another, they do not really provide the precision which is so essential to word distinction.

CONCISE OXFORD DICTIONARY

It is appropriate to start with the *Concise Oxford Dictionary (COD)*[31], the doyen of middle-sized dictionaries. It is based on the source material amassed for the OED and its supplement and the supporting work by its readers in the Bodleian Library and elsewhere. The first edition came out in 1911 when the *New English Dictionary* had only reached 'Sc'. In the earlier editions slight differences could be discerned between the style and presentation of the definitions up to 'Sc' and those for the later letters. As the Fowler brothers who edited the first *COD* were working in Guernsey, they did not have access to Dr Murray's source material in Oxford[32].

There has been a total of eight editions of the *COD*, the most recent being in 1990. Addenda are published between editions and, as with other dictionaries, the pages of addenda give an intriguing insight into social, commercial and technical developments of the relevant period. The addenda of 117 words added in November 1978 was the most recent, the later editions having no addenda[33]. It included 'ACAS', 'chairperson', 'devolution' (in the political sense), 'index-linked', 'MLR', 'mountain' (in the sense of butter mountain, etc.), 'Ostpolitik'.

The word 'quango' was rapidly assimilated. Its currency in the press dates from early 1978, although Oxford Dictionaries have citations from 1976 (and American references from as early as 1973). A slang introduction in the same addenda was to 'go bananas'. It is entertaining to speculate what this indicates about social trends of the period.

The eighth edition, published in the summer of 1990, sought to be less academically daunting with 'emphasis on ease of use and coverage of contemporary English'. The editors also set out to reduce the amount of nesting of entries

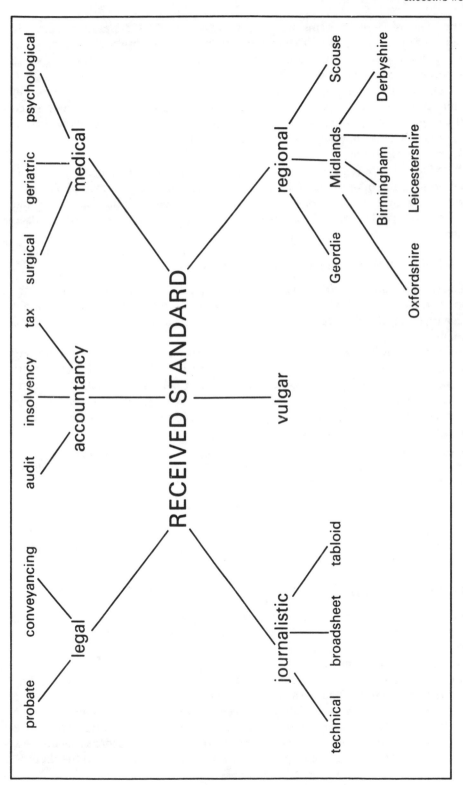

Figure 22   Parts of possible 1992 variation of Murray's diagram

(embedding of derived forms under a headword). This separation certainly makes it easier to read. It still retains a rather cautious approach to change in meaning. For instance the definitions of 'unique', 'hopefully' and 'bullish' are not as generous as in many other dictionaries.

The staff of Oxford dictionaries appreciate a greater interest in dictionaries and an increasing pace in supporting advertising. A computer has been in use since 1980 and this obviously enables updating to be carried out more quickly. Extensive use is still made, however, of a fascinating card-index system which is the heir of Murray's scriptorium.

The editors do not see the dictionary as particularly conservative. It is, however, less bold than the other three in its extension into the outer reaches of Murray's diagram in Figure 20. It does not embrace the Miltonian, Shakespearean and Scottish usages of Chambers. It stops short of many of the more esoteric words in Collins or Longmans.

CHAMBERS' TWENTIETH CENTURY DICTIONARY

Chambers is produced in Edinburgh. It therefore, quite reasonably, includes more Scottish regionalisms than the others. It also gives more archaic and defunct senses than they do. The report writer must make up his mind if he needs this kind of detail.

Although it may appear peripheral to the field of report writing, it is worth noting that the *Chambers Twentieth Century*[34] is the official reference dictionary for the National Scrabble Championship. Indeed, the editor personally adjudicates at the principal national and regional competitions. This is relevant as it indicates the character and scope of the book. In particular, words linger in Chambers. Betty Kirkpatrick, its former editor, writes:

> Removing words . . . is a perilous exercise, because it is a dictionary used by people who do crosswords and play Scrabble and they have a great love of recherché words. Also one of the strengths of the Twentieth Century Dictionary is that it covers a broad spectrum of the language covering a long period of time as well as many areas of interest. Thus one cannot simply remove obsolete words.[35]

It is a well established reference book and is frequently cited in court by counsel and judges seeking definitions. This point may be remembered by those drafting reports with potential consequences in litigation.

COLLINS ENGLISH DICTIONARY

On publication the *Collins English Dictionary* was aggressively marketed[36] and sold rapidly. A second edition was produced in 1986 and a third in 1991. It attempted to produce a global view of English, including some quite obscure usages of, for instance, Caribbean English.

At the time of its first publication two main characteristics distinguished Collins from the first two described. Firstly, as the only new dictionary of standing for a quarter of a century, a more modern progressive approach was adopted. This is not to the taste of some people and may make the dictionary less suitable for those to whom a more conservative style of report is appropriate. To others this will be a refreshing and entirely welcome approach. Patrick Hanks, who edited the dictionary, says:

. . . we did not deliberately set out to be modish. We did, however, deliberately set out to avoid being old-fashioned in phrasing and arrangement.[37]

Secondly, by the same principle, in the ordering of the sense in a definition they 'did try . . . to start always with a sense that, by consensus, could be regarded as central, modern, and typical, and to work outwards from there'[38]. Hanks adds the essential point: 'Like so much else in lexicography, this called for a literary judgement rather than for statistical analysis'. It is worth remembering this point when the various quantitative systems for analysing style are discussed (and dismissed) in Chapter 7.

Hanks' distinctive attitude to his dictionary is further demonstrated by his observation that he regards 'a citation file as a prompt or aide-mémoire . . . rather than as the central point from which all else flows'[39]. He is quite happy to rely on the opinion of experts in particular fields once a citation or two has prompted his interest in a specialist word.

Collins was the first dictionary to include a selection of proper nouns. Longman has now also incorporated them, but tuck them away into attached sections at the back. The more traditional lexicographers have always distanced themselves from this approach[40]. Johnson even avoided eponymous adjectives derived from nouns[41]. Artistic, political and other important personages are described in some detail; for instance, against the names of writers, their principal works are listed. Countries and important towns are also included, even citing populations. The chosen geographical entries were included on a sliding scale, working away from the English-speaking world. The problems of including proper names are illustrated by their difficulty in producing a distinction between 'Rhodesia' and 'Zimbabwe', for the position in that country had not been regularized at the time of publication. Both terms were sufficiently widely used to justify inclusion. Yet how was it possible to distinguish them without entering the political debate, however inadvertently, in the definition?

In 1987 a further Collins dictionary was produced to complement the mainstream work. *Collins Cobuild Dictionary*[42] is physically large and complex in the layout of its entries. There are, however, nine helpful pages of explanation. Although there are only 70 000 entries, each is discussed and demonstrated in some detail. There are valuable treatments of idiom and usage and the book has an important international approach. Its preparation was highly computerized, probably more so than was the case with any other dictionary at the time.

LONGMANS DICTIONARY OF THE ENGLISH LANGUAGE

Longman's Dictionary[43] is physically broader than any of the others. Its editor Brian O'Kill says that there was undoubtedly a need for a new dictionary based on citational evidence when the dictionary was first produced in 1984[44].

It was based on the Eighth Merriam-Webster dictionary, heavily anglicized and in O'Kill's words rendered 'less austere'. His aim was to produce something less daunting and which included citations in the text. The result is an extremely user-friendly dictionary expressed in a way which means that any user can handle it easily. The presentation removes traditional lexicographical symbols which might be confusing. It has more advice on usage than any other dictionary.

Its shape and bulk may make it unappealing to some users. However it was enthusiastically welcomed on publication, as for example by Philip Howard in *The Times*: 'It is remarkable how the world hunger for authority has forced lexicographers to start prescribing correct usage. Longman does it sensibly'[45]. Nevertheless it has never achieved the consumer acknowledgement that it deserves.

THESAURI

Many people find thesauri helpful. The word 'thesaurus' is derived from the Greek word for treasury. It is therefore aptly named. It is a storehouse of words (without definitions) arranged by association. A thesaurus has the advantage over a dictionary that the words are arranged by meaning rather than in alphabetical order.

The principal British thesaurus is Roget's[46]. The first edition was produced in 1852 by Peter Mark Roget, whose father was a French refugee. The French pronunciation of the name has therefore been retained.

When the 1982 edition was produced, the editor, Susan Lloyd, was criticized in the press, albeit in a light-hearted way, for allegedly removing sexist terms such as 'countryman' and 'mankind' and replacing them with 'countrydweller' and 'humankind'. Clearly 'countryman', with its associations of rural expertise, is not comparable with 'countrydweller' which merely specifies where someone happens to live. She was obliged to correct the misrepresentation in a letter to *The Times*. The changes which had been misdescribed reflect only a change in the headwords of the groups of quasi-synonyms.

The current edition edited by Betty Kirkpatrick (formerly of Chambers dictionaries) has retained the spirit and structure of its predecessors. It has expanded and developed to take account of changes in the language and values.

A word of caution about the use of thesauri is essential. A thesaurus is not a substitute for a dictionary and should never be treated as such. It must be used to jog the memory. A different word may be lurking at the back of the memory and needs to be teased out.

All words selected from the thesaurus in this way must have been seen in use. C.S. Lewis's remark that 'one understands a word much better if one has met it alive in its native habitat'[47] seems an understatement. The shades of distinction will be very fine. The precise suitability of a word can be perceived only if it has been seen doing the job for which it was intended.

RULE OF THUMB

The fundamental guideline is therefore that, faced with the great wealth of the corpus of English, word currency and meaning should be dictated by the most recent edition of a dictionary of the first rank.

CRITERIA FOR WORD CHOICE

Some more guidelines will be helpful to the report writer.
1. Choose enough words to be clear. Ambiguity is almost always caused by inadequate wording.
2. Do not use too many. If every word counts for something, then every word in the sentence must be there for a purpose.

3. Choose words which most precisely convey the meaning. The need for this kind of precision is demonstrated by the microscopic scrutiny to which words in contracts and other documents are subjected in court[48].

4. Coyness and euphemism must be avoided. The elevation of the most basic functionaries to the title of 'officer', 'manager' or 'executive' is harmless. In political handbills and journalism a kind of evasive writing may be appropriate, but a more direct style is appropriate to reports. American companies have a wonderfully disparaging expression: a motherhood statement. The term is derived from 'all motherhood and apple-pie' and beautifully describes a facile type of report full of cosy sounding explanations but, in fact, saying nothing.

5. Exaggeration devalues the word and thus devalues the whole report. If superlatives and extreme forms of description are used too widely, the report and its words will become devalued, just as a currency is devalued. These kinds of slack usages are another infection from journalism. In that more spectacular arena they have their proper place. For example:

'*Incredibly*' has become an understudy word. It is summoned when a more specific word is not available.

'*Interesting*' has become a very loose word. Copes in *Girl 20*[49] describes it as a 'postcard word':

> 'Interesting. That's a terrific postcard word isn't it? Today we saw all round the folk museum; it was very interesting.'

Both words have their use, but they, like many others, have been grossly overused and exaggerated. Another example is 'unique', which was originally faithful to its etymology, Latin 'unicus' (one and only), but is now used in a wider sense[50]. Resisting this kind of change, at least for the time being, is not reactionary. For as usages are understood at present, it tends towards imprecision.

SUMMARY

Words are the raw material of all reports. However technical, diagrammatic or numerical reports are, they will need words. If a report is too long, too obscure, expressed at the wrong technical level or in an inappropriate tone, that is the result of word choice.

The English-speaking manager has a choice of words which is unequalled among users of European languages. Every word means something slightly different. Care must be taken to choose words which are appropriate to subject-matter, context and readership.

To assist in this choice all report writers should use the most recent edition of one of the leading dictionaires. A thesaurus may also be helpful.

6 Writing for non-technical readers

Lord Robens has written 'Communications should be swift enough for decisions to be taken and implemented quickly. They must be accurate and simple enough to survive their passage through the organisation, i.e. they must be so designed that they cannot be misused'[1]. In pursuance of the philosophy set out by Robens and many other people a number of guides to simple English have been published. It is important not to forget the last part of what Robens says: '. . . they cannot be misused'. There must be no ambiguity or misunderstanding. In many cases if a word is simplified, some fine shade of meaning is lost.

One of the most notable of these guides was *Gobbledegook* published by the National Consumer Council in 1980[2]. The authors follow in Gowers' tradition[3] of urging the simplest possible form of writing to achieve maximum possible acceptance. Likewise, the Plain English Campaign does sterling work trying to get Government departments and local authorities to simplify many of their publications which are aimed at a general readership. Indeed the term 'gobbledegook' is derived from American Congressman Maury Maverick who was thoroughly irritated by the obscurity of Government reports[4]. Gowers was himself writing for civil servants who were guilty of adopting an archaic register.

The danger arises if these restrictive principles are extended beyond simple universally read handouts, such as Income Tax returns and national Census forms. (A case in the American courts, *New York State* v. *Lincoln Savings Bank* showed that the English used in a business document could be actionable by reason of its obscurity[5].)

Legal writing poses a particular problem. The need to follow precedent and to avoid risky flirtations with novel forms of words frequently runs counter to producing documents which can be easily understood. Much useful work has been done to produce workable compromises between these two factors. For example, the National Consumer Council's *Plain Words for Consumers*[6] and *Plain English for Lawyers*[7] contain guidelines which can be extrapolated to report writing.

The organization Clarity[8] publishes a quarterly newsletter seeking to circulate and promote new and more acceptable forms of English for legal purposes. Founded in 1983 by John Walton, at that time a lawyer with Rugby District Council, the organization now has a subscribers' list of some 350 of whom 75 per cent are English solicitors. Many of the rest are in other parts of the English-speaking world. Their newsletter contains not only phraseology and pieces of drafting which are of general interest but some more specific items such as book reviews and relevant historical items. Its members have drafted an Interpretation Bill. A full and lively correspondence column is contained in each issue.

An appealing example of a succinct little report was contained in the March 1990 edition of the newsletter. This demonstrates a microcosmic form of the conventional report layout described in Chapter 2. It also shows how tortuous legal technicalities can be reduced to a readable level in a few sentences.

Should CLARITY be a charity?

If it were to apply for charitable status, it would be on the basis that we existed 'for the advancement of education'. However 'education' for this purpose does not include political or propagandist activity.

Advantages
We would be eligible for tax relief. If members covenanted their subscriptions we could raise a little extra. However, the amounts involved would be small and almost certainly not worth the trouble involved.

It might help us beg funds from public and grant-giving trusts. However, in practice we would remain quite low in priority for donations.

Disadvantages
We would need a constitution acceptable to the Charity Commission, and we would be strictly bound by it. This would restrict our activities.

We would have to submit annual accounts to the Commission.

The trustees would have a high duty of care with personal responsibility and the committee (whether the trustees or not) would not be allowed to benefit from their position. [At present, the committee are volunteers, who work free of charge in their own or their firm's time, often using their own resources. Sometimes, as in the work on the conveyancing protocol or in lecturing, individual committee members are paid by outside bodies for work introduced through CLARITY. It is possible (but not certain) that we would be expected to surrender those fees.]

Conclusion
We would probably not qualify as a charity but in any case the game was not worth the candle.'[9]

An entertaining and relevant article appeared in the legal publication *Counsel*[10] towards the end of 1987. In it Mr Justice Staughton, who, it happens, is Patron of Clarity, set out ways of encouraging similarly direct performance in a barrister's spoken performance in court.

Some ranges of publications (not strictly reports) are particularly successful in this way. ACAS Advisory Booklets, e.g. *Job Evaluation* (No. 1) and *Introduction to Payment Systems* (No. 2), are very good. Their codes of practice are generally satisfactory as well, when they manage to steer clear of legal terminology, which is difficult. The Health and Safety Executive booklets, e.g. *Noise and the Worker* (No. 25) and *First Aid in Offices, Shops and Railway Premises* (No. 48), are successful in their use of vocabulary. Some of their sentence structures are somewhat tortuous for a general readership however.

These simplistic principles must be applied very warily to reports. It is more relevant to consider what Swift called 'proper words in proper places'[11]. Nevertheless there must be ways of presenting complex issues in a comprehensible way for the less informed. The function of changing gear is the second facet of the register problem, on which the rest of the chapter concentrates.

GLOSSARIES

It may not be practicable to issue two levels of report to suit different types of readership because of restrictions of cost, time and because it is essential for all the intended readers to study the whole paper. Yet various levels of technical awareness will exist and must be recognized. In this case a Glossary should be added. A Glossary will serve two functions:

1. It will explain the meaning of terms to the uninitiated.
2. It will sharpen definitions where it is necessary to give a general or household term a more acute meaning, e.g. 'Draught beer' or 'Lager'. Most British readers will be familiar with these as consumers but in a report a more precise meaning may be necessary[12].

This type of sharpening will be particularly appropriate in documents with a very direct legal significance, for example these definitions in the Glossary of the Stock Exchange Revised Draft Service Agreement:

Business day Any day the Stock Exchange is open for business unless otherwise stated;
Cash benefit Any benefit entitlement relating to money arising by way of any dividend, interest payment, capital distribution, premium distribution or such other benefit of a similar nature;
Certificate Any document of title issue by, or on behalf of, the issuing company which evidences the Account Holder's or, as the case may be, a Nominee's legal title to the securities comprised therein.
Foreign currency Any currency other than sterling.

There are two pitfalls awaiting the compilers of Glossaries:

1. Providing so much information that the description becomes an encyclopaedic item with details well beyond the need of the reader.
2. Defining the word in technical terms which still keep the meaning well beyond the lay reader's understanding.

The following selected examples from a Council for British Shipping paper on marine fuel oil terminology clearly demand a knowledge or, at least, understanding of petrol by the reader:

API gravity An arbitrary scale adopted by the American Petroleum Institute for expressing the relative density of oils. Its relation to relative density is:

$$\text{Degrees API} = \frac{141.5}{\text{Relative density at } 60° \text{ F}(15.6°C)} - 131.5$$

Asphaltenes Those components of asphalt that are insoluble in petroleum naptha but are soluble in carbon disulphide. They are hard and brittle and are made up largely of high molecular weight polynuclear hydrocarbon derivatives containing carbon, hydrogen, sulphur, nitrogen, oxygen, and usually, the three heavy metals – nickel, iron and vanadium.

In this case the likely readership justifies this level of explanation. Such technical explanations would not work if any laypersons were to read the paper.

The same paper illustrates the occasional need to distinguish between the same word when it occurs in two different contexts:

Base (Chemistry context)   One of the broad class of compounds that react with acid to form salts plus water. This includes alkalies as well as other chemicals that have similar chemical behaviours. Water-soluble hydroxides ionise in solution and form hydroxyl ions ($-OH_2$), which result in characteristic chemical properties of bases.

Base (Petroleum context)   Term relating to the chemical nature of crude petroleum. Crude oil may be paraffinic, asphaltic or mixed base, according to the paraffin wax and bitumen in the residue after distillation. Naphthenic base is approximately synonymous with asphaltic base.

These principles also apply when preparing a formal definition in a Glossary and when defining a term in a more discreet way in the course of a report, where the more heavy-handed approach of a complete Glossary will be less appropriate. In either situation there are three phases:

1.   Before writing the Glossary;
2.   Defining the term;
3.   After drafting the definition.

Before writing

See if the term is in one of the more conservative medium-sized dictionaries and follow the sequence in Figure 23. (The *Concise Oxford Dictionary* is ideal as it is less ready to accept abbreviations than the others.) The question as to whether the likely population will understand the term is deliberately phrased as '100%'. If there are even one or two potential readers who may not understand the term, it should be defined. More knowledgeable readers need not refer to the definition.

Writing the definition

A good definition will always consist of two parts and sometimes of four:

> Always: what it is (for example: it is a payment)
> Always: What it does (which provides protection against fraud)
> Sometimes: Where or when it does it (paid annually)
> Sometimes: (up to a point) How it does it (by providing payment
>   of up to 105 per cent of the sum lost).

The bracketed examples above are imaginary. Real illustrations are generally less precise but many are reasonable. The format is well demonstrated by the definition of 'cash tender offer' in the investigation report into the County NatWest affair[13].

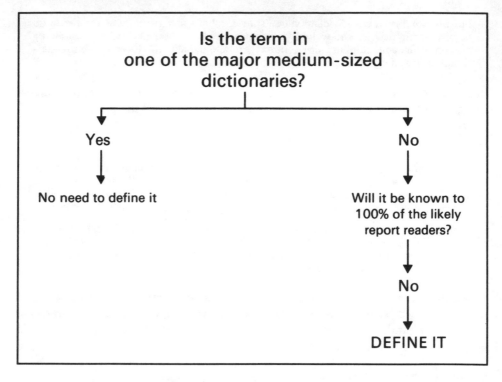

Figure 23   Sequence of decisions in preparing a Glossary item

Offer procedure used in the US to implement a cash offer for the shares of a public company

and these examples from the Black report[14]:

ADVANCED GAS COOLED REACTORS (AGR)
Nuclear reactors operating at high temperatures (over 1000° C), cooled by gas and utilising enriched Uranium oxide fuel.

CLADDING
The covering on nuclear fuel. Designed to resist physical and chemical effects thus preventing corrosion of the fuel and escape of products of the reaction.

After writing

1. Check by eye that the definition is not too long.
2. Check that it has avoided using more technical terms in the explanation. (Following a spiral of cross-references from one technical term to another is always frustrating and can be totally confusing.)
3. Check that the definition has avoided repeating the words being defined in the definition. A definition defining a 'shift controller' as 'a man who controls a shift', is just repeating the original phrase, with no value added, as it were.
4. Check that the term is being defined in the particular way in which it is being used. Ensure that the word in the dictionary has the same sense as that used in the report.

PRESENTATIONAL ASPECTS

Besides these important controls on vocabulary, in order to ensure maximum readability by the non-technical reader:
1. Make extensive use of appendices.
2. Where possible, present numerical detail as ratios or percentages.
3. Use management summaries.
4. Show sequences by flow-charts and algorithms.
5. Make generous use of headings.

SUMMARY

Many subjects will demand a technical treatment and also presentation for non-technical, often senior, readerships.

A non-technical version should avoid technical terminology, but if it is necessary to use technical terms they should be defined in a Glossary. Extensive use should be made of appendices. A layperson's summary may be helpful. (This is discussed in more detail in Chapter 9.) Copious use should be made of illustrations and suitable forms are described in Chapter 10.

The key is to identify the level which is appropriate to the readership.

7 Style

A singer, a politician or a hotel may be said to have style (presumably meaning – when judged against some indeterminate criteria – good style). Many companies and individuals quite understandably seek to improve the style of their reports. The aim is to choose an appropriate style rather than seeking perfection.

Reports are frequently returned to the writer surmounted by the all-embracing condemnation 'poor style' or, perhaps slightly more constructively, 'improve your style'. Usually little or no attempt is made to specify the stylistic improvements being suggested.

Another comment often seen is 'This is not in this company's style'. Sometimes companies produce helpful rule books covering aspects such as paragraph numbering and section heading, but little more.

Newspaper style books often take the matter much further. In 1981 Keith Waterhouse produced a most entertaining analysis of the *Daily Mirror's* style[1]. This is not a style book in the conventional sense, for it does not lay down precepts by which *Daily Mirror* contributors had to produce their scripts. Rather, it is a descriptive analysis of the style of the *Daily Mirror* over a set period. Not only is the book amusing, it indicates the trends of tabloid journalism, which in turn affect the style of the tabloid readers.

Since then his *Waterhouse on Newspaper Style*[2] has taken the theme further and wider. It lampoons almost all the clichés and bad habits of tabloid journalism in a readable and highly entertaining way. It is easy to become numbed to the lack of meaning which excessively used forms of words will have. Waterhouse brings the reader up sharply and report writers would do well to heed his strictures. Some commentators urge writers indiscriminately to use 'everyday words'. There is a tendency for 'everyday words' to mean the patter of big-circulation newspapers. This means phrases which lack novelty or impact. Indeed if a word is used every day, it is scarcely surprising that the report lacks impact.

Analogies of dress are sometimes helpful. Certain forms are definitely unsuitable for a dinner party. Others are definitely unsuitable for the ski-slopes or the football field[3].

STYLE AS PERSONAL MANOEUVRABILITY

Style is all the manoeuvrability that exists between any set of undisputed conventions. Such a set of conventions may be virtually universal within English usage, such as the requirement for every sentence to contain a finite verb and to end with a full-stop. It may be a national convention such as the American love of compound words, one-sentence paragraphs and heavy punctuation. It may just be a set of company conventions such as those in Ford Motor Company favouring initial capital 'C' for 'Company', and in Price Waterhouse for initial lower-case letters for appointment titles. Everything else is a matter of individual style.

Several reports examining English usage in education and in the workplace have responded to criticisms of contemporary standards. Usually they have managed to counter the critics, pointing out that a 'golden age' in standards of English is generally a myth. Newbolt in 1921 and Bullock in 1975 both did this. Kingman was the most recent in 1988.

The Queen's English Society[4] provide a framework for the expression of disquiet over change. Its Vice-Chairman, Peter Bassett, is cynical about the reports of those who do not share his view that there is a general decline in the handling of English. Of the reports just mentioned he says:

> I do not doubt that Lord Bullock is entirely sincere in his belief when he contradicts the contention that standards are falling, but I question whether he is in touch with the problems of communication within industry. In my own industry (power generation) these problems were serious enough to necessitate various expensive and time-consuming steps to be taken, and I presume that this experience is general.
>
> The main weaknesses (and there are many, in our opinion) in the Kingman Report, and in the more recent Cox Report and the Report of the National Curriculum Council, is that it fails to emphasise the supreme importance to school-leavers of being able, when required, to speak and write standard English . . .[5]

In a wonderfully comprehensive and yet descriptive book about Australian English, Sidney J. Baker[6] says:

> The odd idea that there is a definable something called Good English which is pure and beautiful and eternal . . . seems to have grown out of man's puny illusion that he can stop evolution in its tracks.

He goes on to describe 'Good English' as a 'clumsy misshapen monster patched up by all the petty Frankensteins who infest classrooms and pulpits and editorial chairs'.

Two particularly important points emerge from Baker's observations. Firstly, many people delude themselves that there is, or has been, a point at which the written word reached an unsurpassable standard. This has also given Latin its appeal over the last two or three centuries[7]. Because it has run its course, Latin offers standards that are permanent and unchanging. They are, however, standards that are entirely irrelevant. This is now being made abundantly clear as business affairs come to be controlled by a generation of managers who are largely ignorant of the principles of Latin grammar. Secondly, in certain environments, such as the classroom and newspaper offices that Baker describes, rules will be inevitable in the interests of consistency. Newspaper style books will lay down criteria to be respected by all correspondents. *The Times* style book, for instance, specifies the level of a disaster before it can be described as a shambles[8]. *The Economist's* style book[9] published in 1986, which is described in Appendix II, provides strict discipline over such things as use of abbreviations and descriptions of currencies.

Public interest in the subject of grammatical propriety was given a boost during June 1989 by the Prince of Wales commenting on lack of discipline in this respect among his own staff. True to precedent this unleashed the usual modest flood of comment in letters to the press. One correspondent wrote:

> I long to have one day a week designated as a prepositionless day (the BBC) could benefit from one, too) [10]

Another[11] correspondent, a secretary, complained that her employers frequently recorrected her own corrections of the grammar in their letters.

CLICHÉS

While massive blocks cribbed from other reports are – because they are second-hand and therefore not quite appropriate – bad style, so individually clichéd words are to be avoided for the same reasons. Clichés are groups of words that have become gummed together.

'Pressure' is too often 'tremendous'. A 'search' by police is usually 'massive'. These are the obvious expected couplings. Because they are obvious and unoriginal, they can be anticipated and contribute nothing to the report. Longer clichés will also 'have a hypnotic and final effect, the sound of revealed truth'[12]. They take on an undeserved authority.

'Cliché' is a French technical term from the printing trade meaning a print block. In other words it is a block of information which goes about the place together, indivisible.

Clichés tend to be used more lavishly when times are hard or when there is something to hide. A report that is thick with them must be treated with suspicion.

The definitive work on clichés is Zijderveld's *On Clichés*.[13] This merits study by anyone interested in this serious malaise in modern communications. He makes much of the important distinction between a cliché and a slogan: a slogan has a mobilizing role[14]; a cliché has lost its mobilizing power. A rather less strident and more friendly examination of clichés is to be found in Nicholas Bagnall's *In Defence of Clichés*[15]. The principal vocabulary of these iniquities is Partridge's *A Dictionary of Clichés*[16].

NUMERICAL RULES

Numbers have a natural appeal for those seeking guidance on almost any subject. They are definitive and precise. They are not encumbered by what many people see as the woolly vagueness of semantic interpretation. To this end many have sought at least to analyse and frequently to regulate style by numerical rule.

Gunning's Fog Index investigates the fog and, conversely, the clarity of a piece of writing by analysing the number of words per sentence and the number of syllables per word. It was first widely published in the 1940s and, after a while, Gunning recognized that the system was more complicated than it need be[17]. At about the same time Flesch was developing his Reading Ease Score which relied on similar arrangements.

North American commentators have been more prolific in this type of innovation than British. One of the most elaborate devices of this kind is Fry's Readability Graph, produced at Rutgers University Reading Center, New Brunswick[18].

More recently J.O. Morris popularized the Clear River Test which uses the analogy of a boat's passage down a river. Various literary excesses[19] are measured numerically and as the numbers increase they take the form of barriers across the river, obstructing clear communications. The analogy is a good one, but the guidelines can only be general.

This is true of all these gimmicky systems. They are just intended to offer the most general guidance. Gunning makes it clear that this was always the intention. Morris says that the Clear River Test is 'not a precise mathematical test'[20]. He goes on: 'In measuring readability such a test would be burdensome to use and probably pointless'. Frequently, these concepts fall into the wrong hands. To take their numerical generalizations as literally as many report writers and, more often, training managers do, is unrealistic and restrictive.

Such rules have their appeal in a kind of simplistic magic, but style is not measured or improved by magic tricks. However comfortably they may fit glib training objectives, they are far too crude to offer guidance for routine report writing.

The United States Department of Agriculture makes extensive use of such systems in elaborate procedures to evaluate the readability of their documents. Representative samples of at least 100 words are taken. The number and type of words are considered in relation to the number of sentences. Their system applies other rigorous questionnaires to the planning of the document for its printed format, the annotation of tables, typographical markings, pagination, credits and references and many other aspects, both general and particular.

THE CHARACTERISTICS OF STYLE

To analyse the style appropriate to a particular reader or a particular company or a specific report, it is necessary to identify the characteristics of the style, or style-markers as Nils Erik Enkvist calls them[21].

A traveller journeying from Didcot to Reading may look out of a train window and feel that the countryside looks like that of north Germany. This simplistic judgement is the equivalent of saying that a report is in the wrong (or the right) style. For more constructive comments, it is necessary to consider what makes it seem like German landscape. What items would have to be changed to make it seem less Germanic? He then identifies well-defined woods on the hill-tops, isolated farms in small clumps of trees and roads with no hedges.

Words have already been described as the raw material of written communication. So they are the fundamental feature of style. It is appropriate to begin with some brief points on them.

Words

The style implications of word choice was discussed elsewhere in this book and, indirectly, in the discussion of clichés earlier in this chapter. Apart from the actual choice of words, the following points of style are important in this connection.

Repetition of words

Repetition is annoying and confusing. It irritates the reader rather like the recurrence of blocked letters on an ill-maintained typewriter. Journalists necessarily work under pressure, and sometimes great discomfort, so that they can be excused for some infuriating repetitions. The prince among duplications in *The Times* at the time of the 1990 Cabinet reshuffle was:

> Contrary to *expectations* Mrs Thatcher is not *expected* to split the Department of Environment.[22]

The word 'moreover' has its uses but it can seem grotesquely prominent if it occurs more than once in the same paragraph.

> Naturally in periods of pressure one looks to see where time might be saved but every complaint must be given proper attention. Obtaining remedies for complainants after I have issued an adverse report is important but also time-consuming. Moreover, the time it takes to achieve a remedy is often far too long, for this reason I welcome the proposals which the Government advanced in the White Paper responding to the Widdicombe Report and now embodied in the Local Government and Housing Bill. If these proposals become law they will not only speed up the process of obtaining a remedy but also help councils to think more carefully before they reject my recommendations. In previous annual reports I have drawn attention to the regrettable fact that a council's response is often conditional by the fact that my report has been considered in the first instance by the very service committee which I have criticised. Moreover, the reports to council members on my report have sometimes been compiled either by officers who were criticised by me or by their superiors in the same department. The Bill may go some way to diluting the sort of bias, or appearance of bias, which denies a complainant a just remedy.[23]

Statements of the obvious

Prefacing Conclusions with words such as 'After considering all the various possibilities', are ponderous and sometimes seem pompous. The Conclusions would be a poor thing indeed if they were prepared without having considered the possibilities.

Inclusion of redundant words

Each writer must identify his or her own vogue-words – be they the favourites of a moment or the habits of a lifetime – and trim their use so that they do not irritate readers.

Contradiction

Contradiction is also irritating, as when an introductory line reads: 'The companies that have submitted quotes are . . .', to be followed by '. . . declined to quote'.

Archaic phrasing

Some phrases – entirely appropriate in the business correspondence of Victorian England – give a ponderous or old-fashioned look to a modern report. They may have a place in legal writing, if the precedents make it inevitable but just one of them can completely distort a page of a report. Examples include:

notwithstanding
hereunder
aforementioned
hereat
wherefore
heretofore
foregoing

Meaningless statements

No report should ever begin 'I have taken the opportunity'. The opportunity does not exist at that stage. The report has only just begun.

Sentence length

There are two extremes:

1. The Victorian length which was favoured by a generation reared on Latin structures rich in subordinate phrases and clauses, as in:

   The talk to-day, as the brown brandy, which the paler cognac has not yet super-seded, is consumed and the fumes of coarse tobacco and the smell of spilt beer and the faint sickly odour of evaporating spirits overpower the flowers, is of horses.[24]

   It is a style that Cyril Connolly called 'Mandarin English' which presumes that the reader has a classical education, a private income and unlimited time[25].

2. At the other end of the scale there is a Peter and Jane style appropriate to the authors of children's reading primers[26].

Both extremes are represented in reports. For example this sentence length is rather uncomfortable:

Together with a sustained growth in female participation rates, the admission to the EEC of the new countries with cheap excess labour, and the fact that British manufac-turing industry is looking to a hard core of employees in order to increase producti-vity, with the tendency not to replace those who leave or retire – all these trends will act towards increasing the level of unemployment.[27]

The following example, taken from a Price Waterhouse manual which is intended to explain complex examples of international financing to clients, is grotesque. It is comprehensible only with great effort. The phrase 'and the fact that' is an indicator that a new sentence may be required. Exceptions (such as the last 16 words) can often be segregated into separate sentences to advantage:

It would follow that a Hong Kong company subject in full to Hong Kong tax at 18.5% but under the rules conclusively presumed to be subject to a lower level of taxation, would if the conditions as to non-UK residence and UK control were satisfied, be automatically a CFC, and the fact that its profits had borne tax in Hong Kong at a rate exceeding 50% of the corresponding UK tax would be irrelevant except that the Hong Kong tax would be taken into account in calculating the creditable tax.

The ideal lies somewhere between the two extremes. The following paragraph from an Argos Distributors Ltd report shows suitable sentence lengths in an internal report on supervisor training:

> When the trainee supervisors have been selected they will receive a training scheme on supervisory techniques at present carried out by the Warehouse Training Department. On the completion of their training course they will enter into a department which has an established supervisor leading it. The trainee will then work alongside the supervisor, learning about the department and how supervision works. This 'in the field' training will be carried out for approximately one month. When the month is completed the established supervisor is then trained in another department for a period of time. This training is carried out by the supervisor of the department he is entering. The supervisor trains the supervisor with the assistance of the line trainer, who helps in explaining individual operative functions. Whilst his training is going on his department is covered by the trainee. Also in the event of promotion the company would have trained supervisors ready to supervise departments. If a supervisor were promoted to a manager a replacement is quickly found.

This paragraph is complete and it is taken directly from a supervisor's project report. There are several aspects of the style which the reader may have found not to his taste. Perhaps the word 'supervisor' and forms of the word 'train' come up more frequently than is strictly necessary or conducive to clarity. Perhaps it sounds a bit strange 'entering into' a department, rather as one might 'enter into' an agreement. Perhaps another comma or two here and there would add to the sense of it. Despite these criticisms, the passage is easy to read. This is because its sentence length is ideal for that sort of subject-matter in an internal report.

It is most important to judge sentence length in relationship to paragraph length. What may have to be rather a long sentence in order to provide continuity of thought, can afford to be more thoroughly divided if those words are in a paragraph on their own rather than being part of a complex paragraph[28].

Sentence structure

Turner[29] admits that 'it would be difficult to exaggerate the importance of sentence structure in the European literary tradition'. This principle can certainly be extended to reports. Here is a sentence from the report of a water treatment consultancy:

> The purpose of this programme is not only to ensure protection and conditioning of both oil and the whole of the oil holding/handling/distribution systems, but to maintain the fuel oil in peak atomising condition by implementing regular and frequent service visits to optimise the excess air levels thus ensuring that the boilers run at as high a level of efficiency as possible, and to further protect the fireside of the boilers from deposition, high and low temperature corrosion, acid smutting, etc.

Not only is this sentence too long for its subject-matter, but its structure is ungainly:

1. It starts clearly enough. 'The purpose of this programme is . . .'
2. The 'not only . . . but to' construction is difficult to follow when there is so much information.
3. The 'not only' section is complicated by including 'both oil and the whole of the oil holding . . .', etc.
4. Oblique strokes as in 'holding/handling' can sometimes be an economical form of expression. Three or more, however, will often make part of the sentence rather top-heavy.
5. The 'but to' section leads into three separate functions ('to maintain . . . to optimise . . . to protect'). These separate infinitives could either be changed to three separate sentences, or three sub-paragraphs if the report structure was suited to sub-paragraphs.
6. The last of these infinitives is, of course, a split infinitive, 'to further protect'. This will annoy many. It does not actually seem to detract from the clarity here.

Report writers seeking a simple method for analysing their sentence structure may find the analogy of a clothesline in Figure 24 helpful. The main beam of the sentence (subject, verb and any part of the predicate necessary to make sense of the whole) lies along the washing line. (In the Victorian example quoted earlier, the main beam is 'The talk . . . is of horses'.) The subordinate phrases and clauses are the linen on the line as shown in Figure 24 (b):

1. There is no precise number of pieces of linen which may be hung on the line. The writer must judge that for himself. That is why the report is written by an intelligent human being rather than a monkey or a machine. There should be enough to enhance the main beam without making the sentence too cumbersome for the reader.
2. Every piece of linen must be affixed by a clothes peg in the form of a preposition ('in', 'upon', 'from'), a conjunction ('while', 'since', 'but') or a present participle (ending in '-ing'). If there is no such peg, the sentence should probably be broken into two (or, most exceptionally, joined by 'and'). A simple example is found in the Argos Distributors report: 'It is also a fact that we have no Trainee-Supervisors at Daventry Warehouse, this could be the link'. The comma could more conventionally be replaced by a full stop. Possibly the context might justify replacement by 'and' to link the two thoughts together or a colon to suggest that, although they are two thoughts, one is the corollary of the other.
3. The writer should watch out for the danger of having too many bits of linen tacked one to another as is shown by the dotted appendages in Figure 24 (b).

Some words and phrases in mid-sentence give a clear warning that a new sentence may be required:

> however
> on the other hand
> and the fact that (see first example on page 86)
> and (following a comma)

While having admirable uses semi-colons may also imply a need to start a new sentence.

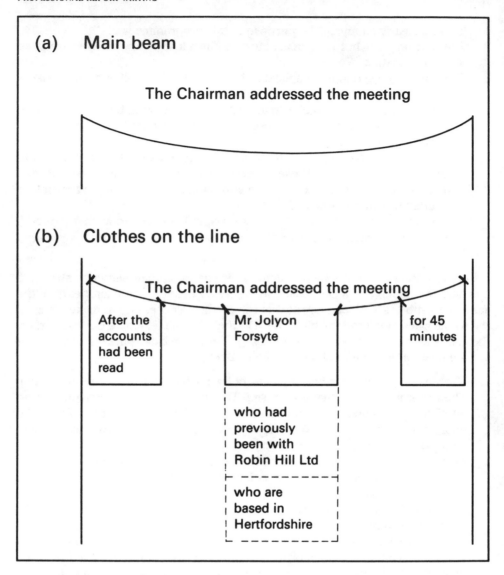

Figure 24 Clothes-line analogy for construction of a sentence

Paragraph length and structure

As with sentence length, two unhappy extremes occur with paragraphs. Some writers feel that a new paragraph is justified at the end of every sentence. The result is an enervating form of mental stepping stones without any sort of grouping of ideas.

The other malaise tends towards grouping the whole document into one gargantuan paragraph. This problem is particularly apparent among writers who work from legal or other similar reference books such as tax handbooks[30]. It is difficult to shrug off a style that may well be justified in the source book on the grounds of legal precedent. Nor are the spectacular descriptive passages in Margaret Drabble's novels[31] or those of Edna O'Brien[32] appropriate for imitation in a report.

The Peacock report on financing the BBC is disfigured by many colossal paragraphs. For example, two consecutive paragraphs (numbers 198 and 199) have 29 and 24 lines each. Paragraph 309 totals a marathon 39 lines[33]. A glance at a report from the 1930s or the 1940s will immediately impress the reader with the fashion for hugely long paragraphs which are extremely unappetising to the modern eye. The Beveridge report, which was the foundation of the Welfare State, is a good illustration of this[34].

Whatever style of paragraph length and structure is chosen, writers must also consider whether or not to give the paragraphs headings. Even if they decide that headings are not appropriate, the character and cohesion of each paragraph should be such that it could be given one. If there is no particular theme to the paragraph and it covers a ragbag of assorted topics, it is badly structured.

Punctuation

There are really very few rules of punctuation. There will, by everyone's acceptance, be a full stop at the end of every sentence and capital initials will be used for proper names. Yet what about a colon or semi-colon, or even the use of stops in abbreviations and acronyms? All these are likely to be a question of style. It may be national, house, or just individual style.

Punctuation has been described as the handmaid of prose. It should be just that. It has been suggested that it was in danger of becoming a stiff-faced chaperone[35]. To use another analogy, there is a danger of the punctuation marks overwhelming the words. Punctuation must always be kept to a minimum commensurate with clarity. It must always be subservient to the words.

This is not the place to provide a comprehensive schedule of possibilities in punctuation. Some excellent general guides are described in Appendix II. Nonetheless it is a good idea to stress some overuses in punctuation style of which report writers should remain keenly aware.

Inverted commas

Use of inverted commas should be minimized. The press have shown an unhappy extravagance with them[36]. Sir Linton Andrews, on seeing inverted commas around a cliché, would ask the journalist from what source they were quoted[37]. Some reports are so heavily laced with them that it is impossible, at first glance, to tell which words are inside and which words are outside the inverted commas. Informal public notices frequently make unorthodox use of them to draw attention to an important word or phrase, as in this illustration from a London Underground station.

PLEASE DO NOT
ENTER
'ASBESTOS'

This is a novel variation of the style which favours greengrocers' apostrophes, as described later in this chapter. It should usually be possible to restrict their use to the points listed which follow:

1. Directly quoted speech:

> For its part the Confederation of British Industry (CBI) has made great efforts to bring the challenges and opportunities of UPAs to the attention of its members and of British business generally, notably through the report *Initiatives Beyond Charity*, published in September 1988. This stressed inter alia, the need to win the involvement of the local community 'certainly including, though not restricted to, the local government authorities themselves'.

This principle can be applied to individual words which have been used. For example in the Fennell report a Police Constable gave evidence which was directly quoted as follows: ' ". . . What I can only describe as a large wall of flame or fire. It was definitely above head high, and immediately following this was like a whoosh . . ." ' Thereafter the report showed the word in inverted commas as: 'The "whoosh" either knocked him onto his back or maybe caught him off balance'[38].

The importance of precise wording is also illustrated by the Jockey Club St Leger report as in:

> Mr Player described the decision in a later written report as 'finely balanced'.[39]

In the Challenger report, quotations are used on various occasions where precise wording is important. Among these are some examples of corporate wording as in those relating to Morton Thiokol Inc who were contractors.

> Thiokol's stated position was that 'the condition is not desirable but is acceptable'.

and later to isolate one word

> . . . and Thiokol was to increase the amount of damage considered 'acceptable'.[40]

All reports of investigations are necessarily very heavy on quotations. The Herald of Free Enterprise report contains extensive quotations of questioning at the inquiry. Likewise the County NatWest report has short paragraphs where the precise wording of witnesses' statements was important:

At that stage as Mr Brown told us:

> '. . . we had a mathematical equation that balanced. We had known buyers and known sellers and they equalled, at which point we told people that the placing was complete. We told institutions that they had received the number of shares they had asked for and everyone thought we had done a very very good job.'[41]

2. Nicknames of individuals in an informal report, or the names of products, promotional campaigns and so on. The principle can also be extended to a rather more formal kind of terminology. The County NatWest inquiry report makes use of inverted commas to describe the argot of the Stock Exchange:

> . . . it had 3.3. million shares under the control of Mr Potashnick. This was

recorded in an account with the reference of 'ITO.1' which Mr Potashnick described as a 'back book'. Third, it had the 31.3 million shares. This was not recorded in the market makers' books at all, although from time to time thereafter this tranche was referred to as being on a 'back back book'.[42]

3. The titles of other reports, books or even exhibitions. In an earlier example under Point 1, a document title was shown in italics as *Initiatives Beyond Charity*. Where office equipment does not provide italics, or for some other reason, it may be desirable to show document titles between inverted commas. This is the traditional format before wordprocessors offered a variety of typefaces. It may also be used for such titles as retailers' ranges as in ' "Mum's-the-word", our range for expectant mothers, enjoyed another year of success'[43].

Exclamation marks

There is no place for exclamation marks in a report. They are a cliché of house journals to indicate a joke (as in the old pantomime boom-boom). It is sometimes argued that they can give emphasis to a sentence. They may indeed do so, but they are a slapdash and careless form of emphasis. (It was originally known as an admiration mark[44].) Greater precision would be achieved by word choice or, if appropriate, commas. If it should ever be suitable to use an exclamation mark in extremis, single marks, thus '!', should be employed. When the exclamation mark was fashionable in private correspondence, multiples of '!!' and '!!!!' occurred, as in this example from a letter of Wilfred Owen[45] in 1911:

> He is a sixth cousin of the great William Morris! has heard Ruskin lecture!! was introduced to Holman Hunt!!!

This hearty type of communication is not suitable in a report in the last decade of the 20th century.

Brackets

Brackets send readers into a siding. They stop their progress through the report and distract them with semi-relevant information. Sometimes this is both helpful and inevitable but it may be used to excess. For example the three sets of brackets in the following report seem to divert the reader too much and too often.

> During the year, the committee discussed matters as diverse as humour in analgesic advertisments (when it reaffirmed that jingles in TV advertisements for home medication products should not be permitted), promotion of advertising controls (a campaign was conducted between November 1984 and January 1985) and the advertisement of VD Clinics (the Authority accepted that the advertising of appropriately controlled VD clinics should be accepted experimentally though monitored closely for complaints).[46]

Frequently these kinds of structures are the result of additions during editing and review; a type of mischief which is addressed in Chapter 11.

Dashes

Dashes were also in vogue in the private correspondence of earlier decades. John Simon[47] recalls that they are associated with 'schoolgirl correspondence of a bygone era'. Sir Ernest Gowers describes them as 'seductive'. This is most apposite. If they are used too loosely they will appear when a more specific form of mark should be used. In reports they should be used only as a form of parentheses stronger than a pair of commas, and less powerful than brackets. The following part-paragraph shows the style:

> . . . However, even in the absence of the difficulties as to enforceability and enforcement which, as there mentioned, we believe would exist in respect of the Deed – or even if a further Deed, in the same form, were to be executed by the Government of Kuwait, and were capable of enforcement by the Secretary of State – we do not consider that it would go far enough. The exercise of voting rights of 14.9 per cent of the issued capital (some 16.1 per cent of the effective voting rights after taking into account the non-voting element) would still leave the Government of Kuwait with a dominating shareholding at general meetings. In our view Kuwait would still be able to defeat, or make it difficult to pass, ordinary or special resolutions of which it disapproved, particularly in combination with other shareholders. Further, the total size of the holding – 21.6 per cent – would continue to dwarf all other holdings, and would be one that could be a constant distraction for the management of BP.[48]

The passage demonstrates all three types of parentheses; the stronger form of brackets, two pairs of dashes (the first of them arguably too long) and at least one pair of commas '. . ., or make it difficult to pass, . . .'.

The audit practice of Price Waterhouse demonstrates this well. At the beginning of the 1980s pairs of dashes used in this way were completely out of the question, being perceived as too informal. Now, they are quite widely used as in this sentence.

> The major new products – an application development system (S B 4) and an accountancy suite (S M 4) – were completed and launched late in 1987.

They are a very common and helpful form of punctuation in the Challenger report:

> for the first several days after the accident – possibly because of the trauma resulting from the accident – NASA appeared to be withholding information about the accident from the public

and

> . . . the carrier would provide the thrust for liftoff and flight through the atmosphere, then release its passenger – the orbiting vehicle – and return to Earth.[49]

An interesting example, in a report which is possibly more formal than any of the others, occurs in a foreword to a housing report by Mr David Trippier, the Housing Minister.

> The theme of this report – housebuilder and rural communities working together – is a welcome one.[50]

Whilst avoiding overuse of these marks, the report writer should make full, imaginative and unabashed use of the entire gamut of English punctuation. The whole range of parentheses should, be applied from the heaviest '( )', through the intermediate '– –', to a simple pair of commas ', ,'. Likewise the range of stops should be employed from full stop, through colon and semi-colon, to a comma. A gin advertisement appeared on the London Underground during late 1970s which suggested that there was something unpleasant about semi-colons. Nothing could be further from the truth[51]. Each of these stops represents a slightly different level of weighting: a different level of pressure which may be important.

Hyphens

Hyphens have become increasingly popular in recent years. Geoffrey Wheatcroft has written of 'the advance of otiose hyphens'. On some occasions they have added clarity: on other occasions they have added nothing. The long-standing convention established by Bernard Shaw[52] and others is that as few should be used as possible and then only to remove ambiguity. Various expressions are shown in, for instance, the *Concise Oxford Dictionary*, with hyphens:

> *hair-line*, but *hair shirt* and *hairspring*
> *long-range*, but *long haul* and *longhand*
> *red-handed*, but *red pepper* and *redhead*

Tony Augarde, senior Editor of the Oxford Dictionaries, has explained that this is only a guide to received practice[53]. It can only be that. The old law applies: as few as possible should be used and then only to remove ambiguity.

Apostrophes

There are areas where reduced usage is to be encouraged in the interests of fluent unhesitating style. It is one punctuation mark where the extended popular use is not only mischievous but actually wrong. Many are the corner post office shops displaying signs:

IDENTIFICATION REQUIRED FOR ENCASHMENT OF GIRO'S

or

BANANA'S 25p EACH

Nothing is omitted from the 'Giro's' or the 'Banana's'. There is no possessive. They are straightforward plurals. It is most important that this infectious and misleading aberration should stop finding its way into reports.

Question Marks

Certainly anything that is a question must conclude with a question mark.

> What would be the consequences of this course of action? How would this compare
> with results in the financial years 1985–1989?

Yet this sometimes produces rather a fierce, button-holing style. It may produce an emotive tone which is too hectoring for a serious commercial report.

A report which makes extensive, and probably excessive, use of these is the Longford report on *Pornography* in 1972[54].

Questions are posed in the text:

How can it be, that human beings can set out to attack others even in the most sensitive realm of being, while we can all be vulnerable to such assault?

and the marathon

Yet any examination of printed material that might be described as bordering on hardcore (illegal) pornography revealed that such a line has become almost impossible to draw, and is frequently as hypocritical as that opposed to relatively innocuous material widely accepted; where is the line to be drawn between a fetishist display of boots, or 'spanking', for example, and the portrayal of one human being inflicting pain (frequently depicted with exaggerated evidence of blood or physical distortion), on another, by using the same boots or whip?

as well as sub-titles both philosophical:

What is Advertising?

and practical:

Does pornography influence behaviour?

Grammar and idiom

Likewise, grammar is largely a matter of personal choice and highly individual style. As Philip Howard says in *New Words for Old*, 'English is not a drill yard for grammarians'[55]. Enkvist sees it as a framework of rules. Grammar defines the possible and impossible. Style is a choice of possibles[56]. Some writers[57] may find the analogy of a game of chess to be helpful. There are numerous possible permutations within a number of possible directions of movement. Perhaps the most colourful metaphor is that of John Simon[58] who sees style within grammatical convention as the actor's right to interpret Hamlet in the way he pleases but not going as far as 'a woman, a flaming homosexual or a one-eyed hunchback'.

In the 18th century many classically based shibboleths were devised by Chesterfield and his friends and contemporaries. In particular the rhetoricians, Campbell, Kanes and Blair, who lectured at Scottish universities on the arts of rhetoric and English composition, took general principles to unsatisfactory extremes of dogma[59]. These have now sunk back to their more proper position of broad guidelines.

Well-established conventions such as the use of a singular verb with *none*, is less rigidly followed now. This sentence from an annual report of the Independent Broadcasting Authority reads entirely comfortably.

Of the nine complaints against ITV adjudicated upon during this year, none were upheld in full: three were rejected outright and six upheld in part.[60]

although its 'none were' is strictly a solecisim.

In particular, these are noteworthy:

Litotes

Litotes means using understatement, or negatives. For example, 'not unpleasant' is a perfectly valid expression. A not unpleasant experience may be far removed from a 'pleasant' one. When the Chairman of Taylor Woodrow was quoted as describing the year's performance, in view of the different economic situation, as 'almost not unsatisfactory'[61] he may have been giving a more precise and more accurate description of his company's position than he could have done with a more straightforward expression. But such convolutions should be used sparingly.

George Orwell required users of this figure of speech to memorize 'A not unblack dog was chasing a not unsmall rabbit across a not ungreen field'[62]. Used excessively it is an irritating habit. In any case, each individual phrase in that example would be difficult to justify. In isolation, it can be a wholesome and harmless form of description.

Split infinitive

The mystique of the split infinitive has also largely been dispelled. It is based on the impossibility of splitting an infinitive in Latin because it was all one word, e.g. 'amare' (to love), 'audire' (to hear). Its almost superstitious preservation into 20th-century English was ludicrous. Many reputable writers have cheerfully split infinitives. Shaw puts this strangely sensitive phenomenon into perspective. He wrote to *The Times* in 1907:

> There is a busybody on your staff who devotes a lot of time to chasing split infinitives. Every good literary craftsman splits his infinitives when the sense demands it. I call for the immediate dismissal of this pedant. It is of no consequence whether he decides to go quickly, or quickly to go, or to quickly go. The important thing is that he should go at once.[63]

Splitting the infinitive has become commonplace in broadcast reports. This has infected, usually harmlessly, contemporary written style. An example of this was to be found in description of the United Kingdom's former partial membership of the European Monetary System. Statements such as 'it is now time for us to fully join the EMS' represented the most comfortable way of expressing that position.

Notwithstanding the general fall from fashion of this particular form of nitpick, there are many people who will still be irritated by it. That is sufficient reason for exercising caution.

Active or passive voice

The question of active or passive voice has been less definitively resolved. It has generated a great deal of excitement in recent years. It is a fashionable bogey for those in search of a simplistic rule to use for improving reports. Some insist on the active, 'Three departments have not submitted monthly returns', as opposed to the passive, 'Monthly returns have not been submitted by three departments'. There is a substantial difference of emphasis.

If no particular emphasis is required, the active generally reads more naturally. The passive can be a very convenient alternative to an irritating repetition of the first person 'I' at the beginning of every sentence. Like any grammatical form or any expression, if it is used to excess, it becomes wearisome and tedious.

The passive voice will often lead to uncomfortable constructions such as in the American bank report: 'This matter is to be arbitrated on by . . . (such-and-such a)

Court'. The juxtaposition of 'on' and 'by' is unsatisfactory. It would read better as: '. . . Court will arbitrate on this matter'.

There are occasions when the fact that something was done is more important than who did it. There are others when it is not known who did it and the active is impossible, as in: 'The alarm was raised.'

The passive provides a useful and discreet foil to accusations of sexist writing: '. . . when the cause is discovered' rather than 'when he discovers the cause' (in circumstances when the discovery could be made by somebody of either sex). It also circumnavigates the rather affected 'One will discover the cause'.

In his King's Cross report, Fennell used the passive, as in:

> He had been told it was on the Northern line escalator

where it was of no importance who the informant was:

> Further alarm was raised by another passenger, Mr Benstead.[64]

In this latter case what mattered was that further alarm had been raised. It was incidental that it was raised by a passenger (and of little consequence that his name was Mr Benstead).

Dennis Baron, Professor of English and Linguistics at the University of Illinois has recently produced an eloquent and witty defence of the passive[65]. He points out that the loathing for this voice comes partly from the current vogue for keeping writing as brief as possible and a belief that there is something unacceptably new and trendy about the passive. Neither is true. The passive can be shorter than the active. The passive was in common use long before the time of the prescriptive 18th-century grammarians who did nothing to discourage it.

Dangling participle

Various dangling participles have entertained students of English for years, such as 'Coming round the corner, the police station came into view'[66]. These have been obviously and blatantly ludicrous. In most reports the danger is more subtle as in the American Airlines report 'Having considered and itemized our requirements, tenders were examined'. Here the suggestion that the tenders did the considering is more dangerous, as the ambiguity to which it gives rise is less obvious to the writer.

Starting sentences with 'And . . .'

For many years starting sentences with 'And . . .' or even 'But . . .' has been considered unacceptable or at least reprehensible. (It is often overlooked that they occur in, for example, Galsworthy[67].) The reason, unknown to most protagonists of the discipline is that, just as a split infinitive as impossible in Latin, so in classical Latin at least, these words were disallowed as openings. Nowadays, taking a lead from journalism such as this business comment in *The Times*:

> A merger would not have created anything approaching a monopoly which is why it was cleared – after some thought – by relevant anti-trust authorities. But it would

have led to further polarisation in the auditing of major companies, which is already tending to concentrate around less than a dozen international firms. And it could well have led to further defensive mergers among competitors.

it has come to be more and more acceptable in reports.

The Bishop of Salisbury's report *The Church and the Bomb* contains the passage:

> In this context, some of the agreements relating to particular types of armament are significant achievements. Biological weapons have been forsworn. Nuclear weapons have been banned from outer space, the seabed and Antarctica . . . And, of course, within the UN, nations have voted for the resolutions which envisaged the eventual elimination of all nuclear weapons.[68]

For those who may feel that this is the handiwork of trendy, liberal clergymen and, as such, is atypical of business writing, a less progressive source is offered. *The twenty-sixth report from the Committee of Public Accounts* includes in its conclusions:

> The very serious frauds which have come to light in recent years would be cause for concern in any organisation, but they are intolerable in a government department. And the fact that only half of them were detected from within PSA increases the suspicion that much more fraud may have remained undetected.[69]

The 1990 Defence White Paper – a serious formal document – uses the same format.

> The Eastern countries are at last actively cooperating in a range of arms control negotiations (progress on which is described in paragraphs 106 to 127). And most dramatically of all, the countries of Eastern Europe are emerging from forty years of political stagnation and beginning a period of fundamental political change, which NATO hopes will lead to the extension of democratic values throughout Europe.[70]

Person

A separate question of style which may not be considered as strictly part of grammar and idiom, but is closely related to them, is the person in which the report is written.

In a business letter, the person may legitimately be varied within the same document, as in: 'It is our practice to offer 10% off all orders over £10 000', but later, 'I shall arrive on the 6.15 train from Euston'.

With a report, the person should be consistent. The writer must make two choices. The first, as shown in Figure 25 (a), is whether the first or third person is appropriate. The third person is clearly impersonal, but it gives the report (and more especially the recommendations) a formality that may make it more forceful.

With reports in which the personal observations and attitudes of the writer are important, the first person singular 'I' will be appropriate. For example, in a railway accident report the writer's experience during the course of preparing the report may be recorded:

> Subsequently I was advised by Mr A Revitt, the Area Signal and Telecommunications

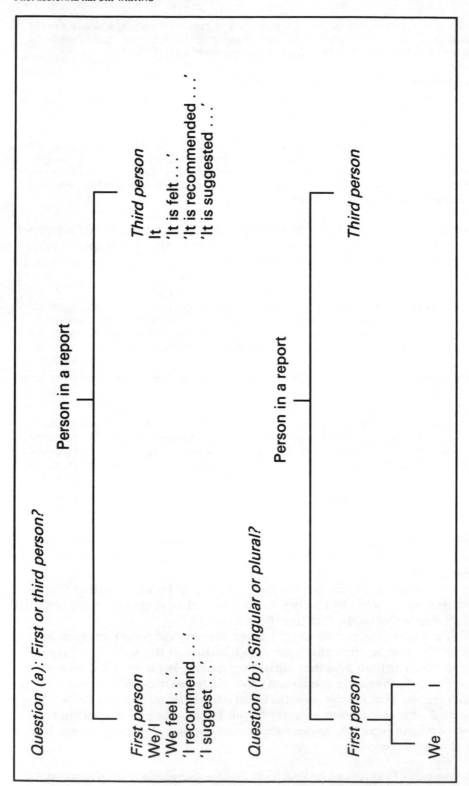

Question (a): First or third person?

Person in a report

First person
We/I
'We feel . . .'
'I recommend . . .'
'I suggest . . .'

Third person
It
'It is felt . . .'
'It is recommended . . .'
'It is suggested . . .'

Question (b): Singular or plural?

Person in a report

First person
We
I

Third person

Figure 25   Choice of first or third person and singular or plural

Engineer that the wiring was stripped from KG8 and physically examined for insulation defects, none were found.[71]

After the Inquiry I rode over the route and in a single round trip from Euston to Watford observed three separate irregular operations of the equipment at different locations.[72]

Equally it may represent a personal view which the author is including as a comment:

The foregoing are all unsatisfactory features and clearly drivers have had just cause to complain about the day to day functioning of the signalling over the route. However, I am satisfied that none of the faults I observed or that have been brought to my attention had any bearing on the accident but clearly drivers should be urged to report faults as soon as they observe them . . .[73]

In other cases it will be the writer's personal experiences which are the whole essence of the paragraph. In such cases, as in this paragraph, from the annual report of one of the four local government ombudsmen, the first person singular is entirely appropriate.

I am sometimes asked what I achieve as a Local Ombudsman. One of the most important facets of my work is settling complaints. I settled 228 in the year under review, 13% of all complaints considered. Some councils, such as Birmingham City Council, have shown a refreshing willingness to make an early settlement and this saves time and expense all round. The substance of such settlements differs little from the remedies I obtain after the issue of a formal report. It may involve an apology, a cash payment, remedial action having money value, procedural changes, or a combination of these elements.[74]

Here is a paragraph from a perfectly respectable internal report from the Airline QANTAS. It is easy to imagine the writer addressing a senior manager in this way in conversation. Yet a written report in this vein does not lose dignity or clarity:

Peak caps and shopping bags are being re-ordered through Regional Headquarters. Personalized book matches will be ordered and I would appreciate simple calling cards for this exercise. With regard to the matches, you may not be aware that the initial order was only on a limited basis at the request of UK/1 (United Kingdom/ Ireland) management to gauge the effectiveness of the idea.

In all cases the writer must consider the tone in which he would address the recipient orally. The ludicrous Victorian pomposity, 'the writer', must be avoided. At the same time, if an informal personal style is adopted, it must not become so matey and colloquial that it loses precision. Two centuries ago, Hazlitt pointed out that 'It is not easy to write a familiar style'. He went on: 'You do not assume, indeed, the solemnity of the pulpit, or the tone of stage-declamation; neither are you at liberty to gabble on at a venture, without emphasis or discretion, or to resort to vulgar dialect . . . You must steer a middle course'[75].

Sexist writing

Avoidance of sexist bias is an example of such a current trend. While awareness of the need to avoid sexual discrimination in writing, just as in any other aspect of business practice, goes back many decades, it was in the 1980s that acceptance of this need became widespread. Impetus was given to this by the increase in the number of women in the workplace. For example, many schools and colleges teach non-sexist writing.

There has been no legislation on the subject. The BBC has produced a code of practice for its own staff outlawing sexist assumptions. This has been greeted with enthusiasm and approval by the Equal Opportunities Commission.

It seems reasonable that where there is an overwhelming majority of one sex in the report's readership, the use of pronouns should reflect this.

The title 'Ms', which first featured in the mid-1970s, came to be adopted even in formal reports extremely quickly. For example, in the biographical sketches at the front of the Challenger report:

> Ms McAuliffe was born in Boston and raised in Framingham, Massachusetts, where she graduated from Framingham State College.[76]

Nevertheless, it is not easy to prepare a long document which is entirely sexually neutral. To do so tends to produce immoderately long sentences, excessive use of the passive and, sometimes, ambiguous writing. Judith Byrne Whyte of the Equal Opportunities Commission, recognizing the full 'he/she' was unwelcome attempted the use of 's/he' in one of her publications. This produced resistance from the publishers.

An excellent inexpensive guidebook recommended by the Commission is Casey Miller and Kate Swift's *The Handbook of Non-Sexist Writing*.[77] This book is constructive, lucid and not in any way strident. It is further discussed in Appendix II.

Capitalization of whole words

The employment of capitals for headings and in other types of layout is covered elsewhere. Certain special uses call for use of capitals or other script. In the report on the loss of the Herald of Free Enterprise the name of the ship

HERALD OF FREE ENTERPRISE

its sister ships

SPIRIT and PRIDE

other vessels such as those that took part in the rescue

RIVER TAMAR
BURGEERMEESTER VAN DAMME

and test programs

NMI FLOOD

were written in capitals[78].

The Jockey Club report on the 1989 St Leger meeting shows horses' names in upper case.

ABLE PLAYER had been galloping along the line of the stands side longitudinal drain, installed in July.

Between the three and two furlong markers, MADRACO fell, bringing down two other runners, PENDOR DANCER and TOLO.[79]

Use of bold face

The use of bold face, particularly in typescript or word-processed reports, should be considered with caution. Some writers place too much reliance on this style to emphasize particular words. In many typefaces the distinction between bold and normal typeface is slight and the emphasis is lost. Some reports in print use it effectively to emphasize important findings. The Herald of Free Enterprise report employs bold face to show a variety of the types of comment; some recommendations are embedded where they are nestling in the text:

Draught gauges or indicators should, if possible, be suitable for interfacing with a Loadicator so that if weight information for vehicles is fed into the Loadicator a running automatic up-date of the ship's condition could be produced. **It is recommended that the Loadicator be in a suitable central position with, if possible, work stations at the two loading stations and on the bridge.**[80]

Other sentences shown in bold face are just comments perceived to be of importance, such as:

In short, the response of the rescue services and of the Belgian people from the King and Queen and Prime Minister to the ordinary people living in and around Zeebrugge was magnificent.[81]

In his King's Cross report, Desmond Fennell used bold face to distinguish specifically-timed events. As is discussed in Chapter 11, one of his main problems was to put the events in an accurate sequence.

Change in style

Style does not stand still. Like vocabulary, all aspects of style change and develop. Changes are not accepted equally quickly by all report-writing cultures. There is a continuum running from such environments as computer manufacturers at one end, ready to accept new forms of expression quickly to complement their dynamic and progressive product, to the more conservative Civil Service departments and legal practices to whom change is fundamentally alien. All others lie between the two.

Change in attitude is demonstrated by the audit partners of Price Waterhouse. In the late 1970s it would have been unacceptable in that firm to split an infinitive, to start a sentence with 'And', to start a sentence with 'But' or to use pairs of dashes as parentheses. Now all these practices are acceptable to a degree and in the right context. Perhaps 60 per cent of the firm's partners and managers would consider split infinitives to be entirely acceptable.

SUMMARY

John Middleton Murray[82] commented that a discussion of the meaning of style would be impossible in six books, much less six lectures. Style is something of a contradiction. It is a question of using the tools and raw materials that are appropriate. Every raw material (words, sentence length, sentence structure and paragraphing) and every tool (punctuation, grammar and – to a point – spelling) is a function of style and must be chosen with care and judgement.

8 Reviewing and editing

Anyone who cares about the clarity and precision of the written word is bound to want to revise his work. Sometimes this will take longer than time permits. Interviewed on the occasion of his 80th birthday the veteran novelist Anthony Powell said:

> I can't write a letter to my bank manager without reading it through and thinking I ought to have done it in quite a different way . . .[1]

The need to review and edit other people's work arises from three situations.

1. The need to review the work of junior staff before it is released, as happens through the various grades of the Civil Service or in partners reviewing the work of staff in accountancy practices and management consultancies.
2. The need to coordinate the contributions of various writers.
3. The need to check over a writer's own work.

REVIEWING THE WORK OF JUNIOR STAFF

Reviewing is essential in order to ensure that the work reflects the integrity and the standards of the company or the department. It is of no interest to the reader that the task has been used as an exercise for the training of junior staff. The level and competence of the advice cannot be compromised.

The effect of over-severe or imprecise advice on junior staff can be devastating, however the following must always be corrected:

1. Technical inaccuracies
2. Ambiguity
3. Repetition
4. A tone which is entirely inappropriate to the readership (although it must be said that the writer should have had the reader's level and area of interest described in detail before the task was undertaken).

Criticising matters of style is a much more delicate business. The variations between the reviewer's and the writer's style are likely to be the result of different ages, upbringings and educations. These can be changed only gradually and, in any case, it is probably only appropriate to alter it if it is seriously adrift from the style of the organization.

A maximum of one stylistic comment per report is probably going to be effective. The writer can then concentrate on this next time without overlooking anything or being daunted by too long a list. Stylistic comments should always be constructive and specific. A red line through a page with no further comment is rude and time-wasting. The author is left guessing as to a better approach, no more accurately than choosing numbers off a roulette wheel and probably with no greater chance of success.

Examples of the style to be imitated should be produced and the desirable features to be imitated pointed out.

COORDINATING THE WORK OF A VARIETY OF WRITERS

A great deal of time can be saved by circulating specifics of the areas in which consistency is required beforehand. This is a particularly good idea if the contributors to the report are working in different places.

When the report is typed or printed, it should not be possible to tell that it has been prepared by several contributors. Areas calling for coordination through instructions before and editing afterwards include:

1. *Style.* This will be particularly evident through sentence structure. Some may write in huge elaborate sentences and lengthy paragraphs while others will feel drawn towards a note telegraphic form with short staccato paragraphs.
2. *Vocabulary.* Some variation in personal choice of words is inevitable but the extremes can be controlled and, if necessary, eliminated. For example legalistic terms or archaisms can generally be eliminated.
3. *Person.* Every contributor must write in the same person, 'We', 'I' or the third person, producing the somewhat impersonal 'It is'. Whichever seems appropriate must be agreed before anyone puts pen to paper in order to save time in editing.
4. *Perception of the readership.* Again, before embarking on the task a conference of the contributors should be held to agree the kind of reader at whom the report is aimed. Among factors to be considered are:

   age
   technical competence
   understanding of the subject
   seniority
   known bias or prejudice
   known preference of report length
   known preferences of layout.

5. *Structure.* A provisional structure can also be agreed at the beginning of report preparation. This can then be checked at periodic meetings.
6. *Repetition and omission.* However well-planned the structure may be, a

report is almost certain to omit certain things and to repeat others when it is the work of several people.

7. *Balance.* If individual contributors are made responsible for separate sections, there will be a slight variation in the length of treatment, which should be ironed out as much as possible where the contributors are dealing with subjects of comparable importance.

This kind of task is greatly eased by a simple set of guidelines aimed equally at managers and secretaries. Many organizations waste a great deal of time in the preparation of reports by having no house style for the arrangement and coordination of detail in a report.

Such a system should never become burdensome or too restrictive, although it can save time and nervous energy.

1. They ease coordination of work, if the report is being produced by contributors from several offices or departments.
2. They minimize the secretarial instructions necessary.
3. The author does not have to waste time pondering over various options of layout, making it easier to work under pressure.
4. They provide or endorse a corporate image.

COMMITTEE WORK

The coordination of the contributions of a committee also produces wide problems of management. The members of the committee will be working at different paces on different parts of the work. Some will be on a draft of one part at a time when they are required to give their attention to the final proof of another. They will become isolated from one another and preoccupied with their own responsibilities for the time being. If different vested interests are represented or different principles, disagreement is bound to arise and inevitably sometimes bitterness. After the 54 meetings of the committee of 22 which prepared *A Language for Life*, Lord Bullock always required them to lunch together. He placed great importance on these lunches and the harmony achieved and maintained by them[2].

APPROACH

The time available for reviewing should be divided into three phases.

Phase One. Read through the report like a personal letter, ensuring that it is understood and that the arguments are clear and persuasive. Do not be distracted by details.

Phase Two. Examine the structure of the report. Check that the sequence is logical, the report is balanced and the headings represent clear signposts pointing the reader's path through the argument. Check that the whole structure reflects the report objective.

If the report has an adequate table of contents, these points can be analysed from that. If there is none, or if it does not reflect the detailed structure of the document, it is a good idea to rough out the report sections and sub-titles on a sheet of paper, so that they can be examined more easily.

Phase 3. Examine the minutiae. Unlike Phases One and Two which will take a finite period, this is an open-ended task. The extent to which they can be completely examined will be a function of time available.

The precise emphasis of this phase will depend on the purpose and readership of the report. It is likely to include:

1. Technical symbols used.
2. Abbreviations and the point at which they are introduced.
3. Cross-referencing both to paragraphs and appendices.
4. Reference to documents.
5. Digestible sentence length.
6. Consistent paragraph numbering (if used).
7. Consistent and logical use of paragraph headings.
8. Consistent expression of numerals.
9. Spelling.

SCISSOR-AND-PASTE JOBS

It will sometimes be expedient, or just unavoidable, to stick bits of earlier reports or other documents into a report. A first attempt may be cut up quite savagely, but with certain paragraphs usually salvaged. All the editorial problems described above apply here. In addition particular care must be taken with pronouns: 'it', 'he', 'these', and so on. Do they refer to what is intended? Should the full noun be introduced?

CONTROL OF THE MANUSCRIPT

Great care must be taken to ensure that the manuscript and, later, the typescript is circulated safely during its preparation. It is rare for the whole document to go astray, although such things have happened. More likely dangers to guard against include:

1. Pages becoming detached by accident. Pages of a draft should therefore be numbered, contrary to the routine in many offices, and the total number of pages should be shown on the front of the draft; even if such a total number would not be appropriate on the end-product.
2. Specialists detaching their sections, while the rest of the report goes on its way. Such practice should never be allowed. It is almost impossible to keep track of a draft if it starts to be dismembered.
3. Circulating several copies of a report in the mistaken view that it is likely to save time. This should be allowed only if each recipient is to be responsible for amending a different section of the draft. If differing revisions are submitted independently without conference, the versions will be so diverse that they will be almost impossible to reconcile.

For control of a draft, many organizations use a proforma. Figure 26 shows the

JOB PROGRESS SHEET FOR GENERAL WORK

JOB NO ....

DATE RECEIVED ....

TITLE/NO .... INTERNAL/EXTERNAL ISSUE

COST REF ....

AUTHOR/DEPT ....

DATE REQUIRED ....

SPECIFICATION

PAPER (SIZE/WEIGHT)   A4/FOOLSCAP   70 g/85 g

COVER .... BINDING ....

NO OF COPIES ....

PROGRESS	DATE
(1) TEXT	
EDITING	
TO TYPIST	
PROOFREADING	
TYPIST FOR CORRECTION	
FINAL PROOFREADING	
TO AUTHOR FOR APPROVAL	
RETURNED BY AUTHOR	
TYPIST FOR AMENDMENTS	
FINAL PROOFREADING	
TO OFFSET/XEROX	
COLLATING & BINDING	
COMPLETED AND PASSED TO AUTHOR	

TOTAL NO OF PAGES .... TOTAL NO OF FIGURES ....

Figure 26   National Nuclear Corporation's job progress sheet for general work

job progress sheet employed by the National Nuclear Corporation. The progress table should have enough columns or boxes to allow for the maximum possible number of retypings. For several dates and signatures to be crammed into one slot is confusing and likely to defeat the object of the control which the form is intended to provide.

9 Summaries and concise writing

In *Richard III*, the murderers en route to murder Clarence give Brackenbury a very terse factual reply to his question. 'What, are you so brief?' asks Brackenbury. 'O Sir', one of them replies, 'it is better to be brief than tedious'[1].

Conciseness has been described above as a fundamental characteristic of written communication. However there are degrees of conciseness. Sometimes a summary or abstract will be required, which may take the form of a summary to surmount a complex document as a guide to its content. Such a need was described in Chapter 5. It may take the form of an abstract to stand on its own independently of the report. In either case the general principles are the same.

One-page summaries are extensively used in commerce, industry and government. Much use is made of them in written briefings for senior executives in the Ford Motor Company, for instance. General George C. Marshall placed great emphasis on one-page summaries[2]. Eisenhower and Churchill were similarly disposed.[3]

Figure 64 from the Black report shows a complex cycle of activities in a way which is manageable even by the non-scientific reader.

The principles described here also apply in the preparation of summaries to appear at the front of many reports, as required by many house styles.

SUMMARIES

Many companies have established the rule that all reports must be surmounted by a Summary or even a 'reader's (*sic*) synopsis (as though the rest of the report was written for the benefit of the writer). If the reader is not going to read the rest of the report, who is? This policy is based on the view that the reader is likely to be very busy. Indeed he may be so, although sometimes 'busy' is a euphemism for 'idle'.

These are helpful uses of a Summary:

1. To consolidate the findings of a huge report. In such cases it is unreasonable to expect every reader to study every word even of the Conclusions and

Recommendations. So a Summary can provide a valuable service in drawing out the main points.
2. To act as the blurb of a book and to indicate to the reader whether it is desirable to read the rest of the report or not.
3. To provide an opportunity to change technical gear and to present the main implications for the general reader who does not wish to become embroiled in the esoteric detail.

Certain dangers must be noted:

1. In no circumstances should the Summary be drafted until every word of the report has been written. Otherwise the writer is in danger of justifying the Summary in the report.
2. No information or description which is not in the main body must be included in the Summary.
3. Most important, the Summary should not regurgitate the Introduction, Conclusions and Recommendations. Readers could – or should be able to (if the report is well structured and clearly labelled) – find these for themselves.

Good examples of helpful and concise summaries can sometimes be found near the front of annual reports. Provided they are restricted to a modicum of salient information they will be a useful quick guide to the affairs of the reporting company. They will probably be about 12 lines and will comprise a simple comparison of the current and previous year's figures.

Organizations that make routine use of summaries often develop proformas for this purpose. These set out the salient points in a configuration to which the readers have become accustomed.

Excellent systems have been evolved by Shannon Free Airport Development Company. If a report makes definite recommendations, these appear on the front sheet. All their reports over three pages long call for a synopsis at the front, but sometimes it may be possible for it to be extremely brief.

A simple and very helpful form of this type of cover-sheet summary is found in the internal auditors' investigation reports of Coca-Cola Southern Bottlers. These are very thorough reports involving many detailed observations. The one-page summary sheet therefore sets out

> REASONS FOR INVESTIGATION
> MAIN FINDINGS
> MAIN RECOMMENDATIONS
> ACTION:
>> ALREADY TAKEN
>> TO BE TAKEN

The semantics of this type of abbreviated description can be muddled. A summary of a different kind under the title 'Abstract' is found in the Communications Studies and Planning Ltd/Equal Opportunities Commission report, *Information Technology in the Office: The Impact on Women's Jobs*[4]. The summary just expands briefly on the table of contents to give a bit more guidance to the reader as to the content of the sections.

APPROACH

The preparation of such abstracts of longer documents is commonplace. Most people use abstracts to prepare notes for their own use, even if they do not produce them formally for other people.

It is most important before setting out on the task of sifting and editing the minutiae to identify the main theme or purpose of the original, for this must always be borne in mind when producing the abstracted report, just as it must in writing a report from scratch. The message of a report is like the plot of a novel. In order to understand the story, it is important not to miss out the main twists and developments.

An abstract is essentially selective, but it must be balanced. It is easy and tempting to concentrate on the unusual, the amusing and the bizarre. This happens in the press and it may well be a proper part of a newspaper's obligation to sell copy and its duty to entertain, but it has no place in the preparation of abstracted reports.

GUIDELINES TO PREPARATION

Emphasis

The emphasis in an abstract is a balance – possibly even a compromise – between the original writer's aim and the abstract reader's interest and requirements. The abstractor must keep asking himself what parts will be particularly relevant to the reader. Some of this will be dictated by the reader's responsibilities or scope of trade. For example:

1. If the company is a multinational, a section of the original dealing with companies employing under 100 people will attract little or no coverage in either the abstract or the summary.
2. If the company brews lager and light ale, a section on stout is likely to merit little space.
3. If the company's sites are all in the Midlands, details of housing policies in North Yorkshire are unlikely to be of interest.

Key points

The principle of emphasis described above is the most important. It overrides all other considerations.

The abstracter must next look for key points in the original. An illustration is given by the Department of Transport/Home Office Green Paper on Road Traffic Law [5], which was a provocative and far-reaching publication, from which many abstracts must have been made. In it the departments concerned proposed a simplification of road traffic law by the introduction of a points system.

Headings

The headings in the original paper indicate the way in which the writer has tackled the subject. The table of contents will give a good idea as to the sequence of headings and the balance of the paper:

> Fixed Penalty System – Improvements to Present Machinery
> Fixed Penalty System – Extension to Other Traffic offences
> A Points System
> Costs and Benefits

These explain the four divisions of the writer's treatment. In most abstracts all four parts will have to be represented. However, the abstracter must take the process a stage further and look at individual headings and determine which parts are relevant; for example, in the section on the Points System:

> Classification of offences
> Points values
> Disqualification
> Other penalties
> Wiping the slate clean
> Driving while disqualified
> Vehicle penalties vis-a-vis a points system
> Legislation

Here some elimination may be possible. Most employers will not be interested in the paragraphs on 'driving while disqualified'. In most companies where there is a high standard of vehicle maintenance, it should not be necessary to take up any space in the abstract on 'vehicle defect and traffic sign offences'.

Annexes, of which there are 13 in this case, must be checked for relevance. Their very nature means that they are unlikely to justify any inclusion in an abstract. There will be exceptions. A computer manufacturer, for instance, might be interested in Annex N: Capital and setting-up costs. This goes into the mechanics and equipment for introducing the new system.

Introduction

As was seen in Chapter 2, the introduction to the original is likely to be heavily weighted with important material. It is the same here. The background, purpose and method of working are set out in the five introductory paragraphs and will merit quite detailed explanation in the abstract. Some parts of the introduction can be ignored, for example:

1. A paragraph describing the sequence of the report.
2. Another explaining how the authors kept in touch with a comparable Scottish committee (unless, of course, the abstract is prepared for a reader in Scotland).

Important points

Certain points are likely to be deserving of detailed scrutiny before the abstract-writer dispenses with them. That does not mean to say that they all have to be included, but each must be considered carefully before it is discarded:

1. Listed matter, particularly if marked with bullet points. The authors of the Green Paper give six reasons why the anticipated behaviour of motorists can not be directly extrapolated from current reactions.
2. Anything that the original author has prefaced by numerical adverbs: 'first', 'second', 'third', and so on. This indicates that these are separate aspects to the problem which the writer considers important.
3. Proper nouns. In this case certain constabularies and certain government departments are named. The sources of the experiences and comments should be identifiable.
4. Acts of Parliament and regulations. These may have an important legal implication on the reader's business. It may be dangerous to avoid this. Sections and sub-sections are unlikely to be necessary.
5. Numerical detail. For example, 'Costs are based on the assumption that a new style minicomputer capable of handling 20 000 tickets a year will be required by each manually operated office'. In many abstracts the figure 'will give a helpful indication of the size of the problem.
6. Comments on future developments. In most cases, the future is likely to be even more important than the background.

METHOD

Mechanics

The following approach will usually ensure conciseness:

1. Read the original passage in its entirety to ensure an overview.
2. Strike out material which it is not relevant to abstract (as, for example the paragraph mentioned above on disqualified drivers).
3. Re-read the first paragraph, then put aside (or close) the original and note any relevant points on a piece of rough paper.
4. If no points come to mind as being important, re-read to ensure that the paragraph is irrelevant.
5. Continue with subsequent paragraphs. (It is a good idea to note the paragraph or page numbers in the margin of the rough notes, to check detail subsequently.)
6. Write out the rough notes as a fair copy, without looking at the original.
7. Check the fair copy of the abstract against the original for accuracy.

Direct copying

Direct copying of prose from the original is unlikely to be justified. However important two or three sentences may seem, they will almost certainly take up a disproportionate amount of room in the final abstract. What looks like an insignificant amount of material in a few lines of the original might take up nearly half of the one-page abstract if copied directly. Similarly it is unlikely that there will be room to reproduce tables. It may be possible to restate totals from the bottom of tables in the original.

Quotation

The dangers of copying, due to the importance of the original sentences or sloth of the abstract-writer, have been discussed. It should also be unnecessary to quote even single phrases directly from the original. Exceptionally, they may constitute an important theme in the original and quotation would be justified.

For instance, in an abstract of the White Paper, *Industrial Democracy,*[6] which followed Bullock, the following would be a reasonable paragraph:

> The authors see such a system as providing a framework for satisfying the various parties' differing objectives, so that conflict can be avoided. They use the expression 'partnership rather than defensive co-existence' to illustrate their principle.

A quotation should never be included just because the writer cannot think of an alternative more concise form of expression.

Style

Long sentences are particularly inappropriate in abstracts. On the other hand a telegraphic style without main verbs is likely to lead to ambiguity. Very short headings will sometimes help conciseness.

Comment

Imposition of the abstracter's own comment should be clearly identified in one of two ways:

1. By change of style, possibly even introducing the first or second person ('I feel . . .' or 'You will note . . .').
2. A sub-heading 'Comment' before the remark.

Attributability

As shown above, examples may often be identified by source, although it is less likely that the abstracter will be able to afford the luxury of attributing observations to individual commentators in the original paper. Exceptionally, the commentator's background may make it particularly important to name him. He may have experience of the trade, area or company concerned.

Caveat

However good the abstract, something is bound to be lost if the original has been well written. Every word should have been included in the original for a purpose. When wording is removed and reduced, some fine shade of meaning or detail will go also. As Benny Green[7] said: 'If you are going to sum up Marcel Proust in four lines you are not going to get very profound.'

Examples

The Monopolies and Mergers Commission report[8] on the Kuwait Investment Authority's acquisition of a substantial shareholding in BP has an excellent summary. It is further enhanced by sub-titles and some useful cross-references. The report is 100 pages long and the Summary consists of 1½ pages (eight paragraphs). It is broken down into:

> The merger situation
> The issues
> Assurances and undertakings
> Our conclusions on the public interest
> Our recommendations

Cross-referencing from Summary sections is extremely useful. Firstly, it provides pointers to the reader who may question some general claim in the Summary. Secondly, it can act as a useful discipline to the writer to ensure that all the points in the Summary are supported by passages in the main text.

The Kuwait/BP report does this:

> Despite this disclaimer, the Commission gave due and careful consideration to the provisions of the Deed and to the assurances previously given embodied in it and concluded that limiting voting rights to 14.9 per cent would not in the circumstances remove the ability to influence the policy of BP and that the overall size of the shareholding gave cause for concern. The Commission's reasons appear fully in the report (paragraphs 8.32 to 8.39 and paragraphs 8.123 to 8.125).

and

> The Commission have concluded (Chapter 8) that the merger situation may be expected to operate against the public interest.

Also, unusually, there is a cross-reference to an appendix.

> On 3 May 1988 the Secretary of State for Trade and Industry required the Commission to investigate and report on whether a merger situation had been created and, if so, whether it operated or may be expected to operate against the public interest.[8]

This is unusual as most readers will wish to refer from the Summary to the main entry in the report before going to the detail of the appendix. In this case, however, a pointer to the precise, albeit legalistic and ponderous, terms of reference is justified.

As a guide, probably no more than two cross-references should be made.

The audit practice of Price Waterhouse often make valuable use of this idea in their Salient Features section, where one or two pages of the main points will be reproduced. A particularly wise comment from a Price Waterhouse audit partner suggested that the Salient Features should contain no more information than the client Chairman can memorize and carry into the meeting in his head. These are often helpfully cross-referenced to the body of the report as in this Salient Feature from an acquisition report:

The current circulation list comprises approximately 15 000 of which only 10 200 are mailed each week. Both these figures include a duplication of some 1 260 rotated addresses (paragraph 29).

This passage from the Monopolies Commission report on BP/Kuwait Investment Authority[9] is another example.

1.4 The economy of Kuwait, which has vast reserves of low-cost oil, is heavily dependent on oil extraction, refining and marketing and Kuwait is one of the founder members of the Organisation of the Petroleum Exporting Countries (OPEC) and plays a leading part in that organization. The state-owned Kuwait Petroleum Corporation (KPC) operates on a world-wide basis in all sectors of the oil industry.

1.5 BP, and Kuwait through KPC, are therefore major participants and competitors in the oil industry, both in extraction and downstream activities. The oil policies of OPEC and Kuwait have diverged and still diverge from those of HMG and BP.

The KPC and OPEC abbreviations used in Paragraph 1.5 were introduced in Paragraph 1.4, as can be seen above. The HMG (Her Majesty's Government) and BP (British Petroleum Co plc) were introduced in an earlier paragraph.

The 248-page Fennell report into the King's Cross Underground fire[10] has a five-page Executive Summary. Paragraph 1 poses three questions:

(i)   How did the fire start?
(ii)   Why was there a flashover?
(iii) Why did 31 people die?

Paragraphs 2 to 10 provide a summarized answer to these. Paragraphs 11 to 26 give an overview of the sequence and format of the report in the following terms:

In Chapter 13 I consider London Underground's approach to passenger safety both before and after the King's Cross fire. That approach was particularly important in the light of London Regional Transport's view that safety was principally a matter for the operating company, London Underground. Although I accept that London Underground . . .[11]

TECHNIQUES OF CONCISE WRITING

1. Identify the main points which it is intended to make (if necessary noting them down on a piece of paper).
2. Allocate a paragraph to each (or, in a highly concise document such as a memo, a sentence each).
3. Keep the sentence as brief as possible without being staccato or disjointed.
4. Keep the sentences to scale with the size of the paragraphs.
5. Embellish the sentences with carefully chosen words (particularly adverbs and adjectives) to give them greater life.
6. Ensure that padding words which add nothing to the sentence are pruned out.

SUMMARY

Some information can be struck out of the original as being irrelevant to the subject-matter. The abstract should never be drafted straight from the original: a set of rough notes should be used as a half-way stage.

Certain details such as itemized information, numbers and proper nouns are likely to be worth preserving in the abstract. Direct copying should never be undertaken, quotation very seldom.

The purpose and theme of the original should always be borne in mind.

10 Visual illustrations

'A minute of maths is worth an inch in *The Guardian*', explained Kingsley Amis in *I Want It Now*[1]. Graphic and sometimes numerical presentations can add enormous clarity and great precision to a report. On the other hand very often it is a spurious enlightenment. The picture looks good at first glance, but adds nothing.

It is easy to ignore individual differences and distinctions in order to produce an attractive simplistic display. A few years ago the Soviet Union expressed an enthusiasm for quantifying everything: steel, petrol, shoe production and the rest. It was a convenient way of comparing pre-and post-revolutionary performance. Thus the Tula region could be shown to boast 42 writers, as opposed to one previously. No mention was made that the one was Tolstoy[2].

These days there are few reports which are not enhanced by some illustration, that is, everything which is not prose.

PLACING

Some illustrations will be better in appendices. Some will be more conveniently accommodated in the body of the report. There are four reasons which may suggest that information should be relegated to appendices:

1. *Relevance* It should never be essential to look at an appendix. The report should always stand on its own: the journey from the Introduction to the Conclusions and Recommendations should always be possible without reference to the appendices (see Figure 19).
2. *Size* Larger illustrations will interrupt the reader's flow and should be placed in appendices. Clearly this is sometimes going to contradict the principle of relevance. A compromise must be reached. Very large tabulations, however important, must be attached as appendices. They can, if necessary, be summarized quite generously in the body of the report. Conversely, a very small illustration (such as a table of three columns and four lines) is probably better placed in the body of the report. It is unreasonable to expect the reader to turn through 40 or 50 pages of text just to refer to such brief information.

3. *Complexity* Sometimes the technical complexity of the information will have the same disturbing effect on the flow of the report as very lengthy data. This kind of detail is more comfortably placed in an appendix.
4. *Number of times to which it is referred* If an illustration is referred to a number of times, it is more satisfactory to have it at the back as an appendix. It can then be referred to more conveniently as the reader works his way through the report. Ideally it should be on a larger sheet of paper, say A3 if the report is on A4. It can then be left sticking out as the report is studied. If the inner surface can be left blank as shown in Figure 27, the reader does not have to keep turning the pages back. Examples of this may be such things as organization charts, maps, plans or sometimes financial statements. A detailed layout of the sister-ship *Spirit of Free Enterprise* was attached at the back of the *Herald of Free Enterprise* report[3]. This was essential to an understanding of the detailed accounts of the events.

The Fennell report[4] on the Kings Cross Underground fire effectively has 13 figures treated in this way. Most of these illustrate minutiae of layout of the underground station. Two of them provide useful information on organization: one on the London Underground management structure (with those who gave evidence to the inquiry and their reporting times highlighted in red) and the other showing the safety organization hierarchy.

Wherever possible, tables should be orientated the same as the text. If it is expedient to lay a table on its side so that it can take advantage of the shape of the paper, the diagram, titles and key must all be the same way up. The appendix number should be the same way up as the main paper so that it can be found easily (Figure 28).

Although an illustration is supportive of the report, it must stand on its own. It must be comprehensible without reference to the text.

PURPOSE

When considering the inclusion of illustrations, the writer should question their purpose. Focusing directly on this will raise two issues: first, whether the picture is necessary at all, and secondly what form is most appropriate. There are three reasons for including an illustration in a report. Each will suggest a different range of formats:

1. To clarify a general impression.
2. To permit the reader to take specific readings.
3. To demonstrate a relationship.

CLARIFYING A GENERAL IMPRESSION

The old cliché, a picture is worth a thousand words, is true in many kinds of reports. In particular, all annual reports, and those which are produced with a non-technical readership in mind, benefit greatly from simple illustrations. If they are to retain their impact, they should be kept simple

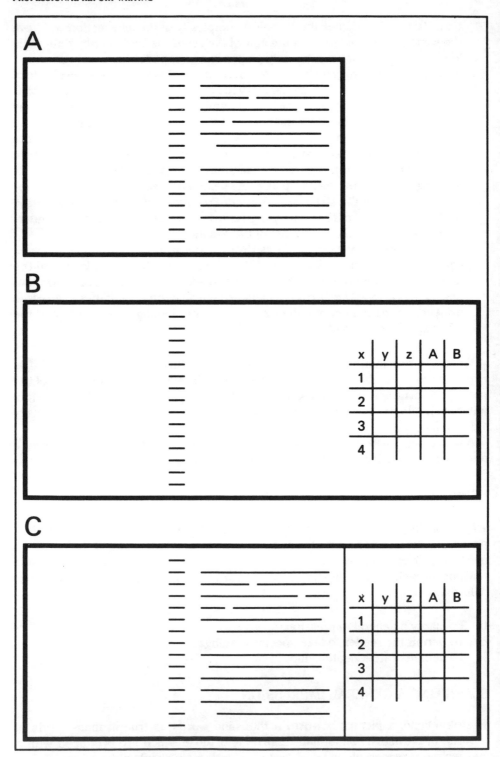

Figure 27   Use of fold-out appendices

APPENDIX D

STAFFING LEVELS MIDLANDS

SITES AS AT 1 SEPTEMBER 1990

	Managers	Supervisors	Warehousemen	Secs	Clerks
Birmingham					
Leicester					
Loughborough					
Nottingham					
Solihull					

Figure 28   Alignment of titles in a table in an appendix

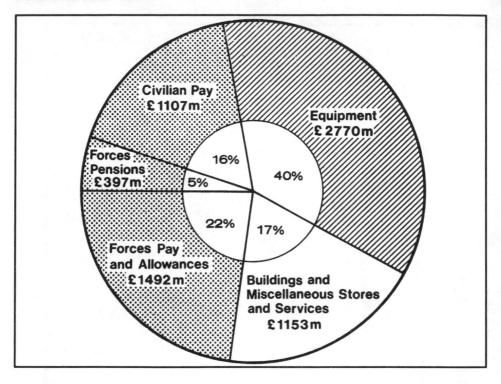

Figure 29   Clear pie chart which could be improved by more distinctive shading

Pie charts

Among the most popular (and, by some, the most derided) of the types of picture which create a general impression are pie charts. They are greatly enhanced by use of colours. If colours are not available the styles of shading used must be distinct. The pie chart in Figure 29 has much merit. At first glance the segments on 'Forces Pay and Allowances', 'Forces Pensions', 'Civilian Pay' and 'Equipment' appear to be similar, yet 'Buildings and Miscellaneous Stores and Services' appears to be entirely different and indeed to have something in common with the percentages which are also on less shaded fields[5]. Three distinct shadings for the sectors are required.

Pie chart segments should be sufficiently large for the type of shading to be easily distinguished. When the segments are very thin, there is not enough shading in the segments for the spots, hachures, lines or other markings to be distinguished.

A pie chart is appropriate only where the whole item is being represented. This may be something such as expenditure (as in Figure 29) or sources of pollution or types of raw material. A pie chart should have at least three segments and eight or nine will normally be the maximum.

A good pie chart with distinct shadings and with the percentages clearly labelled is shown in Figure 30[6]. Perhaps the distinction of shading between lactose and sucrose could be a bit more pronounced but in the main it is a clear illustration.

If, when two adjacent pie charts are displayed to demonstrate a total increase

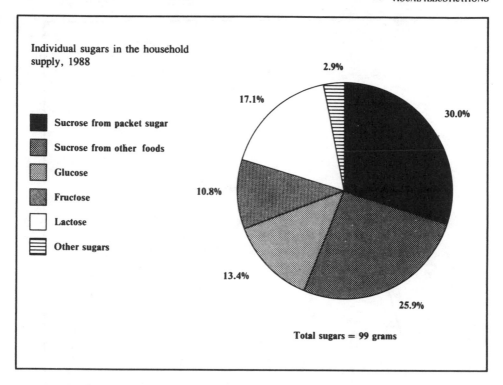

Individual sugars in the household supply, 1988

- Sucrose from packet sugar
- Sucrose from other foods
- Glucose
- Fructose
- Lactose
- Other sugars

2.9%
17.1%
30.0%
10.8%
13.4%
25.9%

Total sugars = 99 grams

Figure 30 Simple pie chart

from, say, £2.5 million to £4.9 million (in other words about double), the area of the pie chart is doubled, the area of the diagram will increase as a function of π and will become disproportionately large and thus misleading.

The inclusion of a spurious third dimension to many diagrams is becoming increasingly fashionable. This vogue adds no precision to the picture but is generally quite harmless. An example, from an annual report[7], is shown in Figure 31. This is not misleading but if the segments extended out of the pie formation, it might be. For example the Marine and Aviation segment, which is only 6 per cent, might look disproportionately large if it stuck out more. There is a danger of the size of the slice giving the impression of a much greater proportion.

Fanciful attempts to show pie charts with crusts, knives poised above them and even birds flying out must be resisted. Certainly a pie chart is intended just to show generalizations and these ludicrous embellishments can only be a distraction.

Bar charts

The same urge to add an irrelevant third dimension is found in the preparation of bar charts. Frequently, in annual reports and similar documents, bar charts will take the form of some relevant symbol. Recent Burton's annual reports have shown various aspects of performance as strips of cloth, squared off at the top. All these are entirely innocuous, but a bank in the Middle East showing its turnover as

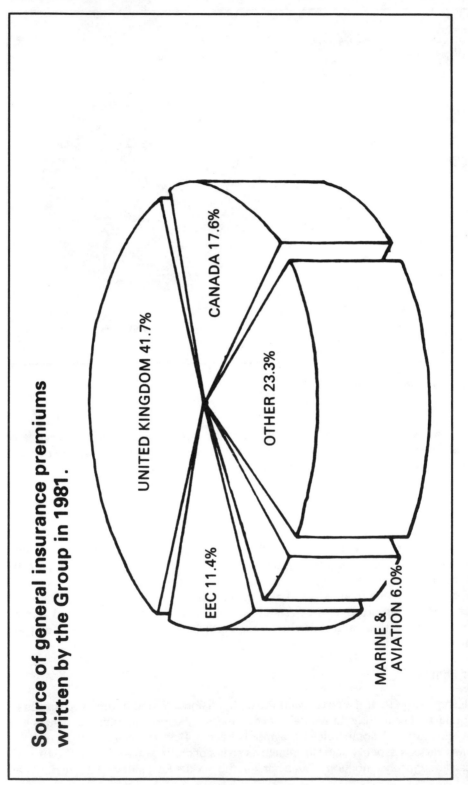

Source of general insurance premiums written by the Group in 1981.

UNITED KINGDOM 41.7%

CANADA 17.6%

OTHER 23.3%

EEC 11.4%

MARINE & AVIATION 6.0%

Figure 31   Pie chart: Insurance group's premiums

a series of palm trees runs the risk of confusion. The imprecise shape of the tree makes for uncertainty. There are four types of bar chart:

Simple bar chart

Bar charts are particularly useful for showing a succession of figures which do not have any sub-categories (Figure 32)[8]. Frequently the figures will speak for themselves and the inclusion of a diagram is an unnecessary encumbrance.

Compound bar chart

These will show sub-divisions of a total, such as that in Figure 33 from the Cleveland Child Abuse report[9]. They are admirable for showing a general impression, but if the reader wants to take specific readings (for example the number of 13 year-old girls in Figure 33) it is not easy to do so even if the y-axis is marked in detail. This is often colloquially known as a stack-bar.

Multiple bar charts

Multiple bar charts in which the bars are bundled together so that they have a common start-point at 0 will permit individual bars to be read without losing the general impression. An example is given in Figure 34[10]. It shows seven types of household, each of which is represented by a bundle of four bars, one for each income group. Many readers find the horizontal dotted lines a useful aid to reading the table (particularly if the y-scale is shown only on one side). Sometimes where very fine calculations are involved figures can be shown on top of the bars. The same approach can be used if tackled carefully to show raw data and percentages. Figure 35 from the Black report[11] does this with percentages in the y-axis and numbers of children on top of the bars.

Compound-multiple bar chart

Figure 36 shows how a compound bar chart can be combined with a multiple bar chart. The figure is able to show a great deal of information in a restricted space. The type of shading for meat products could be better distinguished from carcass meat, however[12].

All broken scales should be broken as near the end as possible and in as pronounced and obvious a way as possible.

The widths of the pillars should not vary except to illustrate intentional differences in volume.

Pictograms

Straightforward pictures may often both enliven a turgid explanation and clarify points. A very broad comparison such as that in Figure 37 can be demonstrated by a pictogram[13]. Figures are rounded and the simplistic presentation accounts only for quantity. There is no representation of quality or performance. Nevertheless the general impression survives effectively.

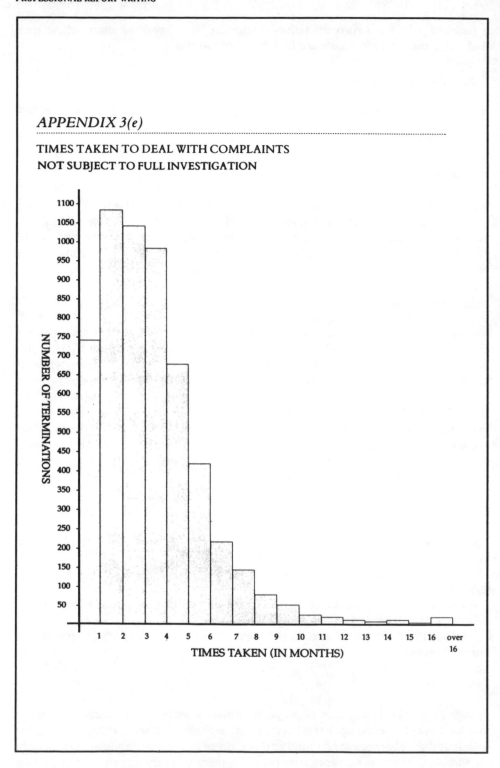

APPENDIX 3(e)

TIMES TAKEN TO DEAL WITH COMPLAINTS
NOT SUBJECT TO FULL INVESTIGATION

Figure 32   Simple bar chart

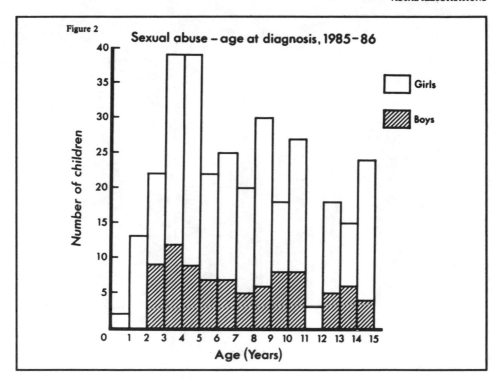

Figure 33   Compound bar chart

Tables enabling the reader to take specific readings

Graphs

The most commonly used figure is a graph. Where more than one variable is represented the lines must clearly be distinguished by the way in which they are marked.

Ideally the y-axis should be marked on both sides, particularly on highly informative and quite detailed graphs. It ensures that the reader's ruler is straight when taking readings. Sometimes this can be achieved by using feint horizontal lines.

If a graph shows positive and negative quantities, it is usual to show 0 as a distinct horizontal line, as in Figure 38.

False zeros sometimes generate strangely emotive comments. There is no reason why the y-axis need start from 0, any more than the x-axis tracing monthly production need start in January. If most of the figures plotted are percentages or functions of an index of 100, they may well produce most of their readings between 80 and 120. In such a case, starting the y-axis at 0 would waste space, cramp the detail and generally be silly. The scale must not, however, distort the information in a way that is misleading.

The intervals on the axes must represent the level of detail in which the reader is likely to be interested. No other criterion is relevant.

Logarithmic scales cannot show 0 or negative quantities. They can be justified

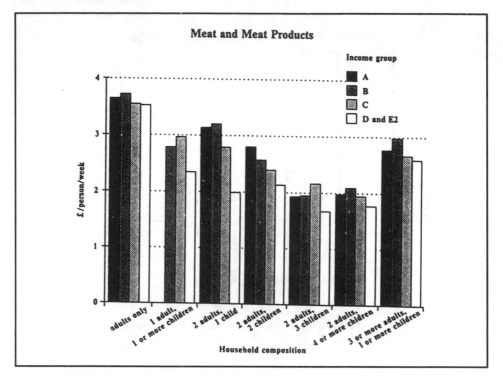

Figure 34   Multiple bar chart

where it is necessary to show two widely differing variables on one graph, but they can be misleading and should be used only where essential.

Columnized tables

Columnized numerical detail or other tables are an important part of many reports.

Examples are shown in Figures 39–41. Figure 39 from the Agricultural Department of the States of Jersey shows how a simple table on tomato yields can be inserted in the text with no surrounding boxes. On the other hand Figure 40 from the same report in which there are seven columns and more detail demands some columnization. In particular the grouping of grades CB, D and E under a parent heading is important.

Figure 41 is from a medical report produced for the States of Guernsey. Here vertical lines are even more important to disentangle three types of data. The figure demonstrates the importance of inserting a dash or zero where there is no detail. Without these, it would be difficult to follow horizontal lines across. For example, in the area of Feet, Spine, Epilepsy for Juniors a substantial blank space would occur without these dashes and readings would be difficult. The abbreviation 'N/A' is ambiguous. It can be used but it should be made clear if it means not available, not applicable, not acknowledged, not answered.

Tables with a √ or a 'X' configuration to show whether a particular variable is present or not have become increasingly popular. They have merit, particularly in

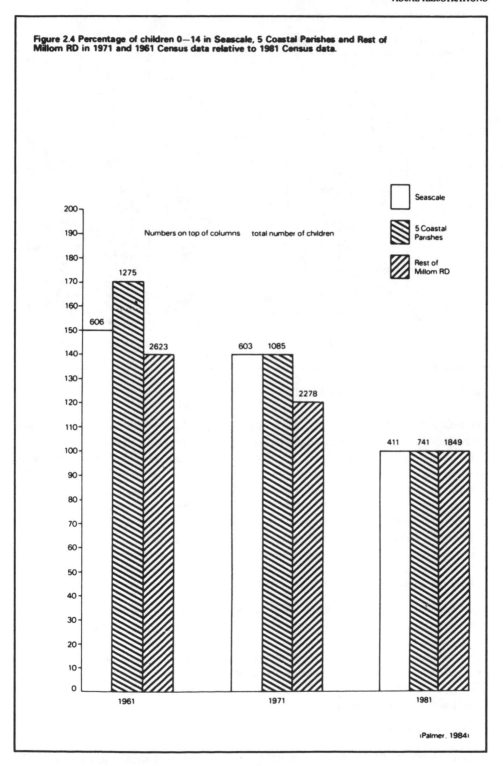

Figure 2.4 Percentage of children 0—14 in Seascale, 5 Coastal Parishes and Rest of Millom RD in 1971 and 1961 Census data relative to 1981 Census data.

Numbers on top of columns   total number of children

Seascale

5 Coastal Parishes

Rest of Millom RD

1961   1971   1981

(Palmer, 1984)

Figure 35   Multiple bar chart complemented by further readings on top of the bars

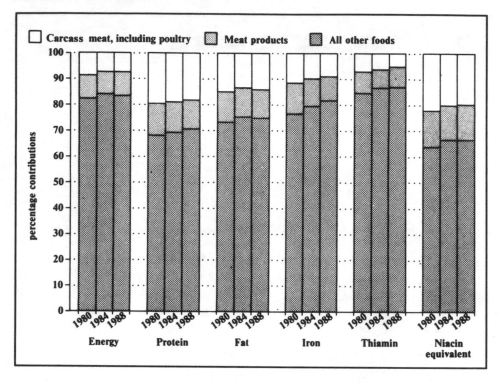

Figure 36   Compound multiple bar chart

providing a simplified summary for a committee of laypeople, most of whom are unaware of the details and unlikely to be much interested in them.

Problems arise where more complicated options are represented in this way. Categorized classifications, often a rating scale of stars '★ ★ ★', '★ ★' and '★', and so on, are sometimes used. Generally these represent judgements which are too simplistic. A simple descriptive phrase augmenting the symbols is likely to clarify the meaning. An example of this is shown in Figure 42 where the rather bland ticks are well supplemented by further explanations[14].

It should never be a physical or an intellectual effort to read a table.

Diagrams demonstrating a relationship

It will frequently be necessary to illustrate a relationship. This may be an organizational relationship, such as would be shown in an organizational tree. It may be a mechanical relationship; a photograph or cross-section of the equipment serves this purpose. It may be a sequential relationship, such as can be shown from a procedural flow chart. It may be a physical relationship, illustrated by a map or office plan. It may be a financial relationship, illustrated by a diagram of a complex shareholding at the time of a merger.

Organizational structures

Management structures are traditionally shown in genealogical tables. The basic structure is often amplified by:

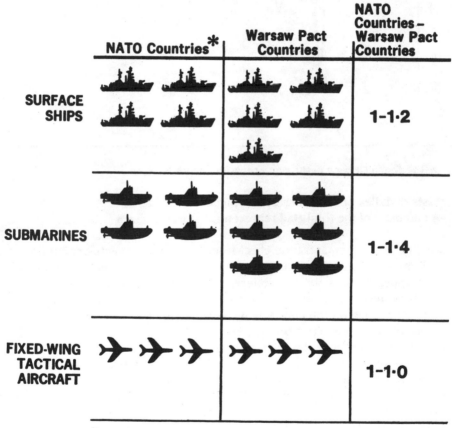

DEFENCE POLICY

FIGURE 3

The CURRENT BALANCE of FORCES in the EASTERN ATLANTIC

	NATO Countries*	Warsaw Pact Countries	NATO Countries – Warsaw Pact Countries
SURFACE SHIPS			1-1·2
SUBMARINES			1-1·4
FIXED-WING TACTICAL AIRCRAFT			1-1·0

*Including the French Atlantic Fleet

Figure 37   Pictogram making very simple comparison

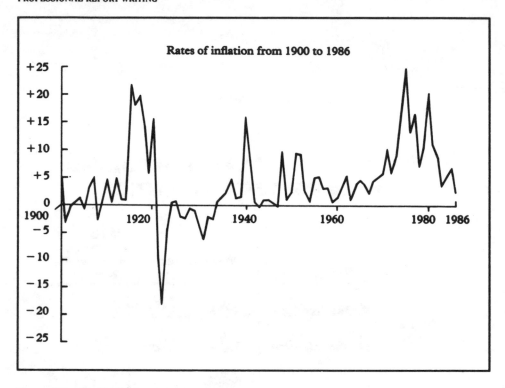

Figure 38   Graph showing positive and negative quantities

1. Lists of duties or areas of responsibilities.
2. A summary of the total staff represented in the diagram.

Figure 43 shows an organization chart from the Kuwait Investment Authority/BP report[15]. An interesting bonus in this presentation, which is taken from one of the report's appendices, is the back-reference to the paragraph in the main report where the diagram is discussed. This is particularly useful in a long report. A reader may chance on the appendix while thumbing through the report and will find it useful to be guided to more detailed explanation.

Sometimes, as in Figure 44 – where there is a great deal of wording in the body of the tree – it may be helpful to enclose the detail in boxes. This example is taken from the County NatWest inquiry[16]. It is noteworthy that it demonstrates the technique of inserting a diagram in the text with a lead-in sentence and no figure number. This is satisfactory as far as it goes but it deprives the reader of any means of referring to the figure. The lead-in sentence has an important caveat: '... the NWIB Group in so far as it is relevant to our Investigation'. It is desirable to restrict organization charts to components relevant to the subject-matter and it is essential to state that the description of the organization has been curtailed in this way.

Elaborate shareholdings may often be usefully set out in a similar way. Figure 45 shows an example. It is taken from a Monopolies Commission report on a proposed merger of a Canadian-based multinational distiller and The Highland Distilleries Company Ltd[17]. This illustration appears to be extremely complicated at first

Sylvana gave highest overall marketable yields with 15.35 tons/vergee, 15% of which were Class I. In size grade out, % size D was also high at 63%.

A condensed summary of yields is given below.

Factor	Position			
	1st	2nd	3rd	4th
Total marketable yields	Sylvana	Primset	A85239	Shirley
Highest % Class I	Sylvana	Shirley	Estrella	Primset
Highest % Size CB	Andra	Estrella	Primset	Atlas
Highest % Size D	Criterium	A85239	A85236	Sylvana

As it can be seen, it is the already established varieties that performed well. Promising new varieties seem to be Primset and A85239.

It must be remembered that 1986 was a poor season for the outdoor tomato crop and fruit quality was poor throughout much of the season. The varieties would require further trialling in a dry summer to accurately assess their performance.

Figure 39   Very simple table containing words rather than numbers and helpful prose interpretation

glance. It is, however, no more than a reflection – and a clear picture – of a very complex structure. Shareholders who are not discussed in the accompanying paragraphs are, of course, omitted. There is no need to encumber the diagram with them.

Illustrations of machinery

Diagrams of machinery in cross-section are often appropriate to reports in the same way as they may be to technical manuals. Most systems must be simplified if the report is aimed at laypeople. It must be labelled in simple terms. The schematic representation of a pressurized water reactor shown in Figure 46 is a very good example.

Photographs are often an essential complement to the prose, especially in accident reports. The Hillsborough reports[18] and the investigation into the Clapham Junction accident[19] have a great many photographs, both coloured and black and white. Some of the more routine reports on lesser accidents do not have so many, although a brief investigation into a railway accident at Crewe[20] necessitated some to show the extent of the damage, the crushed cab, the detached bogeys and so on. The Eminent Persons' report on Southern Africa[21] contains many photographs showing the committee going about their investigations in the field, in Port Elizabeth, in Lusaka and elsewhere.

The Challenger report[22] has copious pictures, including numerous photographs.

Variety	Total marketable	Tons/Vergee Total Class I	%	% of Class I		
				CB	D	E
Atlas	7.57	0.55	7.3	20.3	53.6	17.9
Sylvana	15.35	2.39	15.6	11.9	63.3	23.6
A85236	12.58	0.61	4.8	6.6	74.4	17.5
A85239	14.70	1.09	7.4	17.5	76.0	6.5
Andra	10.78	0.94	8.7	44.1	45.5	6.2
Primset	15.24	1.55	10.2	40.8	42.5	15.8
Criterium	11.55	0.88	7.6	7.6	87.9	4.5
A85238	11.90	1.06	8.9	9.2	60.9	23.5
Shirley	13.86	1.85	13.3	9.6	59.1	29.3
Estrella	10.21	1.24	12.1	42.4	46.8	9.7

Figure 40   Table showing numerically expressed results of tomato trials

Table 3	Defects noted at the Periodic Medical Examinations											
	INFANTS Boy	Girl	1986 Total	1985 Total	JUNIORS Boy	Girl	1986 Total	1985 Total	SENIORS Boy	Girl	1986 Total	1985 Total
Oral Hygiene	3	2	5	22	–	–	–	34	3	–	3	24
Skin	2	1	3	24	2	1	3	9	2	1	3	40
Vision	1	–	1	74	2	–	2	55	3	8	11	147
Squint	–	–	–	15	–	–	–	4	–	–	–	12
Hearing	51	40	91	69	6	9	15	29	4	6	10	30
Otitis Media	16	6	22	52	–	–	–	17	–	–	–	32
Neck Glands	–	2	2	59	–	–	–	11	–	2	2	16
Speech	6	5	11	40	1	–	1	28	–	–	–	18
Lungs	6	8	14	19	3	–	3	6	1	1	2	16
Heart	4	1	5	2	1	–	1	8	–	–	–	8
Abdomen	1	–	1	3	–	–	–	9	–	–	–	5
Testes	20	–	20	12	4	–	4	–	–	–	–	7
Posture	–	–	–	7	–	–	–	2	1	1	2	17
Feet	1	–	1	8	–	–	–	8	–	–	–	16
Spine	1	1	2	–	–	–	–	–	–	3	3	–
Epilepsy	–	–	–	–	–	–	–	3	1	1	2	2
Other	5	3	8	1	7	–	7	1	9	8	17	–
Development	8	2	10	9	1	3	4	12	2	–	2	8
Stability	4	–	4	1	–	–	–	8	–	–	–	21
Enuresis	2	–	2	9	3	–	3	16	–	–	–	7
Under weight	–	–	–	–	–	–	–	–	–	–	–	1
Over weight	2	4	6	7	6	1	7	8	5	7	12	41
Blood Pressure raised	–	–	–	–	–	–	–	–	1	–	1	4
TOTALS 85/86	133	75	208		36	14	50		32	38	70	
TOTALS 84/85				433				268				472

Figure 41   Complex tabulation

Diagrams of sequence of events

Systems are often best illustrated by a flow chart, algorithm or simple tree. For instance the presentation in Figure 47 was used by Currys Limited to show the accumulation of cost involved in a scheme of management training.

A plan of a circuit diagram is shown in Figure 48, describing the life of a returnable bottle sold over the counter in the off-licence trade[23]. It may appear rather elaborate, but it shows, by a consistent system of symbols, how the bottle enters or re-enters the circuit, is sold to the retailer, is sold by him and the various points at which it may become lost. To explain the same procedures in words alone, even if it could be done in the same space, would certainly be less easy to follow.

Figure 49 from the Black report[24] shows a complex cycle of activities in a way which is manageable even by the non-scientific reader.

Maps and plans

Maps and plans require special attention. They generally serve one of two purposes: to set an area in context or to show its detail. Examples of the former are to be found in the Amnesty International annual report[25]. Each national section opens with a simple map of the relevant region with national boundaries marked

-71-

Table 10   Plans for introducing further office technology

Case number	Description	Communicating WP	Stand alone WP	Combined WP and DP	Shared logic WP	OCR	Phototypesetting linked to WP	Computerized telex
1	Head office of oil company	√ now	√ now	√ now	√ probably	√ later in 1980	√ now	√ now
2	Finance organization	√ now						
3	University department		No - dispensing with present WP					
4	Organization sponsoring research		√ later in 1980					
5	Headquarters of chemical company	√ in 1-2 years	√ now	√ in 1-2 years		√ now		√ in 1-2 years
6	Division of chemical co.	√ in 5 years					Possibly in 1981	
7	Public administration departmental office	√ in 2-3 years	√ now	√ now	√ on order	√ next year	√ (probably)	
8	Research consultancy							
9	Public administration dept. office	√ in 5 years	√ progressively	Possibly in 1983	√ in 2-3 years			
	TOTAL	6	5	4	3	3	2	2

Figure 42   Comparative tabulation offering useful supporting comments

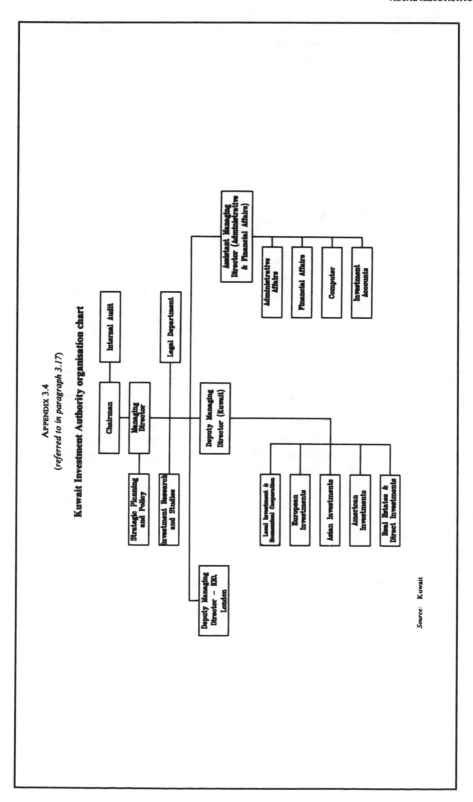

APPENDIX 3.4

(referred to in paragraph 3.17)

Kuwait Investment Authority organisation chart

Source: Kuwait

Figure 43   Organization chart

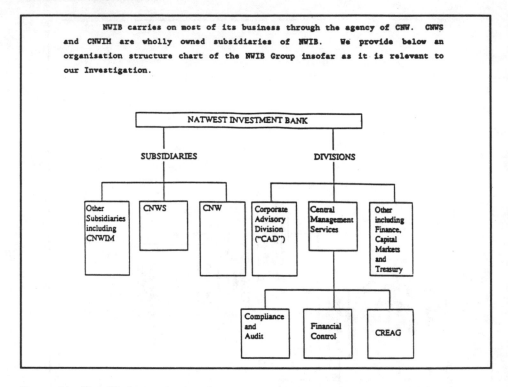

Figure 44   Simplified organization chart

and the relevant country blocked in. Similar maps are shown in, for instance, the Devon & Cornwall Chief Constable's report at the beginning of each Divisional Report to show the local authority districts involved[26].

An Oxford City Council map showing the shopping hinterland of the City in relation to district and county boundaries[27] is given in Figure 50. Careful use has been made here of different line-forms to denote the various boundaries, district, council and so on, as colours were not available. Likewise a map from the Cleveland Child Abuse report showing the layout of the area in relation to relevant local boundaries (police divisions, health authorities and so on) is reproduced as Figure 51. The reference points, Loftus, Greatham, Egglescliffe, are particularly important here.[28]

Detailed maps call for more careful preparation. They must always have a north-point and a scale. Maps are sometimes too busy or overcrowded. This is often the result of taking part of a large-scale ordnance survey map and reproducing it with added technical data but not eliminating irrelevant matter.

Additional checks

Sources

Sources for illustrations must always be cited.

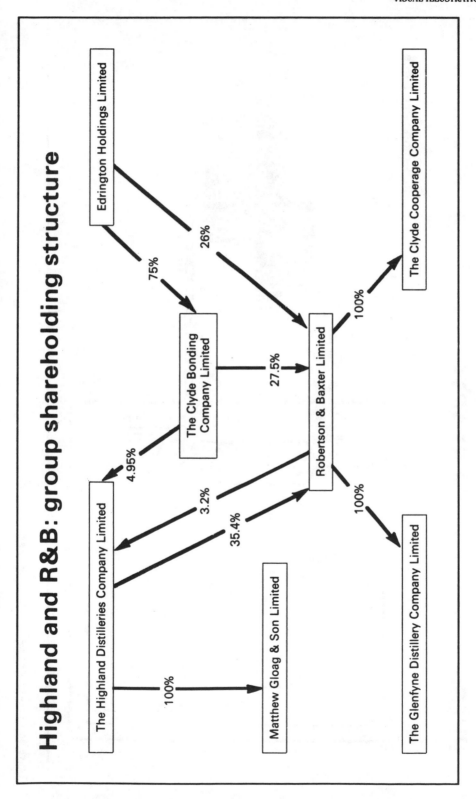

Figure 45   Explanation of complex shareholding structure

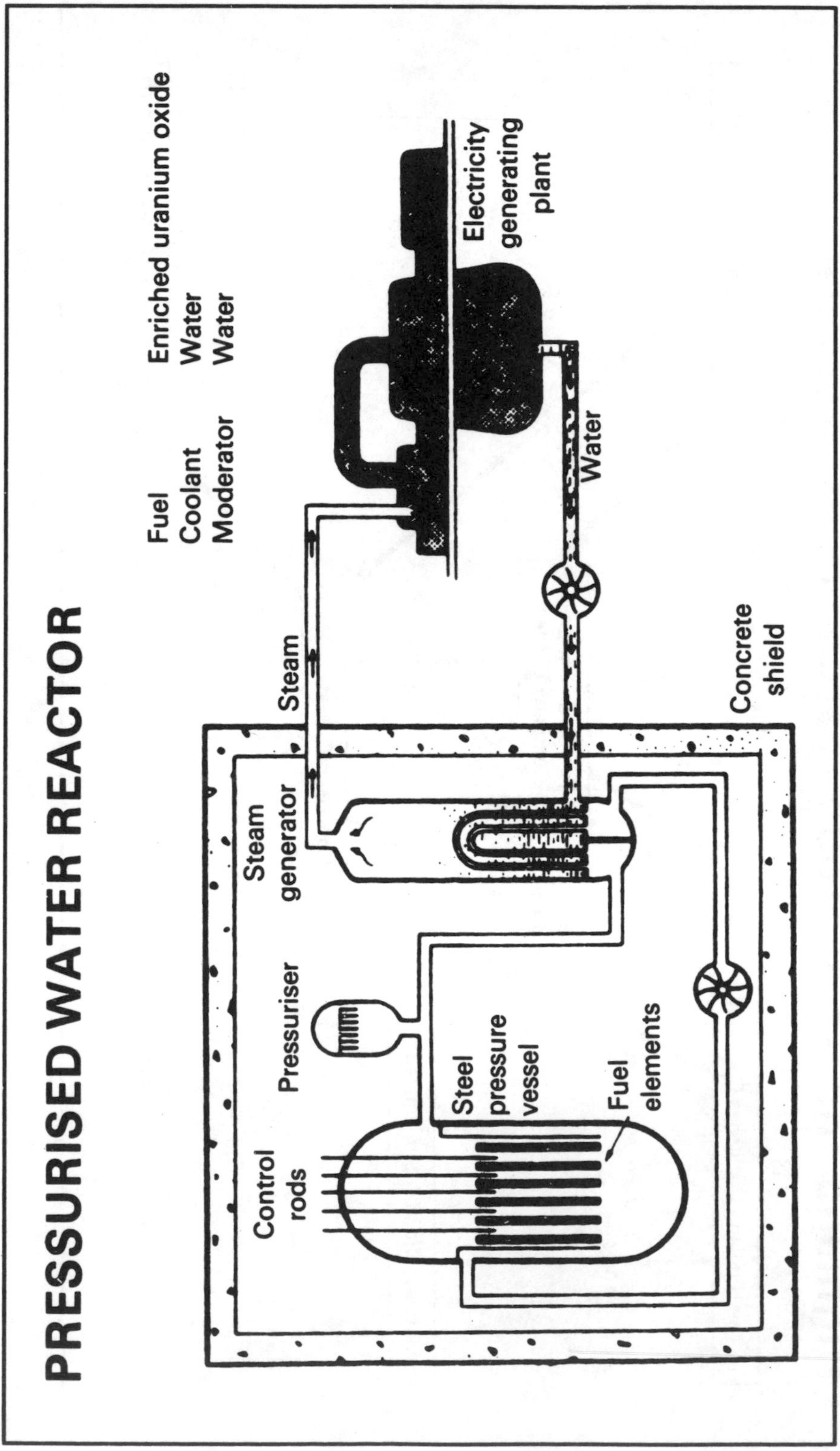

Figure 46   Pressurized water reactor in simple diagram

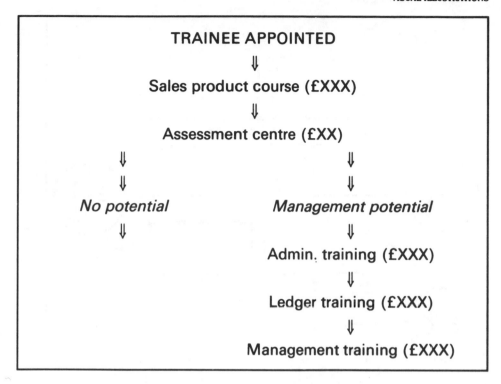

Figure 47　Genealogical tabulation (or tree) of accumulated costs

Updating

Illustrations taken from elsewhere must be checked to see that they are up to date. More recent detail may have to be added. If projected figures were shown on the original, they may have to be replaced by actual data.

Projections

If projections are shown, either on a graph line or as figures in a table, they must be clearly distinguished from past information.

Continuous or discrete displays

A discrete display is appropriate if the variables are separate distinct packages. Where there are an infinite quantity of variables which may be plotted, a continuous display is needed. For example in Figure 52, it should in theory be possible to take a meaningful reading at any point along the x-axis, anywhere between 1919 and 1986. The same does not, of course, apply in Figure 36 which shows discrete information.

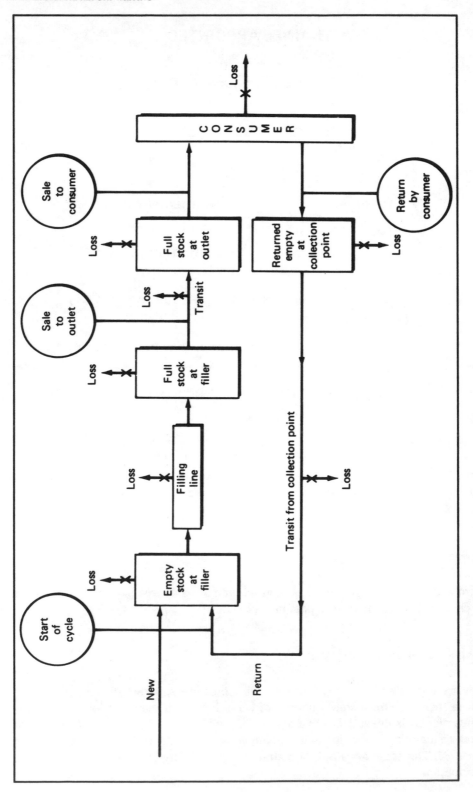

Figure 48 Circuit diagram of the life of a returnable bottle

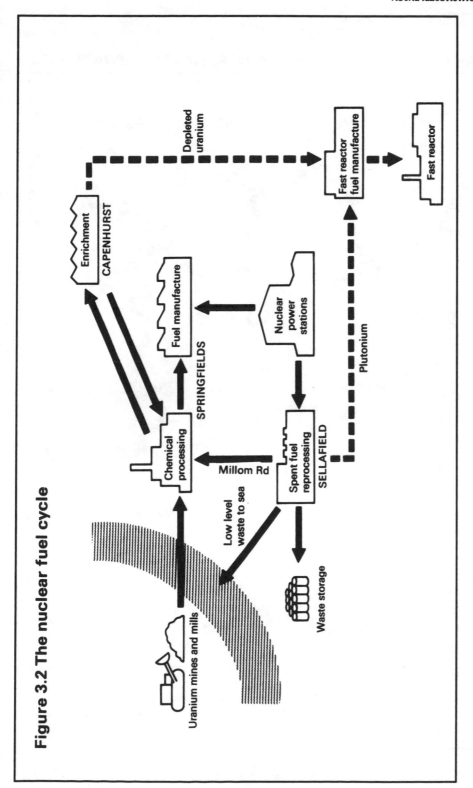

Figure 3.2 The nuclear fuel cycle

Uranium mines and mills

Chemical processing

Enrichment
CAPENHURST

Fuel manufacture

SPRINGFIELDS

Nuclear power stations

Depleted uranium

Fast reactor fuel manufacture

Fast reactor

Plutonium

Spent fuel reprocessing
SELLAFIELD

Millom Rd

Low level waste to sea

Waste storage

Figure 49   Schematic diagram of nuclear fuel cycle

143

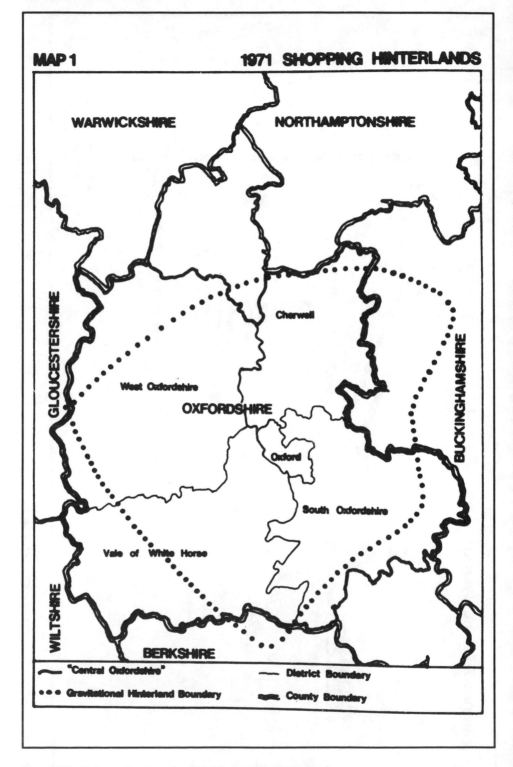

Figure 50   Schematic map of a district council's hinterland

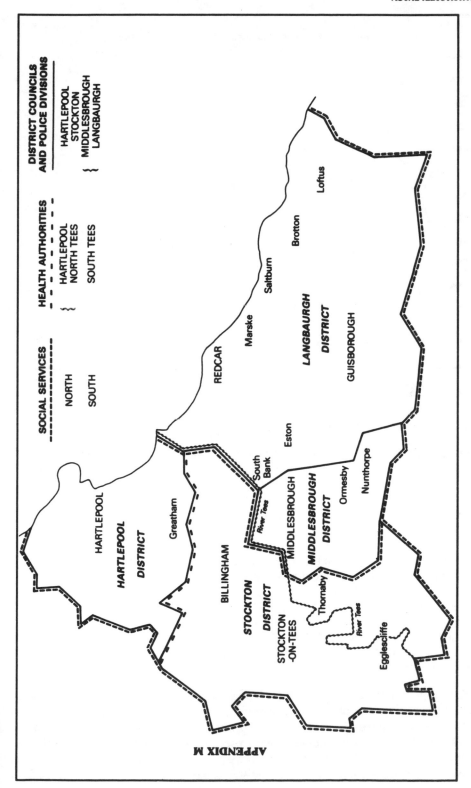

Figure 51 Schematic map of an area with good reference points

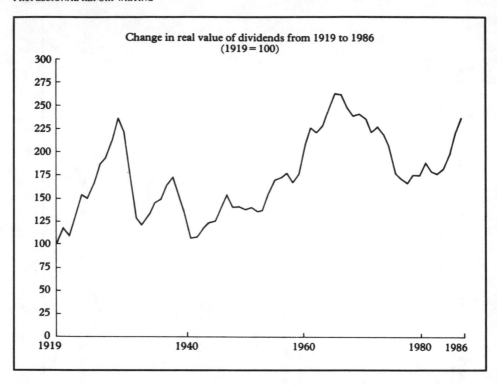

Figure 52   Graph as a continuous display

Introduction of an illustration

When an illustration is shown as an appendix, it can usually be allocated a page of its own. No problems arise. Incorporation of an illustration into the text calls for more care. The following aspects should be considered:

1. Avoid a table running from one page to another.
2. Place the table as near as possible to the text to which it relates.

These two points may sometimes be contradictory but a compromise must be reached in the interests of fluent reading.

The semantics of illustrations

No illustration will stand without words. Line diagrams and numbers require written explanations. Particular shortcomings in the wording associated with illustrations are:

1. Using in a table or diagram a technical or obscure term, which the writer would never dream of using in the report itself without explanation.
2. Using vague expressions such as 'other major companies' to label graph lines. This sort of vagueness conflicts with the kind of numerical precision that a graph or other tabulation seeks to convey.
3. Not specifying the period covered by the illustration.

4. Not stating the base of any percentages shown. The reader will ask: percentage of what?
5. Not making it clear that a graph is double-sided.

Clear, unambiguous word choice is essential for illustration captions and axis labels. Every table must have a title which clearly describes the contents. The writer must never rely on the reader having read the preceding text or, indeed, the reader's general knowledge.

Cartoons

Cartoons have started to feature in reports recently. Provided they are discreetly placed and do not become obtrusive they can enliven reports on serious subjects. The Local Government Ombudsman's annual report has introduced them for the year ended March 1989[29] (Figure 53).

SUMMARY

Illustrations can clarify complicated issues or make even simple information easier to assimilate. Nevertheless illustrations should never be used for their own sake. No magic authority attaches to statistics or any graphic illustration. Sedgwick, in C.P. Snow's *In Their Wisdom*, recalls 'some old mathematician saying that in an air raid he took refuge under the arch of probability'. This fatuous shelter was not enough for Sedgwick[30].

Before including an illustration of any kind, the report writer must ask:

1. What is the purpose of the illustration?
2. Is it necessary?
3. Is the form of the illustration the most suitable for the point being made?
4. Is the display labelled and scaled so that it is quite clear what is being shown?
5. Can the illustration stand on its own?
6. Does this display prove what is intended?

'He had made persistent allegations that women kitchen staff sometimes stood and watched bathers who were semi-undressed.'

'The provision of a low-cost but dignified funeral.'

'Planning permission for a clay pigeon shoot and rifle range.'

Figure 53   Cartoons from the Local Ombudsman's annual report

11 Preparing a report

OUTLINE OF PREPARATION

There are ten processes in the preparation of virtually every report (Figure 54). In many cases these phases will be amalgamated. In some cases, such as where information comes from only one source, they will be dealt with quickly. In others – as when headings are not needed or where there is a standard framework – some of the steps will be almost non-existent. Nevertheless, all steps of the framework should be borne in mind.

IDENTIFY THE PURPOSE OF THE REPORT

The purpose of the report – expressed in the Introduction – must be stated lucidly and unambiguously and should be kept before the writer at all times. Some people go to the lengths of pinning it up physically in front of them. Such an expedient is useless unless the writer keeps referring to it and relating his work to the objective of the report. There is a danger that it will become part of the wallpaper (rather like the heavy quotations and glib maxims with which some offices are decorated).

The purpose (or aim or objective):

1. May have been given to the writer by a superior or another authority.
2. May be a traditional part of a routine, such as a monthly or weekly report or a visit report.
3. May have originated with the writer himself on seeing something going wrong. It is no less important to stick to the objective just because the writer has drawn it up himself.

If the purpose is not kept in mind throughout the preparation and writing of the report, writers will be distracted. Imbalances will occur. There will be a temptation to ramble on about topics the writer happens to find interesting. He will concentrate on aspects for which he happens to have a lot of information. They may be seduced into avoiding subjects which they find tricky. They will avoid issues that are embarrassing or controversial.

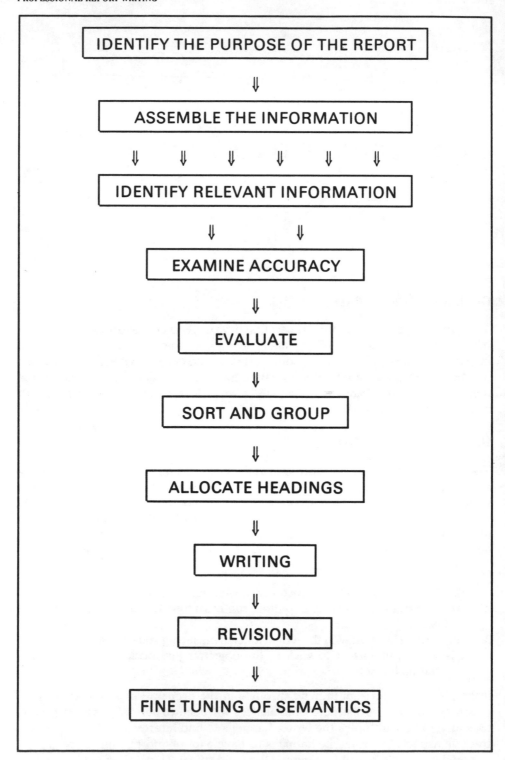

Figure 54   Stages in preparation of a report

An excellent example of terms of reference is provided by the Jockey Club report on the 1989 St Leger meeting.

Reports from the Doncaster Stewards, the Clerk of the Course, the Inspector of Courses, the Stewards' Secretaries and others were received by the Stewards of the Jockey Club. Following their receipt the Stewards of the Jockey Club decided that this Committee of Investigation should be set up with the following terms of reference:

(1) to investigate the circumstances surrounding the abandonment of the Doncaster September meeting.
(2) to recommend such changes as are considered necessary to avoid similar situations arising in the future.
(3) to report to the Stewards at their December meeting.[1]

These terms of reference give a direction to the investigation, stress that it must produce remedial action and give a time frame for reporting.

ASSEMBLE THE INFORMATION

Information and opinion (both the writer's and other people's) will emerge from many different sources for inclusion in the report. It will also come to light on unexpected occasions so a notebook and pencil should be kept in the writer's pocket or briefcase at all times during the preparation of a complex report.

The net will be cast very wide at this stage. The detail will be thinned out later when the relevant items are identified.

The list of possible sources is almost as limitless as the number of purposes for which reports are written. The following are among the most obvious:

Earlier reports
Correspondence
Minutes of meetings
Informal discussions
Technical trials
Fieldwork of every kind
Reference books
Questionnaires
Visit reports
Newspaper coverage

Two examples will illustrate this.

Merchant banker's credit report

Compilation of a credit report for a merchant bank will involve scrutiny and analysis of an astronomically wide diversity of published material: press comment, periodicals of every kind, industrial magazines, stock market reports and annual reports.

Annual reports will be examined not only for the overt claims of the Chairman and directors and the figures of the audited accounts, particular notice will be taken of the notes to the accounts which will give a more detailed idea as to the company's ambitions and problems. The published reports of other companies operating in the same trade will also deserve attention.

A substantial range of unpublished information will also be tapped. The customer will be checked with other banks, possibly even indirectly with other customers. Earlier credit reports may be available. Most important there will be the need to analyse the voluminous details produced by the customer and elicited in discussion with him.

Area sales manager's report

An area sales manager will possibly examine his representatives' reports, reports of competitors' performance, retailers' stock turnover, local, and perhaps national, newspaper comment as well as the observations of periodicals such as *Which*. He will maintain a liaison with the customer relations and press departments so that the feedback through complaints and other letters is reconciled with his performance results.

None of this information will come to light in the most convenient order or the most convenient form. It will probably not even be provided in uniform quantities. In certain circumstances the writer may be able to help himself by suggesting a format for certain types of return or submission. This must be done only if there is absolutely no danger of the form restricting the contributor in such a way that important information is omitted through lack of space.

IDENTIFY RELEVANT INFORMATION

Irrelevant or over-detailed information can be weeded out. While it is unwise to generalize on this very important process, two guidelines will be helpful:

1. Relevance

The writer must apply all sorts of questions to the information he has assembled. For example:

1. Does this apply to this company?
2. Does this apply to these people?
3. Does this apply to these products?
4. Could this statute apply to this situation in the future?

2. Balance

Once the relevance of the information has been established, it must be examined for balance. Aspects of equal standing should be discussed in equal detail. Sometimes a particular bias to the report will be required. An exercise at UAC called for preparation of a general report describing UAC for a foreign reader with a particular interest in motor manufacture. The structure shown in Figure 55 was devised and was absolutely appropriate in the circumstances.

Where persuasive writing on a controversial subject is involved it is usually desirable to show both sides of the argument:

1. Show that both sides of the question have been examined.
2. Avoid the heavily distorted one-sided style, which is characteristic of extreme political journalism and lacks credibility.

1. UAC International

   (a) Location
   (b) Origin
   (c) Shareholding
   (d) Areas of business
   (e) Expansion
   (f) Other interests

2. Divisions of UAC

   (Breweries, Foods, Medical, etc., described)

3. UAC Motors

   (a) Origins
   (b) UK
   (c) Overseas

Figure 55   Structure of a general report for a foreign reader

3. Anticipate counter-arguments and thereby limit tedious extended correspondence.

For the report *Industrial Democracy* to retain some validity despite the near hysterical disagreements which were heard .in the committee, Lord Bullock ensured that arguments both for and against were included[2].

It is at this stage that much of the information will be discarded, or at least set aside. This is indicated by the reduction of the number of arrows in Figure 54.

EXAMINE ACCURACY

Most information can be taken at its face value but there will be some that must be validated. The following questions are typical of those which must be asked:

1. Have figures been irresponsibly and misleadingly rounded?
2. Are ratios meaningful?
3. Are percentages more expensive than bald numbers? (The Catering Manager who said that he had received 60% complaints about the breakfasts was being inaccurate until he revealed that – out of the population of a large private hospital – he had had only five questionnaires returned.)
4. Is the fieldwork up to date?
5. (If names have been mentioned) Are staff-lists up to date? (Have this verified by telephone enquiry. Do not rely on rumour.)
6. Is the information sufficiently specific?
7. Does the information take into account recent legislation, safety instructions and working practices?
8. Does this apply to current equipment?
9. Are prices quoted up to date?
10. Are manuals to which reference is made the most recent editions?
11. Do European Commission regulations of 1992 have any effect?

Lord Justice Woolf in preparing for his inquiry into the Strangeways Jail disorders of April 1990 stated his intention to appoint a team to help him in this way in preparing his report. The team would consist of four former prison governors. Their function would be to provide independent scrutiny of certain facts and claims provided by the Home Office and other sources[3].

EVALUATE

Even when the technical accuracy of all the detail appears to be sound, there must still be some further evaluation:

1. Information from different sources about the same kind of subject must be balanced and comparable.
2. Materials which have come from any biased source must be trimmed back to realism. Such bias may be in the form of dishonest prejudice or it may just be the harmless gymnastics of advertising.
3. Information must be as specific as possible. Generalizations which are the result of haste or of superficial investigation must be sharpened.

This phase is particularly important when preparing a comparison of claims by, say, manufacturers of office equipment, or some service such as office cleaning. The euphemisms of estate agents ('house of character', 'in need of some improvement') have now passed into the lore of situation comedy. Yet the language of other trades is often no more helpful.

What are 'hand-picked staff' in a security firm? Presumably they have been through a selection process like any other employee. A more specific description of employees is helpful: 'All our drivers have been employed by the firm for a minimum of three years. No-one is engaged who has not seen at least ten years' service, with good character, in the Police or Armed Services'.

What is an 'expert service', or, more suspect, 'professional staff'? Do they mean that those providing the service have received some sort of training? Is professional the opposite of amateur here? Some specified achievements or nominated referees who are in a position to give specific evaluation would be preferable and would enable a more accurate comparison to be made.

There is nothing morally wrong or commercially mischievous about these woolly descriptions. They are a healthy part of the exchanges of a competitive economy, they amuse the children and, frequently, help to sell a product or a service. In preparing a balanced comparative report which is leading to a decision, however, they must be eliminated or replaced by more specific information.

SORT AND GROUP

This is probably the most important step of all. The items of information which have been identified must be:

1. Grouped into cohesive packages.
2. Arranged into a sequence which helps the reader.

The order in which a report's sections are sequenced will depend, of course, on the reader's need and interest. It may be appropriate to start with the most interesting or the most important. The subject may be dealt with geographically or chronologically.

Recent Defence White Papers[4] have followed a train of thought from the general to the particular. They start with the global defence issues including the moral issue of arms control, then progress through nuclear defence policy and then conventional policy, particular defence interests such as Hong Kong, community service, down to details of equipment, personnel handling and the details of how it is all funded.

The second report of the Department of the Environment's Working Group of Pop Festivals under Lady Stedman[5] demonstrates an extended chronological approach. First the law is discussed, that is, the framework within which the festivals must take place. Then the evidence submitted to the working group is summarized. The problems (of outdoor and indoor festivals, separately) are analysed. Possible approaches are discussed and then the report ends with the possibility of assistance from public funds, in other words the practicalities of sorting the problem out.

The Franks report[6] has a broadly chronological structure. It is divided into four chapters; the first covers the period from 1965 to 1979 (i.e. until the Conservative government came to power); the second May 1979 to 19 March 1982; the third (including a description of the South Georgia episode) 19 March to 2 April 1982; the fourth analyses the Government's discharge of their responsibilities. The report's terms of reference particularly excluded any occurrences after the invasion of 2 April.

The principal problem faced by Fennell in compiling the King's Cross report[7] was ensuring that the exact sequence of events was identified from the confused accounts of the incident. This then influenced the format of the report[8].

At this stage, definite headings are unlikely to have been allocated. A note as to the character of each group of information will have been made, but this is unlikely to be a sufficiently precise signpost to become the heading in the final report.

Sometimes quite detailed plans may be made. Desmond Fennell compiled a very detailed format for his King's Cross report as a plan before hearing evidence. As soon as he started to assemble the evidence, it became clear that about one-third of this structure would need to be altered[9]. It is inevitable that, however well prepared a report framework may be, alterations will be necessary as the detail evolves.

ALLOCATE HEADINGS

The next stage, therefore, is to allocate headings. The headings must be: clear, unambiguous and different from each other. (If possible no heading should appear twice in the same report and certainly not in the same group of headings.) Sometimes this function can be combined with the sorting and grouping procedure. They will take place simultaneously. Certainly in both processes the author will be guided by the objective of the report. The arrangement of the information and its description by tide will depend on the angle from which the subject is tackled.

Because these two phases are so closely related, and sometimes simultaneous, one set of examples may be used to illustrate these two techniques. They are critical because if the information is not arranged in a logical sequence the reader will have difficulty in following it, the point and conclusion of the report will be obscured or lost altogether and the whole business will have been a waste of time. The second phase is vital because if the signposts are not lucid and precise the reader will not be able to pick out the bits that he wants.

On the Account Officers' Course at the European Training Centre of Citibank NA, a report-writing module has been included. A simple exercise in structuring and tiding a report has been set early in the course to demonstrate and practise the principles described here. The bank officers on the course are drawn from many nations and the authorship of the solutions discussed below is similarly diverse (British, German, Dutch, Spanish, Italian, Zimbabwean, South African and others), but the specifics are not important. They are issued with 30 disconnected points on a general economic issue. In this case it was the economic condition of Greece in a particular year. They work in pairs, to promote discussion, and are invited to sort random details into clearly labelled groups for a report. No guidance is given on the purpose of the report, the number of headings or the desirability of sub-headings. They can devise any purpose for the report provided that the layout reflects it and is consistent in doing so. Six of the solutions are set out in Figure 56. It is perhaps surprising that only 30 pieces of data could stimulate such diverse arrangements.

Figure 56 (a) gives a very simple breakdown so that the sections will inevitably be long and the guidance given by the headlines slight. The headings are indeed very general. The first heading 'Overview' must be distinguished more precisely from the second 'Economic Overview'. What sort of overview does it give? The third and fourth suggest an accountancy approach to the problem. The national budget is compared with the way in which the economy has performed.

The approach in Figure 56 (b) also demonstrates the need for an overview of some kind. Only one other heading of equal status is shown, 'Economy', which is, in fact, the subject of the whole report. The first section calls for no sub-division. On the other hand, the second section contains much diverse information; it is therefore properly and helpfully divided into what the author felt were the most important fields.

Figure 56 (c) also demonstrates an approach based on an analysis of the Greek balance of payments. The external commitments are described first and then the internal difficulties. Care must be taken with a heading 'Statistics'. Is it really appropriate to segregate statistical information in this way? Is it being used as a repository for miscellany which will not fit under any other heading?

The approach in Figure 56 (d) uses a straightforward division into six main headings, more first-rank headings than in any of the earlier examples. 'Employment', 'Energy', 'International Trade' and 'Tourism' are certainly important areas in the interpretation of these authors. 'Monetary', however, was an enormous heading in this answer and became an unwieldy deposit for items they could not place elsewhere.

If there is to be no extensive sub-division, then more first-rank headings are probably necessary, as in Figure 56 (e). In this version each subject is treated discretely. The balance of payments was relegated to a less important placing than in some of the earlier examples, although it was a fairly long section and slightly divided.

Probably the most subtle of the suggested possibilities is in Figure 56 (f). The material is divided into three clear packages and broken down further in a helpful way. The sub-heading 'General' is of course totally uninformative in most circumstances, but is excusable as a sub-heading. The significance of the bracketed adjective ' (Local) ' is uncertain. It certainly adds nothing to the signpost. The heading 'Other Matters' is generally to be avoided particularly if it covers too much information. It has something in common with 'Sundries' in annual accounts; just acceptable if covering small amounts of data but not if there is a lot of it.

WRITING

Ideally, at least one draft will be made before the final copy is produced, although other pressures may sometimes (or frequently) make this impossible. In *I Like It Here*, Garnet Bowen is seated in front of his typewriter, 'his "rough draft" now unavailingly headed "First final draft" '. It had apparently 'got to page 19 again, the point where twice before he had ripped it up'[10].

(a)

OVERVIEW
ECONOMIC OVERVIEW
PUBLIC EXPENDITURE/BUDGET
BALANCE SHEET

(b)

COUNTRY OVERVIEW
ECONOMY
   Employment
   Energy
   Monetary
   International Trade
   Tourism

(c)

BALANCE OF PAYMENTS
EXTERNAL DEBT
INTERNAL ECONOMIC SITUATION
   Production and Consumption
   Budgetary and Monetary Policies
   Statistics
OUTLOOK

(d)

COUNTRY OVERVIEW
  (INFRASTRUCTURE)
EMPLOYMENT
ENERGY
MONETARY
INTERNATIONAL TRADE
TOURISM

(e)

POPULATION
COMMUNICATION
EMPLOYMENT
GNP
ENERGY CONSUMPTION
INVESTMENTS
FISCAL POLICY
MONETARY POLICY
BALANCE OF PAYMENTS
   Goods
   Services

(f)

ENVIRONMENT
   General
   Economic Survey
GOVERNMENTAL POLICY
   (Local) Internal Situation
   International Relationship
INTERNATIONAL TRADE
   Oil
   Tourism
   Export/Import

Figure 56   Six variations of grouping and titling of the same data

A celebrated historian emphasizes that it is vital to start writing, to put something down on paper, however rambling and disjointed it may seem at the first attempt[11]. It can always be changed afterwards. The draft can be read aloud. The passage of time will magically suggest new and improved forms of words. This is wonderful advice. If the report writer does not start writing as soon as he has assembled and sorted all his information, a mental constipation sets in. Indeed the longer the report is left, the more likely it is to assume bogyman dimensions. Quite minor report writing tasks become a bugbear. However it is vital to remember to do the revisions.

Every manuscript should be left overnight and re-examined in the morning. Erratic spellings, repetitions and *double entendres* which were not evident when first written will appear crystal clear the following day. If possible, the writer should read something completely different in the intervening period, in the train on the way home or at least in bed; a chapter or two of a well written novel or a reputable weekly. This will take his mind off the problem preoccupying him and he will look at it in a fresh light in the morning.

REVISION

The report should be scrutinized in fine detail both in manuscript and in type/print. Type has the contradictory effects of:

1. Making a poor report (particularly a windy or vacuous one) appear better than it is.
2. Making spelling mistakes and word repetition appear more obvious. The veteran novelist Anthony Powell wrote in *The Soldier's Art* that manuscript was to be preferred to the typeface, 'typescript imparting an awful bareness to language of any kind, even one's own'[12].

The following points should be borne in mind:

1. Balance between sections.
2. Avoidance of repetition.
3. Removal of contradiction.
4. Consistency of punctuation and accuracy of spelling.
5. Cross-referencing of paragraphs and figures.

Paul Johnson, criticizing an article by Noam Chomsky, is astonished to find a very cumbersome sentence structure. Johnson goes on:

> Of course all of us may produce such horrors as we are setting our thoughts down. But we then cross them out, disentangle the syntax and start again. There is nothing to be ashamed of in getting a sentence wrong the first time. What shows contempt for the reader is the unwillingness to embark on even the most cursory revision.[13]

Just as an oral presentation will be rehearsed, it is highly desirable to try out a report on a suitable reader. It is not always easy to get hold of someone with the time and patience. However the guinea-pig should:

1. Be as near the technical, intellectual and semantic level of the eventual readership as possible.

2. Be prepared to offer constructive and detailed criticism.
3. Avoid nitpicking harmless points just to show that he has read it.
    The task of editing is examined in detail in Chapter 8.

FINE TUNING OF SEMANTICS

Bowen, in *I Like It Here*[14], on looking at a piece of obscure writing, felt that he wanted to stand in front of whoever had written it with 'a peck, or better a bushel, of ripe tomatoes' and then he would throw one at the writer every time he was unable to justify a phrase 'on grounds of clarity, common sense, emotional decency and general morality'. The report writer must be just as severe with his own work, albeit less messy.

No doubt, in view of the strictures of earlier chapters, the writer will have taken great care to choose the most appropriate words available. There will still be scope for further checking before the report is finished. In particular:

1. Words which have been changed in the draft in order to provide variety must be checked to ensure that the sense of the passage has not been changed.
2. Where a word, clause or whole sentence has been inserted into a draft, the whole paragraph should be read (possibly aloud) to ensure grammatical consistency and to avoid repetition.
3. Use of words such as 'recently', 'last year', etc. which relate to a certain point in time should seldom be used unless supported by a specific date. These phrases become meaningless as time passes. However ephemeral the writer intends the report to be, the reader may keep it for much longer than he visualized.
4. Finally the author should check the script and ask the following questions:

    a. Are the words at a suitable technical level?
    b. Do they convey the right tone?
    c. Are any of the words ambiguous?
    d. Are any of the words unnecessary?
    e. Are any words obviously and irritatingly repeated?

Time

Pressure of time is the factor about which the writer can do least. This was certainly a substantial problem with Lord Bullock's *Industrial Democracy*. To complete their task within a year his team had to work long, arduous hours. Bullock himself signed the report in hospital, as a result of a mild coronary[15].

Report writers will always be pushed for time. At the front of Mr Justice Popplewell's report[16] on the Bradford City fire there is a rather sad little note admitting 'Even a High Court Judge has only got 24 hours in a day'. The Challenger report had to be complete in 3 months with the result that much of the evidence had to be taken by telephone[17].

If a report writer has 24 hours to write a report, 24 hours he has. Apart from an initial pitiful complaint, there is generally nothing he can do. There is one aspect of

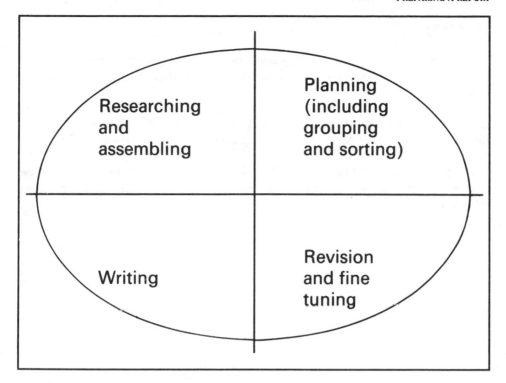

Figure 57   Division of time in report preparation

time that always remains within the scope of the writer and must remain within his control: that is planning.

The allocation of time will depend on the complexity of the report and the amount of effort necessary to discover the raw material. As a very general guideline, the division shown in Figure 57 will suffice. A quarter of the time should be allowed for each of the functions. In most instances this represents an understatement of the time required for writing. As a simple cameo it gives a good indication of the general proportions in a well-planned report.

Even in the best-made plans, there will always be unpredictable problems. A safety factor of 10 or 15 per cent should be built into all planning schedules, even if this means restricting the scope of the report or the number of drafts.

There will inevitably be distractions. Other jobs have to be done in parallel with preparation of the report. The advice offered to Mr Clive Ponting by Lord Strathcona when he was briefly a Defence Minister seems unrealistic. He told Ponting, a high-flying Principal at the time, to get rid of the telephone in his office on the grounds that 'It's impossible to write a report and answer the telephone at the same time'[18].

There will always be sickness, if not among the report writers, amongst word-processor operators, clerical staff, graphic artists and the many others in the chain. Photocopiers and other equipment will break down. Information will be late arriving. The final draft will be drowned in coffee only a few hours before it has to be submitted. It is for these kinds of unwelcome eventuality that allowance must be made in every report plan.

SUMMARY

Not in every report will the ten phases of report preparation be obvious or pronounced. Nevertheless on every occasion, each step should be considered before being disregarded.

Particular care must be taken with the structure of the report in the sorting and grouping phase. If the information is poorly arranged, it will be difficult or impossible to follow. If the headings are carelessly chosen, information will be difficult to identify.

The production of the report must be carefully planned. Sufficient time must be allowed, not just in writing, but for the equally important planning and revision stages.

12 Physical presentation

Whether a report is submitted in manuscript, typescript or print will depend on its importance, circulation, length and expected life. The fine details of presentation are not just a matter of administrative expediency.

Similarly the presentation of a report will affect its acceptability, which may be a question of style and courtesy such as the use of capital initials as discussed in Chapter 7. Reception of the report may be affected by its intelligibility, misuse of abbreviations, a carelessly insinuated diagram or poor spelling. Inconsistent or illogical use of headings and print sizes may have a detrimental effect on the presentation.

All these are the product of the mechanics of typing or printing of the report. They are nonetheless ultimately the responsibility of the author who must make his intentions clear in his dictation or drafts.

PRIVACY MARKINGS

Privacy markings restrict the distribution and handling of the report. Some house styles list a sequence of privacy – or security – markings which all documents produced in the company must reflect. For example, in one professional firm:

> CONFIDENTIAL might reflect the loosest level of marking which covers professionally sensitive material. This would be handled freely within the firm but not divulged outside except to the relevant client.
> PRIVATE would be more sensitive.
> PERSONAL would obviously be even more carefully treated and probably opened only by the addressee, not even by his secretary.

Privacy marking produces a useful measure of control over the processing of sensitive material. Such a scheme has important limitations of which users must be aware. The markings may not be understood outside the company. They will certainly not be accorded the same precise meaning. For example 'Confidential', shown in the system above as the loosest form of restricted marking, will be treated differently in a Government department: the same marking will attract lock and key and will be more limited in its circulation.

There is a danger of being over-cautious in classification so that privacy markings are used to excess. Worse, lack of confidence in the system will lead to a use of superlatives such as 'Strictly Confidential'. Like a word, a form of punctuation or any other feature of written communication, a privacy marking becomes devalued if overused. It becomes clichéd.

Recipients will become blasé about privacy-marked material if it appears on their desks too frequently. Time will prevent them treating genuinely sensitive documents with the protection and security they warrant. In this way, the system either becomes slowed down and clogged by highly classified trivia or the plethora of markings are ignored. The latter difficulty is akin to the products of the cold canvass sales technique whereby unsolicited letters are marked 'Personal and Important'. This is now generally taken to indicate something that can be consigned to the waste-paper basket unopened.

TABLES OF CONTENTS

The need for a table of contents is a function of disparity, rather than extent of a report. A four-page report covering perhaps 20 widely diverse topics may merit a table of contents (by paragraph). An example is a chartered accountant's Internal Control Report, a short report covering internal housekeeping improvements which have suggested themselves during audit. Such a report might cover stock control, cash handling and arrangements for signature.

A 25-page report following one theme may be better off without a table of contents. It may be more appropriate to read it straight through like a letter, and the reader should not be dissuaded from this approach. A report produced on school syllabuses during Sir Keith Joseph's period in the Education Department was prefaced by a prominent note on an otherwise totally blank page to the effect that the report should be read through as a whole. No attempt was to be made to be selective. A very thin table of contents complemented this appropriately.

A table of contents can serve several purposes:

1. It can provide a source of reference to a reader who wishes to look something up.
2. It shows the sequence in which the author has found it appropriate to treat the subject-matter.
3. It can condition the reader to the author's logic and priorities by highlighting particular topics as individual sections (thus the reader will be thinking along the same lines as the writer before he has even read a single line of prose).

If the headings are the signposts to the reader, the table of contents is the gazetteer. It is, therefore, important for the main levels of heading to be represented in it.

The report of Lord Justice Butler-Sloss in the Cleveland child abuse affair[1] had, in effect, two tables of contents. The report was 320 pages long. It started with a one-and-a-half page 'Contents', in (Figure 58), which gives an overview of the structure of the report but is expanded for those who want a more detailed view of the sequence in a nine-page Index. Part is shown in Figure 59.

The Fennell report[2] shows the main components of each chapter in sequence

CONTENTS

Figure 58　Part of detailed table of Contents from long report

INDEX

Figure 59 A more detailed view of the sequence of a nine-page Index

but without itemizing the page numbers, rather like a Victorian book. It shows the contents of each section and certainly gives an overview of the logic of the argument (Figure 60).

INDEX

The amount of detail in the table of contents will depend, in part, on whether there is an index at the back of the report. An index is only suitable for longer reports or those dealing with extremely complex subjects, especially if the report is to be distributed to a wide membership of highly diverse interests.

If an index is included, the table of contents should be reduced to a fairly simple format. The index should never take the form of a slightly expanded version of the table of contents. A table of contents describes the main headings of the report in the order in which they occur. The index draws together every mention of signifi- cant topics. The length of time required to prepare an index and the attention to detail involved must not be underestimated.

In reports in which detailed structure is very important and highly specific selective reading is expected, both paragraph numbers and page numbers can be shown, as, for example, in the three-page table of contents to the Franks report[3]. Moreover both sequences of numbering were shown in the Chapter headings, at the section level within the chapters and in the sub-sections.

CHAPTER

	Paragraphs	*Pages*
I AN ACCOUNT OF THE DISPUTE FROM 1965 TO 1979	15–70	4–20
The Starting Point of the Review 1965–1975	15–32	4–9
The involvement of the United Nations	17–18	4
Assessment of Argentine threat	19	5

Whether it is called an index or a table of contents, overview at the front of a report must give a silhouette of the documents. It can serve several purposes:

1. It can provide a source of reference to a reader who wishes to look something up.
2. It shows the sequence in which the author has treated the subject matter.
3. It can condition the reader to the author's logic and priorities by highlighting particular topics as individual sections.

PAGE NUMBERING

Pages should be numbered in all but the briefest reports. Numbers should be placed centrally top or bottom or on one of the outside corners. Numbering on the inside corners means that the page number is in danger of being hidden by a staple or consumed by the binding. It also gives the reader flicking through in search of a page greater difficulty.

It may be helpful to preface every page number with the chapter or section number. Thus the pages of Chapter 3 will be 3-1, 3-2, 3-3, etc., or 301, 302, 303, etc.

Emergency services training — importance of joint exercises — London Fire Brigade and British Transport Police training by London Underground — recommendations.

CHAPTER 16 COMMUNICATIONS SYSTEMS

Importance of communications — HQ and line controllers — telephone systems — British Transport Police information room — ordering of trains not to stop — logging of calls — public address systems — passengeɪ inquiry points and public telephones — closed circuit television — radio in stations (London Underground, British Transport Police, London Fire Brigade) — train communications — training and practice in use of equipment — recommendations.

CHAPTER 17 FIRE CERTIFICATION

Main legislative provisions governing fire safety — 1903 Paris Metro fire and aftermath — Fire Precautions Act 1971 and Health and Safety at Work etc. Act 1974 — application of 'railway premises' — Opinion of Counsel to the Court — response of Railway Inspectorate and London Underground — the correct view — Fire Precautions Act set a standard for good practice — London Underground relied upon short visits by London Fire Brigade — fire certificate requires adequate means of escape not available at King's Cross before flashover — Midland City exit locked — absence of adequately trained London Underground staff — dangers of smoke known from earlier fires — need for rolling programme of station improvements — identification of possible escape routes following Oxford Circus fire — nearest and best escape route at King's Cross not recognised — subject of certification has wide ramifications — recommendations.

CHAPTER 18 ROLE OF THE RAILWAY INSPECTORATE

Railway Inspectorate's role under railways legislation — inspection of new or altered railway works — agency role under health and safety at work legislation — the Inspectorate's understanding of its responsiblities considered — need for more active role to reflect responsiblity for public safety — drew comfort from London Fire Brigade inspections — decision to stop receiving London Fire Brigade inspection reports — problem of escalator fires identified by Inspectorate in 1973 — the Inspectorate's approach to London Underground considered — inspections of machine rooms in 1987 — adequacy of existing powers — proposed actions — more vigorous use of enforcement powers — improved liaison with London Fire Brigade — recommendations.

Figure 60   Part of table of Contents showing chapter titles and synopsis of chapter

If the material is particularly sensitive the total number of pages can be given as '1 of 14' or '14 of 14', etc.

PARAGRAPH NUMBERING

Some readers are averse to paragraph numbering on the grounds that it is unnecessarily rigid, although it may provide a high degree of precision. It greatly eases discussion of the report at meetings, on the telephone and in informal conversations. It also simplifies amendment if the document is destined for a long life as in:

AMENDMENT

At Sub-paragraph 14 (c) (3)
Delete: 153 skilled 166 semi-skilled
Insert: 281 skilled 210 semi-skilled

There are broadly two types of paragraph numbering system. Both have Arabic numbers for the paragraphs, chapters or sections: variation occurs with sub-paragraphs, etc.

1. *Decimal System* This is sometimes known as the Continental System as it was almost ubiquitously used on the continent before it became fashionable in the United Kingdom. Sub-paragraphs of paragraph (or Section) 1 will be numbered 1.1, 1.2, 1.3; sub-sub-paragraphs 1.1.1, 1.1.2, 1.1.3, etc.[4] The example shown in Figure 61 uses this sytem.
2. *British System* This arrangement may be informally called the old-fashioned British System. It was used throughout the British Civil Service, commerce and industry until the decimal system became popular in the late 1960s. It is now used by only approximately one-third of British companies and is more popular than the decimal system in the USA. It relies on arrangements of Arabic numbers, letter, Roman numerals and sometimes brackets. There is no generally accepted version of the system, nonetheless any document must be consistent throughout all its paragraphs and it is accepted that any symbol in brackets such as (c) is essentially an inferior or subordinate paragraph to the same symbol without brackets, i.e. c.

The advantage of the Continental System is that at no place in the report will the reader have any doubt where he is. It is therefore particularly suitable for reports where sections are very long and perforce extended over many pages. An expression such as:

$$143.7.18.2$$

leaves no doubt that it is part of Section (or Paragraph) 143, sub-section 7, sub-sub-section 18, sub-sub-sub-section 2. If the other system is used, all that may appear on the page is something like:

f. (1)
(2)
(a)

List of recommendations

The following is a list of our recommendations which involve changes in Lloyd's rules or the constitutional framework within which they are made. The list does not record our many judgments and conclusions on various aspects of the regulatory framework of the Society which do not lead us to make specific recommendations.

Number   *Paragraph*

CHAPTER FOUR: THE RECRUITMENT PROCESS

1   The Membership Byelaw (9 of 1984) should be amended as soon as possible to require the disclosure, both to Lloyd's and to the candidate concerned, of any commission or other remuneration or benefit given, as well as received, directly or indirectly, by a member of the Lloyd's community or by a candidate for membership in connection with an application for membership.   4.12

2   Lloyd's should carry out an investigation to ascertain whether there is a commercial justification in any circumstances for the payment of commission for the introduction of a Name and, if so, within what limits.   4.13

3   Lloyd's should prepare a booklet giving detailed information about agents to supplement the revised Applicants' Guide for Underwriting Members. The booklet should include not only a list of agents, indicating whether they are members' agents or members'/managing agents, but should also give brief details of their ownership, their charges and the syndicates to which they have access.   4.17

4   The Council should take the necessary steps to facilitate the disclosure of members' agents' performance by reference to the results of the syndicates to which their Names have had access.   4.21

5   The Council should take steps to extend the regulatory framework, by establishing 'know your client' rules, as soon as possible. The most effective approach is likely to be a code of practice, perhaps supplemented by some specific mandatory rules, designed to ensure that members' agents do make proper assessments of their clients.   4.33

6   Members' agents should be required to produce written statements setting out their policy in relation to the advice given to individual Names about the consequences of membership, and setting out their terms of business, the syndicates to which they have access and their approach to allocating Names to syndicates. Such statements would have to be revised annually. (See also recommendation 39.)   4.34

7   All candidates for membership should be required to sign a declaration to the effect that on the basis of their own experience and knowledge, and in the light of the guidance they have received, they have properly evaluated the merits and risks of membership.   4.37

8   The Rota interview should be so arranged that for some part of it the agent leaves the room so that the candidate can be questioned on his or her own.   4.39

CHAPTER FIVE: SYNDICATE MEMBERSHIP

9   Lloyd's should introduce rules to ensure that agents make available in their annual reports the information necessary to enable Names to judge the competence with which agents' investment management functions are being handled.   5.6

Number   *Paragraph*

10   All underwriting accounts should contain a commentary on the open years quantifying, so far as possible, the anticipated out-turn particularly where a loss is anticipated.   5.8

11   The Accounting and Auditing Standards Committee should carry forward the preliminary work on inception date accounting that has already been done by the Corporation staff and seek ways to introduce this basis of attributing premium income to accounting periods as soon as it is feasible to do so.   5.9

12   Syndicate accounts should present clear, quantitative information on a 'pure year' basis. The Accounting and Auditing Standards Committee should consider how the Syndicate Accounting Byelaw and its explanatory notes might be amended to achieve this result.   5.13

13   There should be a formal requirement for the underwriter's report to quantify the business underwritten according to the various categories commonly used in the market so that Names have a more precise indication of the types of risk they have been underwriting.   5.16

14   The Council should consider whether requirements could be introduced for managing agents to disclose the amount of reinsurance premiums paid for each syndicate by reference to categories of reinsurer.   5.17

15   The Council should consider whether all managing agents should have available on request by Names a written statement explaining the basis on which reinsurance cover is arranged and how the security of the reinsurers is assessed.   5.18

16   The Accounting and Auditing Standards Committee should consider the desirability of further guidance to managing agents and underwriters on the preparation of a statement for Names about the types of risk intended to be underwritten in the following accounting year, together with their assessment of business prospects. They should also consider whether annual reports are produced sufficiently early in the year to enable Names to make considered decisions about their underwriting commitments for the following year.   5.19

17   The Council should impose (either by way of byelaw or through a provision in the standard agency agreement) a general obligation on all agents to draw to the attention of their Names any material information in the agents' possession which may have a bearing on the Names' decision to join or to remain a member of a syndicate.   5.24

18   The 'one agent/one class of business' rule should be abolished.   5.36

CHAPTER SIX: THE LEGAL RELATIONSHIP BETWEEN NAMES, MEMBERS' AGENTS AND MANAGING AGENTS

19   The structure and content of the standard agency agreement and the sub-agency agreement should be considered again in detail from the perspective of the Names, taking into account the specific recommendations and comments made in chapter six.   6.31

Figure 61   An index of Recommendations, using sub-paragraphs

so that the reader who is in search of Section 150 will have no idea whether to go backwards or forwards.

On the other hand, many companies feel that the very long expressions which are sometimes produced by decimal subordinate paragraph numbers are cumbersome and unwieldy. Some compromise by taking the decimal configuration only as far as the third level. Indeed if the numbering needs to be taken beyond that point, the writer should ask if the section or paragraph is not too long. Perhaps it should be further divided with the sub-paragraphs promoted to paragraphs.

Some French and Italian systems use capital Roman numbers as the first level of division.

A selection of paragraph numbering systems is shown in Appendix 1.

NON-NUMERICAL PARAGRAPH MARKINGS

Some writers are tempted to itemize paragraphs without actually giving them numbers. The usual expedients for this approach are bullet points (●), dashes (–) and, sometimes, asterisks (*). A practical problem with bullet points used to be that they were not available on conventional typewriters and are then usually made, laboriously with a pen, by filling in a capital 'O'. Worse, typists were reduced to using a humble full-stop which stands out no more than any other stop on the page. Desktop publishing greatly facilitates this type of marking.

Dashes and hyphens are likewise insufficiently pronounced for this purpose. Like the other markings of this kind they offer no possibility of identifying the item by number for cross-reference or amendment purposes.

The use of asterisks is perhaps even more mischievous. An asterisk is generally associated with a footnote and use as a highlighter will only confuse.

Bullet points

Whereas bullet points and similar markings are unsuitable as notations for paragraphs, they do have a legitimate use. They can be used to particular advantage to stress recommendations. If they are also used at that point in the report they distinguish the separate recommendations, but they still deny the reader any way of referring to the items and are difficult to type.

Ford Motor Company has long used them extensively, in the United States for longer than in Europe. The Challenger report[5] uses 21 to itemize the 21 space missions between late 1982 and June 1986. They are now increasingly used in British reports even in conservative environments such as the audit practice of Price Waterhouse.

They should not be used to excess. The more bullet points used, the less powerful is the emphasis achieved by each point. Research in several organizations in different lines of business has produced a curious uniformity of reaction to bullet points. It was felt that five or six in a sequence was an acceptable maximum.

If bullet points are used:

- They should be used for comparable features, such as criteria, reasons, profit centres and so on.
- The writer must realize that opportunity to identify them by name (point 2 or point C) is lost.
- The items should not be more than two lines long.
- A maximum of five or six in a sequence is acceptable.

The Challenger report[6] makes good use of them to itemize sub-recommendations:

'With regard to the Orbiters, NASA should

- Develop and execute a comprehensive maintenance inspection plan.
- Perform periodic structural inspections when scheduled and not permit them to be waived.
- Restore and support the maintenance and spare parts programs, and stop the practice of removing parts from one Orbiter to supply another.

The SPAD or Systems Performance Assurance Division (i.e. internal audit function) of Rank Xerox is taken further. Very specific guidance is given in their report manual as follows:

Bullets should be used as follows:-

- for the highest level of identification, followed by dashes e.g. '–' for subsequent indentations.

Bullets are treated as the continuation of the sentence from which they started and must be read as such:-

- if within a bullet the sentence is ended, a full stop follows and the next sentence starts with a capital letter.
- If, however, the bullet text does not constitute a complete sentence in grammatical terms (subject, predicate and object), then it is terminated by a semicolon.

Examples of this would be found in bulleted objectives (as they do not have a grammatical subject), for example:-
– to assess the appropriateness of controls;
– to assess the quality of a product.

ABBREVIATIONS

Many generally accepted abbreviations are shown in dictionaries. Those shown in the *Concise Oxford Dictionary* are a good guide. Most of the largest trade unions have been shown since the early 1970s. SLADE was added in the 1978 Addenda, as was ACAS. The small set of Addenda[7] of 118 words also included MLR, NEB (as National Enterprise Board, the same abbreviation as *New English Bible* already being shown) and PLO.

In general the sanction of the dictionary will serve as an indication that an abbreviation may be used unexplained. Inclusion suggests that British readers may reasonably be expected to be familiar with them. Exceptions to this rule are:

1. Abbreviations shown as particularly British or specialist usages which must be explained to American readers or to laymen, respectively.[8]

2.   Abbreviations shown as colloquial, or slang such as 'Trot' (Trotskyist).

If there is no indication of this sort that an abbreviation is generally understood, it is necessary to introduce it. This is usually done by showing it in brackets the first time it is mentioned as

Trade Union and Labour Relations Act (TULRA)

For example:

We use the term 'word processing' (WP) technology to refer to all typewriters with sufficient electronic intelligence and storage to permit the modification and output of stored text . . . For example, there is considerable variation in the claims made for productivity increases achieved through WP.[9]

A (draft) General Council for British Shipping report, *Tanker Safety and Pollution Prevention: Guidelines to Shipowners*, introduces Inter-Governmental Maritime Consultative Organization (IMCO), Crude Oil Washing (COW) and segregated ballast tank (SBT) which are not generally used, but are essential in this particular report.

Some companies use inverted commas as well as brackets:

Enforcement Working Group ('EWG')

At first glance this may appear to be an unnecessary measure. However it is more than that. It is possible that the information which is to be abbreviated may already contain bracketed detail, as

W.H. Smith & Son (Holdings) plc

A distinction should be made between the abbreviation, which the writer wishes to introduce into his report, and part of the original information, thus:

W.H. Smith & Son (Holdings) plc ('W.H. Smith')

or

W.H. Smith & Son (Holdings) plc ('WHS')

Whatever form of introduction is used it must be done on the first occasion that the expression is mentioned in the report. Some writers choose to make an exception of a title: if introduced as part of a title, the abbreviation may pass unnoticed. Just as important, the abbreviation, once introduced, must be used again. Otherwise the reader, who has made a mental note of it on first encounter, reads to the end of the report, notices that there has been no recurrence of the abbreviation and reads the whole thing again.

Of course, some technical abbreviations can be accepted in a paper which is aimed at a strictly technical readership. Some companies take the sensible precaution of publishing a vocabulary in their reports. For instance, the National Nuclear Corporation's vocabulary for the letter C is shown in Figure 62(a). They also produce a separate vocabulary of valve abbreviations (Figure 62(b)).

(a)

C	coulomb
c	curie
cal	calorie
calc	calculated
caps	capital letters (of print)
cc	cubic centimetre
cf	compare
cfm	cubic feet per minute
c.g.	centre of gravity
CHU	centigrade heat unit
CL	centreline
cm	centimetre
cm^2	square centimetre (similarly for square metre, etc.)
cm^3	cubic centimetre (similarly for cubic metre, etc.)
coeff	coefficient
cps	centimetres per second, counts per second
cu	cubic
CW	cooling water, circulating water
cwt	hundredweight

(b)

AIR	air valve
ANG	angle valve
BC	ballcock
BV	butterfly valve
CHV	check valve

Figure 62   Extracts from the National Nuclear Corporation's vocabulary

Exceptionally the reader can be expected to know the meaning of an abbreviation, such as *P&L* (Profit & Loss) in an accountant's report, or *FX* (Foreign Exchange) and *TD* (Term Deposit) in a banker's report. To explain these would be patronising. Abbreviations of this nature should be restricted to internal reports addressed to internal readers whose understanding can be guaranteed. Some writers fear the danger of patronizing the reader with abbreviations with which he is familiar. The danger of using abbreviations unfamiliar to the reader is greater, as is well demonstrated, in environments such as government service. A new minister or a new Permanent Under Secretary may be greatly helped by the explanation of a term which is commonplace to the rest of the department. Nobody was ever patronized by explanations of a symbol or an abbreviation in the same way that they might be with a prose explanation. The *Concise Oxford Dictionary*, whose authors are particularly cautious and discriminating over inclusion of abbreviations, remains the best guide.

Where the plural of an abbreviation is needed it is usual to add the 's' at the end of the whole abbreviation, regardless of logic; as in FOCs (and MOCs, come to that) although the plural relates to the Fathers (and Mothers) of the Chapel (one Chapel)[10].

SYMBOLS

There is a variety of symbols which have achieved general acceptability. In a financial report ( ) indicate deficit figures. For example:

1990	1991	1992
£'000	£'000	£'000
(14)	18	29

shows a deficit of £14 000 in 1990 and credit figures for the next two years. Of course, using colours would clarify this further.

Square brackets [ ] indicate detail that has been inserted into a quotation to indicate a phrase popped in for clarity, e.g. to explain a pronoun:

> He [the West Midlands Sales Manager] explained that he had high hopes for the next 6 months.

Other generally accepted symbols for technical work are to be found in *Hart's Rules for Compositors and Readers*[11].

QUOTATION

The extravagant and slapdash use of inverted commas which is sometimes found in business reports is discussed in Chapter 7, as they are really a function of style. Some points on the reproduction of quotations may be helpful here.

When to quote

Only quote directly as much as is necessary:

1. To show the original writer's precise intentions (as in terms of reference). The Scarman report opens:

On 14 April 1981, . . . you appointed me to hold a local inquiry into certain matters connected with the policing of the Brixton area of South London. The terms of reference were:- 'to inquire urgently into the serious disorder in Brixton on 10–12 April 1981 and to report, with the power to make recommendations'.[12]

2.   To show his precise wording. Later, the same report illustrated this also:

This criticism of harassment was well summarised in the words of Mr Rene Webb, the Director of the Melting Pot Foundation . . . 'We do not object to what they do so much as to the way they do it'.[13]

Direct quotation can be an essential part of an investigation report where precise words may be important. This is extensively used in the Herald of Free Enterprise report[14].

It is necessary to quote verbatim some of the questions put to Mr Ayers and his answers.
Q.   You thought draught gauges were inaccurate?
A.   Yes, sir.
Q.   What tests did you carry out to see whether they were inaccurate?
A.   Personally I have done none. It is just an industry reputation that I am working from.

and so on for a further eight exchanges.

The Fennell report use this approach, as does the Challenger report on which it is modelled. For example, in its Appendix M, there are substantial extracts from the testimony of Mr R.M. Warburton, the Director General of the Royal Society for the Prevention of Accidents. Fennell described this contribution as the 'key to understanding the defects of management and the whole enterprise'. The evidence was of course summarized in the body of the report[15].

In Chapter 3 some shorter passages of the evidence of Sir Keith Bright, Chairman of London Regional Transport, are included[16] even down to such explanations as

after a pause

Describing Bright as 'absolutely crucial to the course of the inquiry', Fennell has suggested that criteria for including exact wording are if it is 'absolutely crucial to the course of the inquiry' and if 'the flavour of the words' is 'absolutely essential to the Conclusion'. He felt that, in this case, 'the reader need to be persuaded by the force of his words'.

Excessive quotation in a report on a technical subject for a non-technical reader must be strictly limited.

What marks to use

There are two systems: double quotes " " as the primary (or outside) quotation marks and single quotes ' ' as the secondary (or internal) marks for quotes inside the original quotation and *vice versa*, single quotes as primary and double quotes as secondary. In the USA double quotes are always the primary set. The same system is strongly advised for wordprocessed reports. Double quotes have only one job to do on a keyboard: the single quotation mark may also do duty as an apostrophe, exclamation mark and various other things. Printing in the United Kingdom is fairly evenly divided between the two practices.

Omission

If parts of a quotation are left out (as in the two Scarman quotations above), dots replace the omitted passage. Among various conventions is one where:
... three dots represent less than a sentence,
...... 6 dots represent a complete sentence or more.[17]

Questionable detail in the original

If a word in the quoted text is questionable, e.g. appears to be misspelt or to represent erratic mathematics, the Latin word *sic* (thus) should appear in brackets (and italics if available) immediately after the item questioned. There has been some jocular over-use of this indicator in *Private Eye* but it can still be used effectively to highlight suspect detail.

NUMBERS

A uniform system for expression of numbers must be agreed for a report, as is often laid down in a company typists' manual. In any case, the system must be uniform throughout the report. Three possible systems exist for cardinal numbers:

1. *Arabic numbers* Arabic numbers (2, 3, 4, . . .) may be used throughout. The word 'one' is usually used for 1 to avoid confusion with capital 'I'. This system has the advantage of being economical on space. Some criticize it on grounds of inelegance.
2. *Words* Numbers written in full may be entirely satisfactory for small numbers, e.g. 'six' and 'sixteen', but become absurd with larger figures such as '*nine-thousand eight-hundred and seventy-four*'. There is a requirement to express numbers in this form in some legal documents, but its general application in report writing is very limited.
3. *Words up to ten* A system which has a rather obscure and puzzling appeal is the use of words up to, say, ten and Arabic numbers thereafter. This weird compromise eases the conscience of those who for some reason are embarrassed by the naked digits for the lower figures without encumbering their reports with unwieldy expressions. It may produce uncomfortable contradictions such as 'It is hoped that between nine and 12 companies will be represented'. The practice is favoured by many newspapers and it produces a somewhat inelegant inconsistency when direct comparisons are being made as in this passage from *The Times* describing an NUM vote:

Those in favour of staying out were; Kent (three votes); Midlands (13); Scotland (12); Yorkshire (59) and Scottish craftsmen (four).

Those for an immediate return were Cokement (five); Colliery Officials and Staff (17); Durham (12); North West (eight); Northumberland (six); Cumberland (one); North Derbyshire (11); North Wales (two); South Wales (22); Durham Mechanics (eight).[18]

In short, any of these systems will do and there seems little wrong – in most circumstances – in using Arabic numbers throughout.

If a number unavoidably occurs as the first word of a sentence, it is usual to write it as a word. This makes for more fluent reading and ensures that the number is not mistaken for a paragraph number.

Numbers over one thousand must be punctuated by commas every three digits. If columnized a space at the relevant position is quite usual. In prose commas are preferable (and essential if there is any danger of a number being split at the end of a line).

EMPHASIS

Words (as in this forceful use of words in the Press Council report on the Sutcliffe Case):

> The Press Council has concluded that in this case the relatives of those at the centre of the story – victim and accused – were subjected to wholly unacceptable and unjustifiable pressures by journalists and other media representatives anxious either to interview or photograph them or to bid for the right to publish their stories. The conduct of journalists who laid siege to their homes in the circumstances described above can best be characterised in the old phrase – watching and besetting. The targets of this attention were people in deep personal grief or grave anxiety and they were harassed by the media ferociously and callously.[19]

or commas as in the Griffiths report:

> That person, regardless of their parent organization, could be given responsibility for providing information to the social services authority about changes in the individual's circumstances that may affect the need for care and support.[20]

Exclamation marks, which have been discussed in Chapter 7, are a blunt form of emphasis covering the whole sentence in a thoroughly crude way. Underlining, BLOCK CAPITALS and **bold face** (the latter is often used indiscriminately and gives only a very indistinct emphasis anyhow) have the advantage of being specific to the word emphasized. They may be over-emphatic and as a result may become confused with headings.

COURTESY

While precision and accuracy have quite properly been emphasized throughout these pages, it is important to remember the allied area of courtesy. The purpose of paying attention to what may appear to be archaic styles of address and fine detail of punctuation is to avoid giving offence. A well constructed, carefully drafted report should not be spoilt by want of a ha'porth of tar which is going to make the report less acceptable to the reader. Such slips occur in the following areas.

Titles of organizations

The titles of organizations, companies, products and other proper nouns should be stated in the same form throughout. If KPMG Peat Marwick McLintock are so called at the beginning of the report, there must be no lapse into the more colloquial Peats later in the report.

Individual titles and descriptions

Such is human nature that inconsistency in forms of address or description can cause offence astonishingly easily. Examples include omitting decorations in one case but not another, and unconventional description of those with any kind of title or professional status.

Those seeking incontrovertible guidance should refer to *Debrett's Correct Form*[21]. While much of it covers charming and, in some cases, possibly old-fashioned information on dinner-table seating and invitation-design, several parts are highly pertinent to report writing. Furthermore, its authority is undisputed, so that its pronouncements will prevent embarrassment in this strangely delicate area.

Use of capital letters

In certain proper nouns the use of capital letters is undisputed. The names of countries and companies warrant them without question, as do months and days of the week, in all but a few Francophile (or perhaps francophile) firms.

The problem arises with such things as appointments. It can be argued that all appointment titles should have capital initials: Managing Director, Sales Manager, Company Secretary and so on. In the 17th century the problem would not have arisen as all nouns were allocated capital letters (as they are to this day in German). Of late, however, a fashion has been advanced for showing appointments with lower-case initials: chief executive, product manager. This unhelpful custom is of American origin and is unwelcome. It does not allow important detail – for such an appointment is – to be picked out at a glance.

Companies will often have their own style in this respect. Some (such as Ford Motor Company) also extend their stipulations to the use of a capital C for the company when dealing with their own company. Those who are not blessed with such specific guidance or who intend to produce such a system are referred to two books which provide general rulings in this area: *Hart's Rules for Compositors and Readers*[22] and *The Oxford Dictionary for Writers and Editors*[23]. Both are revered by lexicographers.

An outstanding document offering this kind of guidance in every respect is the Australian Civil Service's *Style Manual*. First published in 1966, it is now in its fourth (1988) edition[24]. It covers every conceivable editorial function from the minutiae of capitalization to principles of proof correction and indexing. Useful sections and appendices cover descriptions of paper and binding processes.

It must not be forgotten that in many particulars the use of capital initials will mean more than fine distinctions of courtesy. The names of the political parties which are also common adjectives are good examples: a Conservative solution or a conservative solution, the history of Labour or the history of labour, a Liberal Democrat, a liberal democrat or even, in the USA, a liberal Democrat.

SPELLING

Unlike almost any other aspect of this subject, the rules of spelling are finite and, with very few exceptions[25], not open to dispute. Lexicographers admit[26] that if usage insisted on a novel spelling they would record it. Patrick Hanks suggested in 1982 that 'overnite' may soon achieve this recognition[27]. It has not yet done so. For the time being, a particular spelling is certain. Changes are so infrequent that in this connection they may be ignored.

There are three reasons why conventional spelling is important in a report. Firstly, it can change the meaning of a word dramatically by a change of only one vowel such as:

> complement/compliment
> daft/deft
> affect/effect

Moreover, if a word is spelt incorrectly and thus inadvertently creates another word, it calls for almost superhuman vigilance in copy-editing to notice that there is a mistake. Such an error will not be identified by a spell-checker.

Secondly, it damages the credibility of the report. The reader will be entirely justified in saying 'if the word recommendation is spelt with only one 'm' – although it can only spell recommendation whether it has got one m, two ms or three ms – how do I know that the £10 000 in the next line shouldn't be £20 000?' Confidence in the report has been lost.

Thirdly, some readers, once they see a spelling mistake, will search through the rest of the report for more, ignoring the content. Similarly, those who, watching a spoken presentation, on noticing a set of percentages which (for perfectly legitimate rounding of the components) do not add up to 100, will spend the rest of the talk looking for more arithmetical inaccuracies.

Unlike other unconventional aspects of report presentation, such as word use, punctuation or style, irregularities of spelling may therefore be described as wrong. Perhaps for this reason, many report writers deny any need for competence in this elementary field or are anxious to abdicate their responsibility and pass it on to the typist. The more common excuses include:

(a) 'I can always look it up in the dictionary.' Indeed he may, but before he gets round to doing so, there has to be some doubt that the spelling is amiss.

(b) 'It's the typist's job.' It is certainly the typist's job to query suspect spelling. The author's signature appears at the bottom of the report, however, and it is his job to ensure that it is properly spelt. In this respect s/he must give particular attention to proper nouns and various homophones such as

born/borne	led/lead	storey/story
canvas/canvass	licence/license	their/there
complement/compliment	principal/principle	
discreet/discrete	sight/site	
forbear/forebear	stationary/stationery	

He must also check the similarities such as

| allusion/illusion | later/latter | prescribed/proscribed |

The last pair are particularly important as the two words mean the opposite of each other. In Simon Raven's *The Face of the Waters* the publisher twins Carmilla and Theodosia Salinger have an apt exchange about a dubious literary endeavour in which they have become involved:

> '. . . Apparently the typescript will be ready before very long – soon after some trip he's going on to consult what he calls "his principles".'
> 'P,A,L,S or P,L,E,S'
> 'Former'
> 'Pity', said Theodosia. 'if only it were the latter, they might tell him to give the whole stinking thing up.'[28]

The Medical Director of a pharmaceutical company has produced a particularly colourful example of potential confusion when one of his doctors expressed the intention of 'analising' all his patients.

(c) 'Spelling does not matter.' Whether the writer likes it or not, it does matter. Firstly, more and more homophones like those shown above emerge as the language expands. Frequently they have very important differences in meaning. Secondly, few things (not even erratic use of capital initials) irritate so much as misspellings. This type of ignorance, whether it threatens the clarity of the report or not, certainly makes the writer appear ludicrous. Such mistakes destroy the credibility of the report. Indeed because the edges are so well defined, spelling provides a heavy stick with which the critical or truculent may chastise the author.

(d) 'The word processor will sort it out.' It will not distinguish decisively between words of similar spelling although word processors will highlight words which are completely wrong. Furthermore it makes writers over-confident and careless so that they place too great reliance on the spell-checker correcting their work. Then when they produce work in manuscript, they are unable to spell at all.

(e) 'I have never heard of one of these two words and so would never use it.' This makes it all the more important to spell the other word of the pair correctly.

PAPER

Coloured paper can be helpful in segregating parts of a report. Many local authorities use coloured paper for Confidential Sheets.

The Sports Council use coloured paper to denote the documents for different committees, thus:

Gold	:	for Whole Sports Council
Green	:	UK Affairs Committee
Yellow	:	National Resources Committee
Blue	:	Regional Resources Committee
Pink	:	Research and Information Committee
Salmon	:	Policy and Resources Committee.

SUMMARY

The need for attention to detail in the typing or printing of a report cannot be overstated. It covers consistency in the introduction and use of abbreviations.

Symbols and numbers must also be used in uniform and logical system. Quotations should be used only when it is appropriate to specify the precise form of the words used.

APPENDIX I Numbering systems

COMBINATION OF ROMAN AND ARABIC NUMBERS

In continental Europe this system is popular. It is demonstrated by the layout of the Organization for Economic Co-operation and Development Road Research report, *Traffic Control in Saturated Conditions*[1]. The first part of the table of contents is shown below to demonstrate the Continental preference for using Roman numerals for chapters or sections and then devolving to Arabic.

Chapter 1
INTRODUCTION
1.1   Statement of the Problem
1.2   Scope and Objectives of the Study
Chapter II
DEFINITION, CONTROL OBJECTIVES, PARAMETERS AND MEASURES
II.1   Definition
II.2   Saturation Situations and Parameters
II.3   Possible Action Measures
Chapter III
STATE-OF-THE-ART
III.1   Introduction
III.2   Traffic Control Parameters and Modes
III.3   Computer-based Control Systems (On-line)
III.4   Off-line Optimisation Techniques
III.5   Specific Applications
III.6   Other Traffic Engineering Measures (Non-Signalisation)
III.7   Theoretical Strategies
III.8   Public Transport in Congested Conditions
III.9   Inter-city Traffic Corridors

The breakdown is extended by decimals if required. For instance sub-section III.3 is developed:

III.3
    III.3.1
    III.3.2

III.3.3
III.3.4
III.3.5
III.3.6

European Commission reports make use of Roman numerals for sections even if the numbering is not extensively subdivided. Their report on *How Women are Represented in Television Programmes in the EEC*[2] uses this system. For example, in Part One:

I   NEWS BROADCASTS
II   ADVERTISING
III SERIES AND SERIALS
IV PRELIMINARY CONCLUSIONS

SECTIONS WITH UNIQUE SEQUENTIAL PARAGRAPH NUMBERS

In most reports paragraphs are numbered sequentially throughout the report. Decimal numbering, as described below, reflects the section number in the parent number. The consulting arm of Hacker Young uses a system that divides the report into Chapters/Sections numbered by Arabic numbers and then gives each paragraph a unique sequential number without decimal points. Thus Section 1 will start with paragraph 101, 102 and so on up to, say, 180, 181. Section 2 will run 201, 202, 203, etc. This has the notable advantage that in a speedily-prepared draft the typist does not have the problem of wondering whether there is a decimal point there or not.

For lesser paragraphs, unbracketed Roman numerals and letters are used:

1
   101
   102
      i
      ii
         a
         b

USE OF LETTERS AND SMALL ROMAN NUMBERS

Many house styles use strictly prescribed sequences of letters and in the lower levels of subordinate paragraph, small Roman numbers. Price Waterhouse uses

1.
   (1)
   (2)
   (3)
      a.
      b.
      c.
         (a)
         (b)
         (c)
           i
           ii

A useful format for a simple 24-page report is that in Masterman's *Television and the Bombing of Libya*[3]. The report analysed BBC and ITN news coverage for 2 days: 15 April and 17 April 1986. These are given letters A and B. Thereafter the following sequence is used:

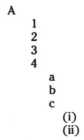

A
- 1
- 2
- 3
- 4
    - a
    - b
    - c
        - (i)
        - (ii)

DECIMAL NUMBERS FOR THE MAIN DIVISIONS

Shannon Free Airport Development Company use similar combinations, but require decimal numbers for the sub-division:

1. SECTION HEADINGS
    1.1 Subsection
        (a) Paragraph
        (b) Second Paragraph
2. SECOND SECTION HEADING

Their instructions then direct small Roman numbers in brackets for further sub-divisions, followed by unidentified dashes for subsequent divisions:

(b) Second paragraph
    (i) Sub-paragraph
        – Sub-sub-paragraph
        – Second sub-sub-paragraph
    (ii) Second sub-paragraph

However, their instructions preface these latter divisions with the caveat that they should be used only 'if it is absolutely necessary'.

The Trustee Savings Banks Central Board system takes the decimal markings a stage further:

3.1
    3.1.1
    3.1.2
    3.1.3
    3.1.4
        (a)
        (b)
    3.1.5
        (a)
        (b)
3.2

The Worsley report[4] on the control of the Institute of Chartered Accountants has a basic format of the decimal system (going up to 3.23 and 5.26) but thereafter lower-case bracketed Roman letters when required and exceptionally lower-case bracketed Roman numerals

```
10.1
10.2
10.3
10.4
10.5
      (a)
            (i)
            (ii)
            (iii)
      (b)
```

The National Nuclear Corporation, which produces long, complex and sometimes massive reports, extends such a system yet further:

```
section      1
sub-section  1.2
clause       1.1.1
paragraph    1.1.1 (a)
item         1.1.1 (a) (i)
             1.1.1 (a) (i) 1
```

ALL-DECIMAL SYSTEM

Since the late 1960s, the most popular scheme of numbering has been the all-decimal system. Such arrangements in their pure form make no provision for any symbols other than the decimal combinations. They are thus absolutely clear and unambiguous, if sometimes a bit cumbersome. They have, therefore, the clarity and precision of a Dewey library cataloguing system[5].

The *Civil Service Typing Manual*[6] now provides for use of a decimal system. A good example of its use is the Griffiths Report[7]. It actually goes so far as to say that Roman numerals should be avoided (although it happily uses a Roman system for its own appendices).

APPENDIX II Suggestions for further reading

Here is a selected list of books suitable for reading by everyone to whom the content of this book has proved to be of interest, unless the notes indicate that the book in question deals with some specialism. The titles of works dealing with more esoteric aspects are to be found in the detailed references in Appendix III.

The notes describing the books explained in detail below contain many superlatives. This is deliberate. The books shown here are recommended, with very few qualifications.

FOR READING (AS OPPOSED TO REFERENCE)

English language

The King's English (H.W. and F.G. Fowler; Oxford)
First published in 1906, it was the work of both H.W. and F.G. Fowler. It enjoyed a second edition in 1907 and a third in 1931. It describes style and custom rather more than giving a clinical glossary of individual words and syntactical functions. It is arranged not like a dictionary but in a series of chapters: Vocabulary, Syntax, Airs and Graces (which includes humour, metaphor and other embellishments), Punctuation and so on. Every chapter is beautifully simple to read and copiously illustrated by examples, albeit, of course, from pre-1931 publications.

Nevertheless, although the Fowler brothers illustrate and describe, *The King's English* is still strongly prescriptive. It is responsible, for instance, for such dogmas as 'Prefer the Saxon word to the Romance'.

Fowler's Modern English Usage (revised by Sir Ernest Gowers; Oxford)
This is, of course, legendary and a work of great scholarship. It was first published in 1926 and appeared under the name H.W. Fowler, his brother having died some nine years earlier. It was revised by Sir Ernest Gowers (*q.v.* below) in 1965. It is a mine of fascinating information, grammatical, semantic and etymological.

It is arranged as a reference book in alphabetical order. The articles are couched in fluent prose and may be read straight through if desired. The entries include individual words with comments on their use, as well as phenomena such as *archaism, criticism, pronouns* and *unattached participles.*

It may be argued that despite its revision it has not really kept pace with the times. Indeed, nearly 20 years have passed since the revision. It is highly prescriptive by modern standards and the business report writer may find that it gets too bogged down in Classical allusion. However it is bliss to the authoritarian and will provide hours of entertainment and distraction to anyone interested in the English language.

The Complete Plain Words (Sir Ernest Gowers; Penguin paperback, HMSO hardback)

Gowers will make easier reading for many people than the Fowlers' books. It was first produced as *Plain Words* in 1948 at the request of the Treasury. In 1954 *The Complete Plain Words* appeared, incorporating *The ABC of Plain Words* which Gowers had produced three years before.

Sir Ernest Gowers was an experienced civil servant who was given the task of improving Civil Service English. The book was aimed at civil servants who had been guilty for several decades of writing in the style of an even earlier era. In other words they were writing in Victorian English at the beginning of the second half of the 20th century. So perhaps the malaise which Gowers sought to rectify no longer applies.

The book reads like a novel. It is full of examples, many of which are hilarious and a few of which defy credibility. All aspects of English usage are covered and there are now nine chapters on word use, as opposed to five in the previous edition.

The original version was updated in 1973 (Sir Bruce Fraser). The third edition was produced in 1986 by Sidney Greenbaum (Quain Professor of English Language and Literature at University College, London) and Janet Whitcut (an alumna of the Longman Dictionary Department). They have made strenuous efforts to update the book to include acceptable modern usages, but the book still retains the flavour of the 1940s to counter malpractices of the 1930s.

The Oxford Guide to English Usage (compiled by ESC Weiner; Oxford)

Weiner makes it clear that this is a book 'intended for anyone who needs simple and direct guidance about the formation and use of English words – about spelling, pronunciation, meanings, and grammar – and who cannot claim any specialist training in these subjects'. It does just that.

It is easy to refer to without prominent clear headings. It is well spaced which greatly facilitates selective reference.

Solecisms and danger areas are helpfully itemized with bullet points. There are four sections of roughly equal size on Word Formation, Pronunciation, Vocabulary and Grammar, as well as some interesting appendices.

Usage and Abusage (Eric Partridge; Penguin)

This celebrated and much published work is laid out on very much the same lines as Fowler's *Modern English Usage*. The articles are shorter and generally less bound up with obscure academic allusions. It was first published in Britain in 1947 (20 years after Fowler). For these reasons, it is more readable to most people.

For all its brevity it still contains a wealth of relevant detail as to etymology, quotation and precedent.

Eric Partridge died in 1979, aged 85, after a lifetime dedicated to the language. Most of the last 35 years of his life was spent in the British Museum library pursuing this great affection. His output was prodigious. About 80 works are attributable to him. Only two can be shown in this appendix. Anyone wishing to sample a wide range of this great man's work should cast his eyes over the tribute anthology *Eric Partridge in His Own Words* (edited by David Crystal, published by Andre Deutsch).

Strangely this magnificent contributor to the understanding of English was never decorated.

The Facts of English (R. Ridout and C. Witting; Pan)

Here is a paperback of the same general nature as Partridge's *Usage and Abusage* but it is very much simpler. It will be particularly helpful to clerical staff, typists and those more at home with numbers than words. This is not intended as a patronizing comment. The book gives good practical explanations of points that the occasional or inexperienced report writer might confuse: use of apostrophes, *affect/effect*, commonly used Latin phrases (such as *ad hoc, per annum, prima facie*).

The authors are a text-book writer and a journalist. They give suitably direct and uncomplicated advice.

The Use of English (R. Quirk; Longman)

This is a particularly readable account of the main issues in English language development. Professor Quirk was the Quain Professor of English Language and Literature at the University of London and was widely regarded as the guru of all aspects of practical English use. The book uses literary rather than commercial examples and is historical in treatment. However, its relevance to report writing is obvious as soon as a few pages have been read.

Comprehensive Grammar of the English Language (R. Quirk, S. Greenbaum, S. Leech and J. Svartvik; Longman)

This is the most complete analysis of English grammar ever produced. It was compiled by four men who could claim to be unsurpassed in learning and authority on the subject. David Crystal, himself a great scholar, compiled the index.

With 1800 pages it is priced accordingly. It is essentially something to dip into.

International English (L. Todd and I. Hancock; Croom Helm)

This comprehensive book by a Senior Lecturer in the School of English at Leeds University (Todd) and the Professor of Linguistics and English at the University of Texas is particularly helpfully arranged. There are alphabetical entries covering articles on words that are misused, parts of speech, types of English and so on. In addition there is a detailed index for those seeking more specific information.

As the title suggests it covers all types of English throughout the world. It is particularly careful not to be judgemental.

New Words for Old, Weasel Words, Words Fail Me, Winged Words and *A Word In Time* (P. Howard; Hamish Hamilton)

These are fascinating and highly readable short essays on semantic usages. Each one discusses a particular cliché, vogue-word or extended expression. Many of the articles appeared in the author's occasional column in *The Times*, of which he is Literary Editor. Others were written specially for these books.

The five books first appeared in 1977, 1978, 1980 and 1988 and 1990 respectively. There is no doubt that the tone of his comments is, in the main, less prescriptive in the later articles.

As to why his views are less authoritarian, Philip Howard suggests a variety of reasons, while stressing that such a complex matter does not permit a quick or simple explanation:

> You could say that I have developed a more realistic and sensible view of the way the language works. You could say that I have been influenced by my friends, in the field like Randolph Quirk and Bob Burchfield. You could say that I have become embarrassed by the shrill tone of voice in the earlier pieces. You could say that I am growing middle-aged and I dare say there would be an element of truth in all the explanations.[1]

The 1988 book *Winged Words*, is a set of 55 essays all characterized by Howard's fluent erudition. It is divided into two parts: new words and new usages. He updates his semantic commentary to take account of the years of 'AIDS', 'Big Bang', 'yuppies' and 'carers'.

The most recent book *A Word in Time* concentrates not so much on trendy words but on eccentric use of existing words and current trends in punctuation and grammar

The State of the Language (P. Howard; Hamish Hamilton)
Philip Howard explained that he was producing a book explaining whether English is dying and what is happening to it[2]. He does this with his usual mind-blowing breadth of example and allusion.

The answer to the question which he poses is a pragmatic one. Howard accepts that language and usage are changing. This was demonstrated by his disapproving response to the Prince of Wales's comments in December 1989.

> When, in his latest populist tirade, the Prince of Wales complains about 'the dismal wasteland' of modern English, he is talking unhistorical and reactionary rubbish . . . It is simply not true that English is being used less well than it was a generation ago . . . What we need now is a sensible middle road between the absurd old rigours that treated language like square-bashing, and the new encouragement of children to express themselves.[3]

The English Language (R. Burchfield: Oxford)
This book by Robert Burchfield, who is referred to in Philip Howard's quotation above, is highly readable, although dauntingly learned. Burchfield recently retired from several decades as Editor-in-Chief of the Oxford Dictionaries. The approach is historical but it remains (published 1985) very much up-to-date.

The Right Word at the Right Time (edited J. E. Kahn; Readers Digest)
This book adopts a popular approach. It has various useful examples of English usage and makes recommendations being descriptive in tone. Extensive use is made of red to denote questionable and recommended usage.

The book is nevertheless large and offers desk rather than pocket guidance.

Dictionary of Differences (L. Urdang; Bloomsbury, London)
A readable book, this was produced in 1988 by one of the most eminent and

experienced lexicographers in Britain. He explains in his Introduction: 'This book came about because over the many years during which I have compiled dictionaries, encyclopedias, and other reference books, I have often encountered people who mix up more or less ordinary things. They have trouble remembering the difference between *cement* and *concrete*, or between a *fission bomb* and a *fusion bomb* (to mention a few 'ordinary' things).' In fact his selection is less esoteric than his slightly mischievous extract suggests. Many commonplace adjectives and verbs are helpfully defined.

The dictionary defines each of a pair of frequently confused words in entries which are agreeable to read. In the main they are between 100 and 200 words long and give detailed and learned treatments.

It is conveniently free of the labyrinth of cross-references which characterize so many books of this kind. It has a full and helpful index.

Put It in Writing (J. Whale; Dent)
An essentially popular book, this takes 34 short articles which originally appeared in *The Sunday Times* between September 1983 and April 1984. None is longer than 700 words.

They cover such topics as punctuation, repetition and gender, all of which may be of interest to some business writers. The quality varies. Some are simplistic and some are authoritarian.

The Joy of Words (F. Spiegl; Elm Tree Books)
Here is a most entertaining book. In it Fritz Spiegl, the broadcaster and journalist, rambles through a huge range of the euphemisms, pomposities, contradictions and absurdities of late twentieth-century linguistic change.

The book is suggestively sub-titled 'A Bedside Book for English Lovers' and this *double-entendre* is representative of the tone of the whole work.

Sometimes Spiegl is sarcastically vitriolic, as when discussing the argot of social work, and some of the pictures – photography and cartoons – which are reproduced in the text are so small as to be tantalizingly illegible. Generally, however, it is difficult to put the book down and the discursive style does not detract from important semantic points wittily made.

Style (sic)

The Economist Pocket Style Book (The Economist)
This book was greeted with great excitement when it was published. It was believed by naive members of the public that it was going to instruct every commercial and business writer to produce punchy, concise, succinct prose as in *The Economist*.

It does not do this and presumably never set out to do so. It does, however, give 90 pages of useful guidelines in an alphabetical sequence. The range of topics covered in the short book is considerable. Commonly mis-spelt words are listed under Spelling. Nearly a dozen pages of organizations, such as ECOWAS (Economic Community of West African States) IATA (International Air Transport Association) and WCL (World Confederation of Labour), are catalogued and explained. *Copious* explanations of measurements are included.

Some guides on style, in the sense of word-choice are given, such as the use of 'gender' as opposed to 'sex' and an exhortation to use 'way of life' rather than 'lifestyle'.

It is however a very useful reference book and not a panacea.

Punctuation

You Have a Point There (Eric Partridge; Routledge and Kegan Paul)
This is an unsurpassed guide to punctuation by the author of *Usage and Abusage* (q.v. above). Every punctuation mark (including such things as italics) is picked up, turned over and examined in fine detail. Examples are shown and trends described.

The book summarizes the various uses with a chapter on 'orchestration' of the marks. This metaphor demonstrates admirably how the various marks must be drawn together to complement each other. Finally there is a chapter by John W. Clark of the University of Minnesota on practices in the United States.

Mind the Stop (G.V. Carey; Penguin)
Carey's book is much simpler and shorter than Partridge (*q.v.* above) (124 pages, as opposed to 226). It is therefore less profusely illustrated. Many find that its advice is more direct and it is therefore easier to consult for quick guidance.

Carey first produced the book in 1939. A revision was published in 1958. The revision showed most commendable sensitivity to even the smallest changes in custom that had occurred since the first version. There is a useful chapter on proof correction.

G. H. Vallins, author of *Good English*, (Andre Deutsch) says in another book that he covers punctuation only loosely as it has been dealt with once and for all by Carey and Partridge.

American English

British and American English (P. Strevens; Cassell)
Strevens's little book is probably the best simple guide to American English for those who need to write occasional reports for American readerships. Seven easy chapters include an explanation of the reasons for the divergence of the two versions and some plain direct guidance on grammatical habits in the two countries. The book ends with a very short pair (American–British and British–American) of 'Contrasting Word-lists' (approximately 200 words each).

What's the Difference?: An American–British/British–American Dictionary (N. Moss; Arrow)
Moss provides much more comprehensive vocabularies (in both directions) than Strevens (*q.v.* above). The author was born in Britain but was educated largely in the United States.

It is a light-hearted paperback which can be read for entertainment as well as used for reference. It is probably more suitable for interpreting American writing than as a guide to word-choice. It contains many colloquialisms. It was first published in 1973 and revised in 1978. Many of the American terms shown have now achieved general acceptance in Britain.

Dictionary of American Slang (edited by H. Wentworth and S. B. Flexner; Second supplemented edition, Crowell)
This book only just gets into the list. Much of it is provocative. Some of it is obscene. Many of the terms included appear to be one-off nonce words of individual writers. There are 22 000 definitions, mostly supported by quotations. These are drawn from a very wide range of sources.

It just squeezes into the list as American reports sometimes contain words hovering on the edge of received language. It is also fascinating in the breadth of its source material. Unless the user is strong-willed or has plenty of time he should be wary of opening it (hence its inclusion under 'Reading' rather than 'Reference'). This original was produced in 1960. The supplement contains items added in 1967 and 1975.

Australian English

A Dictionary of Australian Colloquialisms (G.A. Wilkes; Sydney University)
The author, Challis Professor of English Literature at the University of Sydney, begins his Introduction 'While on study leave in Oxford in 1968, I was asked by an English scholar whether there were any distinctively Australian proverbs. My first response was that there were not . . .' This 470 page book is the result of more leisured reflection.

More detailed than his 1978 version, this 1985 edition covers much of the same ground. Copious illustrations from Australian journalism and literature enliven the definitions.

The Australian Language (S.J. Baker; the Currawong Press)
A book of essays covering in minute and learned detail every imaginable aspect of Australian English.

Baker traces all the argots of Australian English and follows their evolution in bush, desert, farm and town. With extensive notes, many fascinating side streets are employed during the journey. Readers who feel that the youth of Australia means that its linguistic history is shallow should have a look at this book. The briefest glance at its pages will soon disabuse them of this naive view.

History of English language

A History of The English Language (A.C. Baugh and T. Cable; Routledge and Kegan Paul)
This book traces the history of the language from its origins in the Indo-European to the *New English Dictionary*. The chapters are arranged chronologically and end with a long chapter on 'The English Language in America'. The second of two appendices shows how spelling has changed by passages from different eras quoted in quick succession. It is very readable and a detailed table of contents enables the reader, if he wishes, to be selective.

A History of English (B.M.H. Strang; Methuen)
This is another history of the language which is very agreeable to read. Professor Barbara Strang describes it in her Preface as 'a book for beginners in linguistic history'. She sets out to dispel 'the fairy-tale – not to say the nightmare – quality' of

the subject. She succeeds in doing this brilliantly. To add to the relevance, she starts with recent changes and works her way back to the period before AD 370.

The English Language (Volume 1): Essays by English and American Men of Letters 1490–1839 (edited by W. F. Bolton) and *The English Language (Volume 2): Essays by Linguists and Men of Letters 1858–1964* (edited by W.F. Bolton and C.D. Crystal; Cambridge)

These two volumes are ideal source books for anyone who wishes to follow the development of the language in original material. They show important and relevant passages from the period of Caston and the demise of Middle English through the critical phase of Defoe, Addison, Swift, Johnson and the threat of the English Academy, via Webster to George Orwell and Anthony Burgess. There are reasonable, but not overwhelming, notes and every entry has a helpful short paragraph of introduction.

Sexist writing

The Handbook of Non-Sexist Writing for Writers, Editors and Speakers (C. Miller and K. Swift; Second British Edition, The Women's Press Ltd)

This is an excellent book which unlike many works rejoicing under the title 'handbook' is indeed just that. Its size, length (170 pages) and format make it extremely manageable and easy to use for reference.

It covers every conceivable aspect of sexist writing from prefixes and pronouns to generalized descriptions of people and social titles. It carefully and successfully avoids being patronizing or authoritarian.

Although American in origin, there are virtually no traces of this in its text. Only occasionally as in its mini-thesaurus, where it suggests alternative appellations, do certain forms of words appear which seem alien to British ears.

Textbooks

Writing Technical Reports (B.M. Cooper; Penguin)

This is a Pelican original which is deservedly popular and widely used. It was first published in 1964 and has been reprinted many times. Of the seven chapters, the content of the first six could generally be applied to most non-technical reports. The seventh deals with illustrations. There is a useful appendix on various sources of information.

Except for some of the simple comments on word use, the book avoids the temptation of many handbooks on written communication to produce many authoritarian generalizations which do not fit every situation.

Communication in Business (P. Little; Third edition, Longman)

Of all the general guidebooks on business communication, this is probably the best. It is comprehensive, covering oral communication, meetings, essays, notices and non-verbal communication. Three chapters on wording, one on summaries and one on reports are particularly relevant to the subject area in question here. Although the book is so wide-ranging it contains much important specific information. There is, for instance, an interesting appendix on the use of postcodes which is astonishingly interesting for such a prosaic subject.

Business Communication (R.T. Chappel and W.C. Read; Fourth edition, Macdonald and Evans)
This comprehensive book also covers all aspects of communication. One chapter covers reports, but others touch on closely related areas. Two other chapters on the reporting responsibilities of committees are useful. It is a little unimaginative in its comments on style and word use, but provides some first-class guidance for the authors of simple informal communications.

Effective Business Communications (H.A Murphy and C.E. Pack; McGraw-Hill)
This is not useful as a guide to British business report writing. However, it is helpful to those who deal with American report writers or who have to write reports for American readers, as an insight into the way in which the American managerial mind works.

It is not lissome; over 700 large pages. Part 4 (three chapters) covers reports and contains many examples.

The reader must be warned that the authoritative and rather glib style describing some of the comparisons may be misleading. Not only is this a bit high-handed but the lessons drawn from the examples essentially represent American practice and contradict what would be acceptable in Britain.

Specialized Textbooks

The Successful Consultant's Guide to Writing Proposals and Reports (H. Bermont; Bermont Books)
This one is a highly specialized book of 55 (unnumbered) pages. It is not cheap. It gives direct practical guidance on the drafting of consultants' proposals and reports. Good and bad examples are discussed.

The author starts his introduction: 'There are books on how to write a proposal, and there are books on how to write a report. But for the consultant, these books as separate entities are meaningless. In our profession, the proposal and the report are linked in so many ways that they virtually become one process.' He then develops his guidelines to satisfy that need.

Employee Reports (A. Hilton; Woodhead-Faulkner)
Here is a very highly illustrated book which helps in the design of reports aimed at employees. The author, who is editor of *Accountancy Age*, stresses that he does not suggest formulae or models but wishes to stimulate managers into thinking more seriously about employee communication.

His 60 figures run through all the obvious types of illustrating: pie charts, graphs, etc. He also demonstrates cartoons and other less conventional forms of display.

Practical Performance Appraisal (V. and A. Stewart; Gower)
This contains ten chapters on the benefits and mechanics of installing, monitoring and generally using an appraisal system. It is regarded as the definitive study of its subject. Its content therefore has an inextricable bearing on appraisal reporting.

Spelling

The Pergamon Dictionary of Perfect Spelling (C. Maxwell; E.J. Arnold)
This interesting and originally presented book includes common mis-spellings in

red. The correct spellings are shown in black. It provides explanations as to forming verbs, adjectives, etc. It also furnishes exercises for those who have a major problem in this field.

At Appendix I it boasts 'Some spelling rules' and prudently limits them to 24 conventions. Other peripherally relevant appendices include marked maps which are helpful for spelling counties and countries. Others such as those analysing weights and measures are of less obvious relevance to the subject.

The book is not small for a spelling manual, running to 335 pages.

Word Spell (edited B. Wileman and R. Wileman; Harrap)
This acknowledges the problem that those who cannot spell have problems with dictionaries and shows mis-spellings in pale blue. This is sizeable at 371 pages.

The Right Way to Spell (J. E. Metcalfe; Elliot Right Way Books)
This explores various aspects of the derivation of spelling; concentrating particularly on the logic of derivation. Plurals are treated at some length.

The spelling guide *per se* occupies just 20 pages at the back of its 160 pages.

The *Pan Dictionary of English Spelling* (M.H. Manser; Pan)
This first-class book slightly taints its excellence by calling itself 'ideal'. It is nevertheless admirable in content, in presentation and in range. Its scope even extends to technical and obscene terms, unusual in such guides.

Very simple definitions are given and these are entirely adequate for purposes of distinction.

A helpful three-tier format characterizes all entries. The word being defined is shown in bold print, followed by the simple definition and italicized derivatives.

Statistics and tabulations

These books are listed in increasing order of simplicity.)

Statistics for Management (J. Ashford; Institute of Personnel Management)
This is a 400-page tome on the technicalities of statistical method. The book is derived from a self-instruction course in statistics which the author prepared for the National and Local Government Officers Association. It is an invaluable reference book for anyone dealing in detail with tabulations, numerate displays and illustrations. Some parts (such as the explanations of probability and estimation) are not suitable for the faint-hearted layman. Nor are they intended for him.

Wheldon's Business Statistics (G.L. Thirkettle; Ninth edition, Macdonald and Evans)
This is a much revised and frequently reprinted authority on statistical method and presentation. It is highly respected. There are detailed explanations and examples of all the principal forms of visual display. The chapters on Sampling and Surveys are particularly lucid and useful. A detailed system of headings makes the book particularly easy for reference.

Statistics in Action (P. Sprent; Penguin)
This book gives a useful insight into statistical method. It concentrates on statisticians' interpretation of data and does not cover display. It is particularly strong on probability and stochastic processes.

Plain Figures (M. Chapman in collaboration with B. Mahon; HMSO)
A 110-page A4 work published by the Civil Service College in 1986. The authors who are slightly suggestively described on the cover as having collaborated pay what they call 'a humble tribute' to Sir Ernest Gowers whom they perceive as the inspiration of their work. The connection is not immediately obvious.

The book is, however, extremely well presented with extensive relevant and varied illustrations. The book is firmly critical of bad practice and written in a refreshingly frank style.

Use and Abuse of Statistics (W.R. Reichmann; Penguin)
This is an excellent, plain guide to all aspects of statistical handling and display. The diagrams are simple and it is suitable to be read through from beginning to end. Various complicated processes are relegated to appendices. An agreeable, chatty style and plenty of analogies make this book very easy to read.

How to Lie with Statistics (D. Huff; Penguin)
This short book is an entertaining explanation of the principal ways in which statistics and statistical presentations can mislead. It has a wide-ranging (for a 125-page book) selection of simple illustrations and many amusing but relevant cartoons by Mel Calman.

The fringe

The State of the Language (edited by L. Michaels and C. Ricks; University of California Press)
Here is a selection of essays, published in January 1980, of varying appeal and varying relevance to report writers. The editors are Professor of English at the University of California, Berkeley, and Professor of English Literature at Christ's College, Cambridge. They compiled the work of 63 contributors from both sides of the Atlantic. The British ones include Randolph Quirk, Robert Burchfield, Kingsley Amis, D. J. Enright, Anthony Burgess and David Lodge. All aspects of language use are covered including feminist parlance (Angela Carter) and the argot of homosexuality (Edward White) as well as the use of language in politics (Enoch Powell) and broadcasting (Denis Donaghue). Many of the essays are subjective to the point of bigotry. Most of them are instructive and nearly all are entertaining.

The State of the Language: 1990 Edition (edi(ed by C. Ricks and L. Michaels; Cambridge)
Precisely a decade later Professor Ricks and Michaels have produced a brand new version. It takes the same format as the 1980 edition and consists of 62 contributions by 62 authorities. None of them appeared in the 1980 version and all have been produced to represent trends of the 1980s.

There are reappearances by Randolph Quirk and Enoch Powell as well as many welcome new ones by Ted Hughes, Fiona Pitt-Kethley and others considered representative of the decade just finished.

Some themes are new such as the vocabulary of MDS which is covered more than once, while Kingsley Amis returns to his perennial favourite of malapropism.

A Dictionary of Slang and Unconventional English (Edited P. Beale; originally edited E. Partridge; eighth edition, Routledge and Kegan Paul) The 8th edition of this doyen (440 pages) of fringe reference books was produced in its most recent form with two aims in mind. It was to be easier to consult and it was to take account of notes made by Eric Partridge between 1967 and his death in June 1979.

It is a superb work of scholarship written in a lively style demonstrated by some lapses into the first-person singular as in 'of the three, the first term is the least used; also, it arose the latest – not, I think, before ca 1955'.

It has some interesting if highly specialized articles in the appendices; some deal with phonetics, with the language of the Australian underworld, with certain public schools. Others trace in detail the etymology of various bizarre words such as *Kibosh* and *loo*. Another appendix looks at the extensive vocabulary from wars, including the Boer War and the Korean War, although the stock thrown up by the Second World War is disappointing.

Dictionaries: The Art and Craft of Lexicography (S.I. Landau; Cambridge)

This book, which attracted much interest on publication in 1989, is a comprehensive guide to lexicography. Anyone interested in word use, as all report writers should be, will inevitably be drawn into the field of lexicography. In this readable book they will learn the history of the craft, the problems of definition, usage and compilation. The place of preferences and notes are helpfully described and it is acknowledged in detail that no 1990 lexicographer can be without a computer.

Studies in Lexicography (Edited R. Burchfield; Oxford)

These are ten interesting essays edited by the master of lexicography. They are not for anyone who may have found Landau (above) heavy going.

A Dictionary of Obscenity, Taboo and Euphemism (J. McDonald; Sphere Books)

This is a lively and entertaining description of usage and, more intriguingly, usage of words which lie outside the range used in reports.

Nevertheless, for anyone interested in the development of the language, taboos provide a fascinating route to trace shift in word meaning. Words move in and out of acceptability through the centuries for little reason other than fashion in sensitivity.

This book follows these kinds of shift in a most entertaining way allowing hunch and informed guesswork to replace the irrefutable proof of origin on which the more conservative lexicographers insist.

The New Englishes (J. Platt, H. Weber and M. L. Ho; Routledge and Kegan Paul)

This is a very learned yet readable analysis of English forms to be found outside Britain and the Old Commonwealth.

The chapters on the role of English in the various societies where it serves as a second or official language, on word borrowing and usage and the future of the 'New Englishes' are particularly fascinating.

Strangely they do not touch on the Arabic forms of English to be found on the south coast of the Arabian Gulf and elsewhere.

Waterhouse on Newspaper Style (K. Waterhouse, Viking)

In *Daily Mirror Style*, Waterhouse produced a characteristically witty and light-hearted analysis of the peculiarities of the way in which that tabloid is produced.

This equally amusing book is more wide-ranging and more detailed. It not only discusses frivolous aspects of the subject, such as double-entendres of headlines, but also investigates more seriously journalistic use of punctuation, grammar and vocabulary. It also provides a valuable glossary of terms for non-journalistic readers.

Its relevance to report writing is that report authors can be guided to avoid certain, if not malpractices at least eccentricities of journalistic style. Everyone is exposed to journalism but must distance themselves from that style in their more formal craft.

Coffee Table Books

(In case you have a coffee table in your office, these might be more instructive to your waiting visitors than trade journals and travel agents' magazines.)

The Cambridge Encyclopedia of Language (D. Crystal; Cambridge)
This handsome book was published in 1987 and is lavishly illustrated with photographs and diagrams.

The Story of English (R. McCrum, W. Cran and R. MacNeil; Faber and Faber)
Here is another book appropriately illustrated for easy reading. It was published in 1986 based on a television series which at times seemed rather patronizing. The book is less so.

Contact: Human Communications (Edited R. Williams; Thames and Hudson)
With yet more illustrations (379 and 57 in colour) this covers a rather wider range of communications. It is also rather older than the others, having been published in 1981.

FOR REFERENCE

Reference books described in detail in this book

The Concise Oxford Dictionary of Current English (Oxford)

Chambers Twentieth Century Dictionary (Chambers)

Collins English Dictionary (Collins)

Longmans Dictionary of the English Language (Longman)

Collins Cobuild English Language Dictionary (Collins) (Edited J. Sinclair)

Webster's New Collegiate Dictionary (Merriam-Webster)

Roget's Thesaurus (Longman and Penguin)

Debrett's Correct Form (Futura)

The Oxford Dictionary for Writers and Editors (Oxford)

Style Manual for Authors Editors and Printers (Fourth edition) (Australian Government Publishing Service)

Interpreting Company Reports and Accounts (Fourth Edition) (G. Holmes and A. Sugden: Woodhead-Faulkner)

How to Understand and Use Company Accounts (R. Warren; Business Books)

Reference books not described in this book, but of obvious content

Longman's Dictionary of Business English, (J.H. Adam; Longman)

Dictionary of Management (D. French and H. Saward; Pan)

A Dictionary of Economics and Commerce (Edited by S.E Steigler and G. Thomas; Pan)

A Handbook of Management (Edited by T. Kempner; Penguin)

A Dictionary of Foreign Words and Phrases in Current English (A.J. Bliss; Routledge and Kegan Paul)

New Dictionary of American Slang (Edited R.L. Chapman; Macmillan)

The Complete Desk Book (S. Feldman; Hamlyn)

Dictionary of Accounting Terms (D. French; Institute of Chartered Accountants in England and Wales)

Rooms Dictionary of Confusibles (A. Room; Routledge and Kegan Paul)

Newspeak: A Dictionary of Jargon (J. Green; Routledge and Kegan Paul)

Everyman's Dictionary of Abbreviations (J. Paxton; Dent)

Brewer's Dictionary of Phrase and Fable (Revised by I.H. Evans; Cassell)

A Dictionary of Foreign Words and Phrases in Current English (A.J. Bliss; Routledge and Kegan Paul)

Very short simple guides to report writing

Report Writing (D. Wheatley; Penguin)

The Basics of Writing Reports Etcetera (N. Moore and M. Hesp; Clive Bingley)

Report Writing (R. Lewis and J. Inglis; National Extension College)

How to Write a Report (J. Fletcher; Institute of Personnel Management)

How to Write Effective Reports (J.E. Sussams; Gower)

How to Write Reports (J. Mitchell; Fontana)

(Wheatley probably offers the best value for a short book.)

Books that will be helpful to those for whom English is not their first language

Oxford Advanced Learners' Dictionary of Current English (Oxford) (Generally regarded as the leading dictionary for those learning English as a foreign language.)

Chambers Universal Learners' Dictionary (Chambers) (Rather cruelly lambasted by Auberon Waugh[5] when it came out for the unhelpful banality of its example uses. However, many foreign people have found this paperback extremely useful.)

Practical English Usage (M. Swan; Oxford) (Guidelines on grammatical use.)

Current English Usage (F.T. Wood, revised by R.H. and L.M. Flavell; Macmillan). (Good guide to word use and idiom.)

Books of Value to Scientific Writers

How to Write and Publish a Scientific Paper (Robert A. Day; third edition, Cambridge)
The number of reprints is accurate testimony to this excellent little work by the Professor of English at the University of Delaware. All sorts of subjects are covered: references, tables, layout, titling and many aspects of interesting writing.

The book is written and presented in a jolly style which makes it suitable for reading or reference.

The large number of competent, and sometimes eminent, scientists who seek advice on writing for publication will find this invaluable. (The paperback version comes wrapped in cellophane.)

Good Style for Scientific and Engineering Writing (John Kirkman; Pitman)
This is a very handy book of 130 pages which genuinely tackles style and produces some really useful guidelines. What is more, unlike many books which purport to offer guidance to scientific writers, it does so in a scientific context.

Science Writing for Beginners (A.D. Farr; Blackwell Scientific Publications)
This is a helpful book which provides guidance for scientific writers, examining the subject from the standpoint of the various documents which they might produce: essays, science papers for publications, book reviews, dissertations and so on. Some valuable pages are given to writing for the American press (although this section is misleadingly ambitious in its title, which refers to 'foreign journals'). One of the later chapters tackles writing a book and this also gives valuable advice. Like Kirkman its examples and comments are firmly set in a scientific context.

A Handbook of Writing for Engineers (Joan van Emden; Macmillan)
While being a bossy and, at times, rather arrogant little book, this 1990 publication will be of use to many scientific writers whose literary fluency does not match their technical competence.

It does not tackle report format or tabulation except at the simplest level. It does however give useful advice on the elements of style, while rather negatively describing writing as a 'chore'.

Interestingly, the author – despite her sex – uncompromisingly presumes the writer to be male. She makes an apology for this in the introduction; such as was made in the earlier edition of this book, but has now been ruled out of order in this version.

APPENDIX III   References

CHAPTER ONE

1. *Amnesty International Report 1989*, Amnesty International Publications, London, 1989, p. 141.
2. Ibid, p. 224.
3. Devon and Cornwall Constabulary, *Chief Constable's Annual Report 1988*.
4. Department of the Environment/National Water Council, *Copper in Potable Waters by Atomic Absorption Spectrophotometry*, HMSO, London, 1980.
5. Department of Health and Social Security, *Report of the Committee of Inquiry into Human Fertilisation and Embryology* (Cmnd 9314), HMSO, London, 1984.
6. Royal Astronomical Society, *Report on the Scientific Priorities for UK Astronomical Research for the Period 1990–2000*, London, 1986.
7. (Chairman) Sir Douglas Black, *Investigation of the Possible Increased Incidence of Cancer in West Cumbria*, HMSO, London, 1984.
8. Chemical and Allied Products Industry Training Board, *Working at the Future: Strategy for 1977/82*.
9. Cornwall County Council, *Cornwall Structure Plan*, 1st Alteration, Explanatory Memorandum, Truro, 1988, p. 31.
10. R. Warren, *How to Understand and Use Company Accounts*, second edition, Hutchinson, London, 1988.
11. G. Holmes and A. Sugden, *Interpreting Company Reports and Accounts*, fourth edition, Woodhead-Faulkner, Cambridge, 1990.
12. *A Survey of UK Published Accounts 1989–90*. Obtainable from the Institute of Chartered Accountants in England and Wales, Gloucester House, 399 Silbury Boulevard, Central Milton Keynes, MK9 2HL.
13. Home Office, *Supervision and Punishment in the Community: A Framework for Action* (green paper), HMSO, London, 1990.
14. Ministry of Defence, *Statement on the Defence Estimates 1990* (Cm 1022), (Vols 1 and 2), HMSO, London, 1990.
15. Commission of the European Communities, *Completing the Internal Market*,

White paper from the Commission to the European Council, Luxembourg, 1985.

16. *A Language for Life*, Department of Education and Science, Report of the Committee of Inquiry appointed by the Secretary of State for Education and Science under the Chairmanship of Sir Allan Bullock FBA, HMSO, London, 1977.

17. Department of Trade, *Report of the Committee of Inquiry on Industrial Democracy* (Cmnd 6706), HMSO, London, 1977.

18. Department of Energy, *Sizewell B Public Inquiry*, report by Sir Frank Layfield, HMSO, London, 1987.

19. Buckinghamshire County Council, *School Visit to Cornwall by Stoke Poges County Middle School May 1985*, Report of Chief Education Officer.

20. D. Fennell in conversation with the author (November 1989).

21. *Falkland Islands Review, Report of a Committee of Privy Counsellors* (Chairman the Rt Hon Lord Franks OM, GCMG, KCB, CBE) (Cmnd 8787), HMSO, London, 1983.

22. *The Spectator* (22 January 1982), p. 4.

CHAPTER TWO

1. M. Bradbury, *The History Man*, Arrow Books, London, 1977.

2. *Living Faith in the City:* A progress report by the Archbishop of Canterbury's Advisory Group on Urban Priority Areas, General Synod of the Church of England, Church House, Great Smith Street, London SW1P 3NZ, 1990, p. 97.

3. The Social Policy Committee of the General Synod Board for Social Responsibility, *Not Just for the Poor: Christian Perspectives on the Welfare State*, Church House Publishing, 1986.

4. *Concise Oxford Dictionary of Current English*, Oxford, eighth edition, 1990, p. 997; E. Partridge, *Usage and Abusage*, Penguin, 1973, p. 260.

5. The Press Council, *Press Conduct in the Sutcliffe Case*, Press Council Booklet No. 7, 1982.

6. Home Office, *The Hillsborough Stadium Disaster 15 April 1989*, Inquiry by The Rt Hon Lord Justice Taylor: Interim Report Cm 765, HMSO, London, 1989, p. 1.

7. *Report of the Inquiry into Child Abuse in Cleveland, 1987*, presented to the Secretary of State for Social Services by the Right Honourable Lord Justice Butler-Sloss DBE, HMSO, London, 1988.

8. The Football League, *Report of the Committee of Enquiry into Structure and Finance* (Chairman: Sir Norman Chester CBE, MAK), 1983.

9. Department of Transport, *Railway Finances*, Report of a Committee chaired by Sir David Serpell KCB, CMG, OBE; HMSO, London, 1983.

10. Ibid, p. 5. See also *The Times* January 1983, where many hostile immediate reactions were recorded e.g. 'Throw it in the dustbin' (National Union of Railwaymen), 'A blinkered irrelevancy' (Transport 2000).

11. *Child Abuse in Cleveland*, op cit.

12. *Falkland Islands Review*, op cit, p. 1.

13. *Report of the Presidential Commission on the Space Shuttle Challenger Accident*, Report to the President, June 6th 1986.

14. Department of Transport Air Accidents Investigation Branch Aircraft Accident Report 2/90, *Report on the accident to Boeing 747–121, N 739 PA at Lockerbie, Dumfriesshire, Scotland on 21 December 1988*, HMSO, London, 1990.
15. Cabinet Office Advisory Council for Applied Research and Development, *Industrial Innovation*, HMSO, London, 1978, para. 1.4.
16. Department of Trade and Industry, *Insurance Annual Report 1988*, HMSO, London, 1989.
17. Communication Studies Planning Ltd/Equal Opportunities Commission, *Information Technology in the Office: the Impact on Women's Jobs*, 1980, para 1.4.1, p. 4.
18. Ibid, para 1.4, p. 2.
19. Department of Trade and Industry, *County NatWest Limited, County NatWest Securities Limited: Investigation under section 432(2) of the Companies Act 1985*, report by Michael Crystal QC and David Lane Spence CA, HMSO, London, 1989.
20. *Industrial Democracy*, op cit.
21. Health and Safety Executive, *The Accident at Bentley Colliery, South Yorkshire 21 November 1978*, HMSO, London, 1979.
22. Health and Safety Executive, *The Flixborough disaster*, report of the Court of Inquiry, HMSO, London, 1975.

CHAPTER THREE

1. Price Commission, *Whitehead and Company Ltd – Wholesale Prices and Prices in Managed Houses of Beer, Wines, Spirits, Soft Drinks and Ciders*, HMSO, London, 1979.
2. *The Memoirs of General the Lord Ismay KG, PC, GCB, CH, DSO*, Heinemann, London, 1960, p. 146.
3. The Monopolies and Mergers Commission, *The Government of Kuwait and The British Petroleum Company plc* (Cm 47), HMSO, London, 1988.
4. Jockey Club, *Report of Committee of Investigation* (1989 Saint Leger), 10 January 1990.
5. *The Times*, leader, (6 March 1990).
6. Department of Transport, *Report on the Collision that occurred on 11th October 1984 near Wembley Central Station*, HMSO, London, 1986.
7. Health and Safety Executive, *Bentley Colliery*, op cit.
8. V. Bogdanor, *Standards in Schools*, National Council for Educational Standards, 1979.
9. Department of Transport, *mv Herald of Free Enterprise: Report of Court No 8074*, HMSO, London, 1987.
10. Home Office, *Hillsborough* (interim report), op cit.
11. Health and Safety Executive, *Flixborough*, op cit.

CHAPTER FOUR

1. The Institute of Chartered Accountants in England and Wales, *Governing the Institute*, Report of a Working Party under the Chairmanship of Mr F. E.

Worsley, 1985.
2. Communication Studies Planning Ltd/Equal Opportunities Commission, op cit.
3. *Regulatory Arrangements at Lloyd's, Report of the Committee of Inquiry*, Chairman Sir Patrick Neill QC (Cm 59), HMSO, London, 1987, para 2.5, p. 4.
4. Department of Transport, *Investigation into the Clapham Junction Railway Accident*, HMSO, London, 1989.
5. Health and Safety Executive, *Flixborough*, op cit.
6. Home Office, *The Hillsborough Stadium Disaster 15 April 1989*, Inquiry by the Rt Hon Lord Justice Taylor (Final Report).
7. Organization for Economic Co-operation and Development, *Road Research: Traffic Control in Saturated Conditions*, Paris, 1981, p. 6.
8. *County NatWest report*, op cit.
9. *Hillsborough report* (interim), op cit.
10. *Hillsborough report* (final), op cit.
11. Home Office, *The Brixton Disorders 10–12 April 1981: Report of an Inquiry*, the Rt Hon the Lord Scarman OBE, HMSO, London, 1982.
12. Department of Education and Science, *Report of the Committee of Inquiry into the Teaching of English Language*, appointed by the Secretary of State under the Chairmanship of Sir John Kingman FRS, HMSO, London, 1988.
13. Home Office, *Report of the Committee on Financing the BBC*, Chairman Prof. Alan Peacock, DSC, FBA (Cm 9824), HMSO, London, 1986.
14. Jockey Club, op cit.
15. Building Research Establishment (A. A. Ogilvy), *Bracknell and Its Migrants: Twenty One Years of New Town Growth*, HMSO, London, 1975.
16. Department of the Environment/National Water Council, op cit.
17. Education Council, *The Health Divide: Irregularities in Health in the 1980s* (M. Whitehead), 1987.
18. *Scarman report*, op cit.
19. Communication Studies Planning Ltd/Equal Opportunities Commission, op cit.
20. Council for Science and Society, *Childbirth Today*, 1980.
21. Public Health Laboratory Service, *Laboratory Diagnosis of Venereal Disease*, HMSO, London, 1972, p. 25.
22. Ibid, p. 34.
23. *Scarman report*, op cit, p. 95.
24. Ibid, p. 95.
25. The Royal Society, *General Notes on the Preparation of Scientific Papers*, third edition, 1974, p. 10.

CHAPTER FIVE

1. A. Wesker, *Words as Definition of Experience*, Writers and Readers Publishing Co-operative, London, 1976.
2. Note in (particularly) Switzerland, Belgium, Yugoslavia and Canada: E. Hanghanin, J. B. Pride and J. Holmes (Editors), *Sociolinguistics*, Penguin, Harmondsworth, 1972, p. 104; M. Pei, *The Story of Language*, second edition, George Allen & Unwin, 1966, pp. 262 and 273.

3. R. E. Nicholson, *A Literary History of the Arabs*, Cambridge, 1956, p. 159.
4. T. M. Lindsay, *A History of the Reformation*, T & T Clark, Edinburgh, 1933, Vol. 1, pp. 149 ff.
5. C. A. Ferguson in P. P. Giglioli (Editor), *Language and Social Context*, Penguin, Harmondsworth, 1972, p. 239.
6. Central Statistical Office, *United Kingdom Balance of Payments*, 1989 Edition, HMSO, London, 1989.
7. R. Harris, *The Language Makers*, Duckworth, London, 1980, pp. 171 and 179.
8. P. Howard, *Words Fail Me*, Hamish Hamilton, London, 1980.
9. All the works of Simeon Potter are worth exploring for this kind of detail. See also G. Hughes, *Words in Time*, Blackwell, Oxford, 1988 which traces social development of language.
10. J. Goody and I. Watt in P. P. Giglioli, op cit.
11. Napoleon A. Chagnon, *Yanomamo: The Fierce People*, second edition, Holt, Rinehart & Winston, New York, 1968, p. 74.
12. J. A. Sheard, *The Words We Use*, André Deutsch, London, 1970, p. 15.
13. F. W. Westaway, *The Writing of Clear English*, Blackie, London, 1926: 'prefer a word of English (*sic*) origin to a word of classical origin'.
    C. R. Cecil, *The Business Letter Writer*, Foulsham, Slough, 1980, p. 26.
    R. Gunning, *The Technique of Clear Writing*, McGraw-Hill, Maidenhead (Revised Edition), 1968, p. 38.
    W. Strunk and E. B. White, *The Elements of Style*, Macmillan, London, third edition, 1979, does it in a fairly constructive way; B. M. Cooper, *Writing Technical Reports*, Penguin, Harmondsworth, which is excellent in other ways does so on p. 114.
    National Consumer Council, *Plain English for lawyers: Some guidelines on writing and designing legal documents*, April 1984, pp. 8–12 takes the same approach but in a more constructive way. More user-friendly phraseology is suggested for the purposes of legal drafting.
    Even the admirable Robert A. Day, *How to Write and Publish A Scientific Paper* has a similar format in its 'Words to avoid' section in Appendix 4, pp. 186–189.
14. C. R. Cecil, op cit, pp. 26–27
15. C. Connolly, *Enemies of Promise*, Penguin, Harmondsworth, 1961, p. 22.
16. *The Times* (21 October 1981).
17. B. Appleyard *The Sunday Times* (6 May 1990) and also BBC Radio 4, *PM*, (24 April 1990). The columnist Taki shows it (*Spectator*, 12 May 1990) also as a passive and suggests that public figures can be *outed* by involuntarily having their names published in homosexual periodicals.
18. 'Below her a small boat puttered quietly at the landing stage. . .', A. Brookner, *Hotel du Lac*, Triad/Panther, London, 1985.
19. B. Levin, *The Times* (22 November 1978).
20. G. L. Brook, *A History of The English Language*, André Deutsch, London, 1958, p. 180.
21. P. Jenkins, *The Guardian* (9 July 1980).
22. J. Brandford, *A Dictionary of South African English*, Oxford University Press, 1980, p. 125, has 'Kaffir . . . now a punishable offence in some parts of Southern Africa."

23. For example, see H. M. Townley and R. D. Gee, *Thesaurus Making*, André Deutsch, London 1980. A list of recent archaisms: *aliens, blitz, charabanc, Great War, Hackney cabs, motor cars, spivs, wireless sets.*

24. K. M. E. Murray (Sir James Murray's granddaughter), *Caught in the Web of Words: James Murray and the Oxford English Dictionary*, Yale University Press, 1977, p. 167.

25. J. R. Hulbert, *Dictionaries British and American*, André Deutsch, London, 1968, p. 16.

26. R. Quirk, *The Use of English*, Longmans, Harlow, 1978, p. 145.

27. OWLS, on telephone number Oxford (0865) 511544 or, for more leisurely enquiry to them, through Oxford University Press, Walton Street, Oxford 0X2 6DP.

28. For the original version, see *The Oxford English Dictionary*, Oxford University Press, 1933, Vol. I, p. xxvii. The version in Figure 20 is taken from the *Shorter Oxford English Dictionary* p. x and has added Archaic.

29. H. Wentworth and S. Berg Flexner, *Dictionary of American Slang*, Crowell 1975 p. vii. This is further described in Appendix II.

30. *Shorter Oxford English Dictionary*, Oxford University Press, 1973.

31. *The Concise Oxford Dictionary of Current English*, Oxford University Press, eighth edition, 1990.

32. R. W. Burchfield, Presidential Address, The English Association, 1979.

33. *The Concise Oxford Dictionary of Current English*, Oxford University Press, sixth edition, 1978, with addenda pp. 1359–1360.

34. *Chambers English Dictionary*, Chambers, Edinburgh, 1988.

35. E. Kirkpatrick letter to the author (12 August 1982).

36. *The Collins English Dictionary* second edition, Collins, London, 1986. Particularly prominent in aggressive marketing was a campaign of television advertising for Collins *Concise*, not considered here, featuring Frank Muir.

37. P. Hanks, letter to the author (19 August 1982).

38. Ibid. In an otherwise enthusiastic review of the first Collins edition Auberon Waugh (*Spectator* 15 September 1979) took Hanks to task for his subjective, and possibly arbitrary, ordering of the senses. Hanks replied (*Spectator*, 6 October 1979) that historically the first sense of a sock was a light shoe worn by a Roman actor in comedy.

39. P. Hanks letter to the author (17 August 1982).

40. See R. Burchfield, *Dictionaries and Ethnic Sensibilities* in L. Michaels and C. Ricks (Editors), *The State of the Language*, University of California Press, 1980, p. 15.

41. Johnson avoided all eponymous words such as *Arian, Socinian* and *Calvinist.*

42. Collins, *Cobuild English Language Dictionary*, Collins, London, 1987.

43. Longman, *op cit.*

44. Brian O'Kill, conversation with the author (November 1989).

45. P. Howard, *The Times* (5 October 1984).

46. *Roget's Thesaurus*, Longman, Harlow, 1987.

47. C. S. Lewis, *Studies in Words*, Cambridge University Press, second edition, 1967.

48. For example see *Racial* in *The Times Law Report* (30 July 1982): Court of Appeal *Manila v. Lee.*

49. K. Amis, *Girl 20*, Penguin, Harmondsworth, 1980. (See also the quotation from Galsworthy at Note 67 to Chapter 7.)
50. Eighth edition of *Concise Oxford Dictionary* marks the extended use of the marking *disp* to denote a disputed usage.

CHAPTER SIX

1. Lord Robens, *Human Engineering*, Jonathan Cape, London, 1970.
2. National Consumer Council, *Gobbledegook*, 1980.
3. Sir E. Gowers, *The Complete Plain Words*, HMSO, London, third edition, 1985, described in detail in Appendix II.
4. J. O. Morris, *Make Yourself Clear*, McGraw-Hill, New York, 1980, p. 149.
5. *The Daily Telegraph* (1 September 1980).
6. National Consumer Council, *Plain Words for Consumers*, 1984.
7. National Consumer Council, *Plain English for Lawyers*, 1984.
8. Clarity, 35 Bridge Road, East Molesey, Surrey KT8 9ER, Telephone 081–979 0085, Fax 081–941 0152.
9. *Clarity*, No 16, March 1990.
10. *Counsel: The Journal of the Bar of England and Wales*, Hilary, 1987.
11. See also Jonathan Swift, *A Proposal for Correcting, Improving and Ascertaining the English Tongue*, 1712, per W. F. Bolton, *The English Language: Essays by English & American Men of Letters 1490–1839*, Cambridge University Press, 1966, p. 107.
12. Price Commission, op cit, p. viii.
13. Department of Trade and Industry, *County NatWest*, op cit, p. 184.
14. *Black report*, op cit, p. 98.

CHAPTER SEVEN

1. K. Waterhouse, *Daily Mirror Style*, Mirror Books, London, 1981
2. K. Waterhouse, *Waterhouse on Newspaper Style*, Viking, London, 1981.
3. There are numerous examples of the metaphor of dress. Among the most interesting:
   N. E. Enkvist, *Linguistics and Style*, Oxford, 1964, uses the analogy of wearing brown shoes with black tie: its effects vary from the striking through the humorous, the awkward and the rude to the disastrous.
   P. Howard, *The Times*, 9 September 1980 on old-fashioned expressions being like a bowler-hat or rolled umbrella.
   G. W. Turner, *Stylistics*, Penguin, Harmondsworth, 1973, speaks of linguistic as well as sartorial class uniforms.
4. 2 South Side, Pulborough, West Sussex RH20 2DH.
5. Peter M. Bassett, letter to the author (4 December 1989).
6. S. J. Baker, *The Australian Language*, Currawong Press, Milson's Point, 1978, p. 12.
7. J. R. Hulbert, op cit.
8. P. Howard, *New Words for Old*, Hamish Hamilton, London, 1977, p. xiii.
9. The Economist, *Pocket Style Book*, The Economist Publications, London, 1986.

10. *The Times* (letters), Alison Weller (20 July 1989).
11. *The Times* (letters), Amanda Wheaton, (21 July 1989).
12. R. Hoggart, *The Uses of Literacy*, Penguin, Harmondsworth, 1977, p. 103.
13. A. C. Zijderveld, *On Clichés*, Routledge and Kegan Paul, London, 1979.
14. Ibid, p. 7.
15. N. Bagnall, *A Defence of Clichés*, Constable, London, 1985.
16. E. Partridge, *A Dictionary of Clichés*, Routledge and Kegan Paul, London, 1978.
17. R. Gunning, op cit, p. 38. See comments in H. A. Murphy and C. E. Peck, *Effective Business Communication*, McGraw-Hill, second edition, 1976, p. 76. See also J. O. Morris, *Make Yourself Clear*, McGraw-Hill, New York, 1980, p. 122.
18. *Journal of Reading*, December 1977, Vol. 21, p. 22.
19. Words per sentence; words per paragraph; words per punctuation pause; syllables per word.
20. J. O. Morris, op cit, p. 119.
21. N. E. Enkvist, *Linguistics and Style*, Oxford, 1964, p. 35.
22. *The Times* (15 May 1990).
23. The Commission for Local Administration in England, *The Local Ombudsmen, Annual Report 1988/1989*, para. 3.4, p. 133.
24. R. Jefferies, *The Amateur Poacher*, Smith Elder & Co, London, 1889, p. 97.
25. C. Conolly, *Enemies of Promise*, Penguin, Harmondsworth, 1961, p. 30.
26. W. Murray, *Happy Holiday*, 1964, The Ladybird Key Words Reading Scheme Book 7 *et al*, Ladybird Books, Loughborough.
27. National Computing Centre, *Impact of Microcompressors on British Industry*, 1979.
28. See also G. W. Turner, op cit, p. 234.
29. Ibid, p. 71.
30. Such as *Butterworths Yellow (or Orange) Tax Handbook, Tolleys* etc.
31. M. Drabble, *The Needle's Eye*, Penguin, Harmondsworth, 1981, pp. 198–200 and 218–220.
32. E. O'Brien, *Night*, Penguin, Harmondsworth, 1980, pp. 73–77 (1600 words in one paragraph).
33. *Home Office*, Peacock, op cit, para. 198, p. 41, para. 199, pp. 41–42, para. 309, pp. 77–78.
34. Social Insurance and Allied Services, *The Beveridge Report in Brief*, HMSO, London, 1942, para. 25, p. 11, paras 27 and 28, pp. 12–13, para. 242, p. 20 and many others.
35. H. Herd, quoted in E. Partridge, *You Have a Point There*, Routledge and Kegan Paul, 1978, p. 5. (Herd's original work was *Everybody's Guide to Punctuation* 1925.)
36. See P. Howard, *New Words for Old*, Hamish Hamilton, London, 1977, p. xiii on *The Times* rules for them.
37. G. L. Brook, *Varieties of English*, Macmillan, London, 1973.
38. Department of Transport, Fennell, op cit, p. 101.
39. Jockey Club, op cit.
40. Presidential Commission, op cit.
41. *County NatWest*, op cit.

42. Ibid.
43. Burton, *Annual report '86*, p. 38.
44. G. H. Vallins, *Pattern of English*, André Deutsch, London, 1956, p. 149.
45. J. Stallworth, *Wilfred Owen*, Oxford, 1974.
46. Independent Broadcasting Authority annual report 1984–85
47. J. Simon, *Paradigms Lost*, Chatto & Windus, London, 1981, p. 143 quoting a view of Prof. O'Neil of Harvard.
48. Monopolies and Mergers Commission, op cit *(Kuwait/BP)*
49. Presidential Commission, op cit.
50. Action with Communities in Rural England and House Builders Federation, *Affordable Homes in the Countryside*, 1988 (foreword D. Trippier).
51. G. H. Vallins, op cit, p. 149.
52. A. Tauber (Editor), *Bernard Shaw on Language*, Peter Owen, 1965.
53. Tony Augarde conversation with the author (June 1979). See also *The Concise Oxford Dictionary of Current English*, eighth edition, 1990, Oxford, p. xxxiii.
54. *Pornography: The Longford Report*, Coronet Books, London, 1972.
55. P. Howard, op cit *(New Words for Old)*, p. ix.
56. N. E. Enkvist, op cit, p. 19.
57. The analogy of chess is pursued at length by D. J. Allerton, *Essentials of Grammatical Theory*, Routledge and Kegan Paul, London, pp. 11, 33 and 39.
58. J. Simon, op cit, p. 213.
59. A. E. Darbyshire, op cit. p. 95.
60. Independent Broadcasting Authority, op cit.
61. BBC Radio 4 (June 1981).
62. G. L. Brook, op cit.
63. *A Language for Life*, op cit.
64. Department of Transport op cit (Fennell).
65. *English Today*, ET17, Vol. 5, No. 1, January 1989; D. Baron, *Going Out of Style*, pp. 6–11.
66. See also Sir Ernest Gowers, op cit (second edition, 1973), Pelican, Harmondsworth, pp. 207–208. More recently this harmless example occurred in *The Listener*, 17 May 1990. John Swinfield is describing in *Opiates of the People* a physically uncomfortable journey through Peru: 'At last, stomachs churning, backs and necks near breaking, the little town of Yauri swings into view.'
67. 'They felt, besides, that Solstis, an Englishman of Russo-Dutch extraction, was one of those who were restoring English music, giving to it a wide and spacious freedom from melody and rhythm, while investing it with literary and mathematical charms. And one never could go to a concert given by any of this school without using the word "interesting" as one was coming away.' (J. Galsworthy, *The White Monkey*, Penguin, Harmondsworth, 1967, p. 31.)
68. *The Church and the Bomb: Nuclear Weapons and Christian Conscience* (The report of a working party under the chairmanship of the Bishop of Salisbury), Hodder and Stoughton, Sevenoaks, 1982.
69. *Twenty-sixth report from the Committee of Public Accounts* (conclusion), 21 June 1984, HMSO, London, 1984.

70. *Statement on the Defence Estimates 1990*, Vol. I (Cm 1022–1), HMSO, London, 1990.
71. Department of Transport railway accident report, *Report on the collision that occurred on 16th October 1986 at Kensal Green*, HMSO, London, p. 7. para 45.
72. Ibid, p. 8. para. 54.
73. Ibid, p. 8. para. 58.
74. *Local Ombudsmen*, op cit, para. 3.7, p. 31.
75. W. Hazlitt, *Selected Essays* (G. Keynes, Editor), The Nonesuch Press, 1942, p. 474.
76. Presidential Commission, op cit.
77. C. Miller and K. Swift, *The Handbook of Non-Sexist Writing for Writers, Editors and Speakers*, Women's Press Ltd, London, second edition, 1989. Note also an interesting article entitled *Gender-Neutral Drafting in Canada* by Donald Elliott which appeared in the news-sheet *Clarity*, No. 16, March 1990, p. 10.
78. Department of Transport, op cit *(Herald)*.
79. *Jockey Club*, op cit.
80. Department of Transport, op cit *(Herald)*, para. 31, p. 37.
81. Ibid, para. 24.1, p. 32.
82. N. E. Enkvist, op cit.

CHAPTER EIGHT

1. A. Powell, interviewed by K. Amis, *The Sunday Times* (15 December 1985).
2. Lord Bullock, conversation with the author (6 August 1982).

CHAPTER NINE

1. W. Shakespeare, *Richard III*, Act 1 Scene iv.
2. J. O. Morris, op cit, p. 122.
3. Lord Normanbrook in Sir J. Wheeler-Bennett (Editor) *Action this Day: Working with Churchill*, Macmillan, London, 1968, p. 23.
4. Communication Studies Planning Ltd/Equal Opportunities Commission, op cit.
5. Department of Transport/Home Office, *Report of the Inter-Departmental Working Party on Road Traffic Law*, (Green Paper), HMSO, London, 1981.
6. The Prime Minister *et al, Industrial Democracy* (White Paper) (Cmnd 7231), HMSO, London, 1978.
7. BBC Radio 4.
8. Monopolies and Mergers Commission, op cit *(Kuwait/BP)*.
9. Ibid.
10. Department of Transport, op cit.
11. Ibid, para. 16, p. 18.

CHAPTER TEN

1. K. Amis, *I Want It Now*, Panther, London, 1969, p. 180.
2. T. Szamuely, *Spectator*, 12 July 1980.

3. Department of Transport, op cit *(Herald)*.
4. Department of Transport, op cit.
5. Ministry of Defence, *Statement on the Defence Estimates 1978* (White Paper) (Cmnd 7099), HMSO, London, 1978. The more recent Defence White Papers, such as the 1990 version to which various references are made elsewhere in these pages, are much more glamorous in their presentation. Indeed sometimes the illustrations have got a bit too elaborate.
6. Ministry of Agriculture, Fisheries and Food, *Household Food Consumption and Expenditure*, Annual Report of the National Food Survey Committee, 1988, HMSO, London, 1989, Figure 4.4, p. 38.
7. Prudential Corporation, *Annual Report and Accounts*, 1981.
8. *Local Ombudsmen*, op cit, Appendix 3(e), p. 52.
9. *Child Abuse in Cleveland*, op cit, Figure 2, p. 314.
10. Ministry of Agriculture, Fisheries and Food, op cit, Figure 2.27, p. 21.
11. *Black Report*, op cit, Figure 2.4, p. 36.
12. Ministry of Agriculture Fisheries and Food, op cit, Figure 3.26, p. 36.
13. Ministry of Defence, op cit, 1978, Figure 3, p. 8.
14. Communication Studies Planning Ltd/Equal Opportunities Commission, op cit, Table 10, p. 71.
15. Monopolies and Mergers Commission, op cit *(Kuwait/BP)*, Appendix 3.4, p. 86.
16. Department of Trade and Industry, op cit *(County NatWest)*, Para. 2.02.
17. Monopolies Commission, *Hiram Walker-Gooderham and Worts Ltd and the Highland Distilleries*, 1981.
18. Hillsborough reports, op cit (Final and Interim).
19. Department of Transport, *Investigation into the Clapham Railway Accident*, HMSO, London, 1989.
20. Department of Transport Railway Accident: *Report on the Collision that occurred on 7th November 1980 at Crewe*, HMSO, London, 1983.
21. *Mission to South Africa: The Commonwealth Report.* The Findings of the Commonwealth Eminent Persons Group on Southern Africa, Penguin, Harmondsworth, 1986.
22. Presidential Commission, op cit.
23. Department of the Environment, op cit.
24. *Black Report*, op cit, Figure 3.2, p. 40.
25. Amnesty International, op cit.
26. Devon and Cornwall Constabulary, op cit.
27. Oxford City District Plan.
28. *Cleveland Child Abuse*, op cit, Appendix M, p. 320.
29. *Local Ombudsmen*, op cit.
30. C. P. Snow, *In Their Wisdom*, Macmillan, London, 1974.

CHAPTER ELEVEN

1. Jockey Club, op cit.
2. *Industrial Democracy*, op cit.
3. *The Times* (15 May 1990).
4. See any between the simple black and white Ministry of Defence *Statement on*

the *Defence Estimates 1978* (Cmnd 7099), HMSO, London, 1978, up to the more elaborate Ministry of Defence *Statement on the Defence Estimates 1990* (Cmnd 1022, I and II), HMSO, London, 1990. The first volume of the latter moves logically from the security threat to a general treatment of the armed forces to a specific set of comments on procurement, exports and financial management of defence.

5. Department of the Environment, *Pop Festivals and their Problems. Second report of the Working Group on Pop Festivals*, HMSO, London, 1978. (Before Lady Stedman, the Chairman had been Lord Melchett.)

6. *Falkland Islands Review*, op cit.

7. Department of Transport, op cit *(Fennell)*.

8. Mr Desmond Fennell, conversation with author (1 November 1989).

9. Ibid.

10. K. Amis, *I Like It Here*, Panther, London, 1975, p. 81.

11. J. Keegan, conversation with author (March 1977). This is a view shared by J. O. Morris in *Make Yourself Clear!*, McGraw-Hill, New York, 1980, p. 174: he urges writers not to be put off by a bad first draft.

12. A. Powell, *The Soldier's Art*, Fontana, London, 1968, p. 97.

13. P. Johnson, *The Spectator* (24 July 1982). (Chomsky, one of the most celebrated linguists of the century, was Professor of Modern Languages and Linguistics at the Massachusetts Institute of Technology at the time.)

14. K. Amis, op cit *(I Like It Here)*, p. 86.

15. Lord Bullock, conversation with author (6 August 1982).

16. Home Office, *Committee of Inquiry into Crowd Safety and Control at Sports Grounds* (Interim Report), HMSO, London, 1985.

17. Presidential Commission, op cit.

18. *The Observer*, 24 February 1985, publishing extracts from D. Leigh, *Inside Whitehall.*

CHAPTER TWELVE

1. *Child Abuse in Cleveland*, op cit.

2. Department of Transport, op cit *(Fennell)*.

3. *Falkland Islands Review*, op cit.

4. *Neill report*, op cit, p. 86.

5. *Presidential Commission*, op cit.

6. Ibid.

7. *The Concise Oxford Dictionary of Current English*, Oxford, sixth edition, 1978 reprint.

8. *The Concise Oxford Dictionary of Current English* marks peculiarly British usages as UK only. Collins already has the more aggressive *Brit*. Longmans show *Br*. Chambers does not make this particular distinction, although the expression *(Scot)* prefaces many of its definitions.

9. Communications Studies Planning Ltd/Equal Opportunities Commission op cit para. 1.3, p. 3.

10. Presidents of a sub-division of a print union.

11. *Hart's Rules for Compositors and Readers at the University Press, Oxford*, Oxford (thirty-ninth edition 1983), pp. 54–59 and pp. 61–62.

12. Home Office, *The Brixton Disorders 10–12 April 1981: Report of an Inquiry by the Rt Hon the Lord Scarman OBE*, HMSO, London, 1982, para. 1.1, p. 1.
13. Ibid, para. 4.49, p. 60.
14. Department of Transport, op cit *(Herald)*, para. 19.6, p. 28.
15. Department of Transport, op cit *(Fennell)*, Appendix M, p. 230.
16. Ibid, Chapter 3.
17. *Hart's Rules,* op cit, p. 43 say three is enough in any situation. E. Partridge, *You Have A Point There*, Routledge and Kegan Paul, 1953, p. 84, says that six should be used for a complete sentence or more; but three for less than a sentence. This distinction seems useful.
18. *The Times*, 4 March 1985.
19. *Press Conduct in the Sutcliffe Case:* A report by the Press Council, Press Council Booklet No. 7.
20. *Community Care: Agenda for Action:* a report to the Secretary of State for Social Services by Sir Roy Griffiths, HMSO, London, 1988, para. 6.7.
21. *Debretts Correct Form,* Webb & Bower, 1990 (paperback Futura 1976).
22. *Hart's Rules,* op cit. See also G. V. Carey, *Mind The Stop*, Penguin, Harmondsworth, 1958, who describes his own change of attitude over two decades: "I feel less complacent about CAPITALS than when I originally wrote . . . (1939) . . . chiefly because of the present (1958) tendency to treat them as though they are slightly indelicate, or else extremely expensive."
23. *The Oxford Dictionary for Writers and Editors*, Oxford 1981.
24. *Style Manual for Authors Editors and Printers*, Australian Publishing Service, Canberra (fourth edition, 1988), obtainable from Books Express, PO Box 10, Saffron Walden, Essex, CM11 4EW.
25. See G. H. Vallins, *Spelling*, Andre Deutsch, London, 1973, especially Chapter 8, p. 150, for alternative spellings.
26. In 1982, Betty Kirkpatrick (letter to author 12 August 1982) suggested that press use of *tt* in *benefited* might soon give it respectability. It is now shown in *Collins English Dictionary* (second edition) but not in any of the other principal dictionaries identified in Chapter 5.
27. P. Hanks' letter to author (17 August 1982).
28. S. Raven, *The Face of the Waters*, Panther, London, 1985.

APPENDIX I

1. Organization for Economic Co-operation and Development; *Road Research, Traffic Control in Saturated Conditions*, Paris, 1981.
2. Commission of the European Communities, *How Women are Represented in Television Programmes in the EEC,* Part One. Images of women in news, advertising, and serials, European Commission, Luxembourg, 1987.
3. L. Masterman, *Television and the Bombing of Libya: an Independent Analysis*, M. K. Media Press, Newark, 1987.
4. *Institute of Chartered Accountants,* op cit *(Worsley)*.
5. Devised by M. Dewey, 1873.
6. Civil Service Department, *Manual for Civil Service Typists*, HMSO, London, 1974, pp. 13–14.

7. *Community Care: Agenda for Action,* op cit.

APPENDIX II

1. P. Howard, letter to the author (30 July 1982).
2. Ibid.
3. P. Howard, *The Times* (21 December 1989).
4. G. H. Vallins, *The Pattern of English,* Andre Deutsch, London, p. 159.
5. A. Waugh, *The Sunday Telegraph* (27 July 1980).

Index

THE DAVID SOLUTION

Valerie Stewart

How to bust the bureaucracy (and avoid paralysis by analysis)

~~~~~~~~~~~~~~~~

How to empower your staff

~~~~~~~~~~~~~~~~

How to put customers first (yes, truly)

~~~~~~~~~~~~~~~~

How to create an enabling culture

"A great book. Valerie Stewart has hacked away all the nonsense in organizations to reveal the truths and the people at their heart. This is a book full of good sense and good stories, with a nugget of wisdom on every page."
Professor Charles Handy

"Every practising manager will recognize the symptoms described ... there has never been a time when such initiatives were so badly needed."
Sir John Harvey-Jones MBE

A Gower Paperback

HOW WORLD CLASS COMPANIES BECAME WORLD CLASS

Studies in Corporate Dynamism

Cuno Pümpin

How *successful* companies:

- Work to add <u>value</u> to their goods and services
- Find a multiplier to repeat their advantage
- Encourage growth promoters to continue the cycle

~~~~~~~~~~~~~~~~

How *world class* companies:

- Create flexible, empowering structures
- Are people-oriented
- Make the best use of time as a resource

A Gower Paperback

THE MOTIVATION MANUAL

Gisela Hagemann

How to apply modern motivation theory to create shared vision, mutual trust and employee involvement

~~~~~~~~~~~~~~~~

How to use open communication to raise competence and quality

~~~~~~~~~~~~~~~~

How to liberate the true potential of your team through motivation

~~~~~~~~~~~~~~~~

Plus
27 ready to use group and self development activities to help put your plans into action

~~~~~~~~~~~~~~~~

"A fascinating and highly practical treatment"
The Director

A Gower Paperback

PROBLEM SOLVING IN GROUPS

Mike Robson

How to harness the power of the group to deal with problems

~~~~~~~~~~~~~~~~

How to ensure that the group process runs smoothly

~~~~~~~~~~~~~~~~

How to use eight problem solving techniques

~~~~~~~~~~~~~~~~

How to present solutions and evaluate results

Problem solving in groups is the central technique underlying successful **total quality** *implementation and effective* **teamworking.**

Mike Robson, *managing director of MRA International, is one of the world's most experienced consultants in this area.*

A Gower Paperback

PROJECT LEADERSHIP

Michael Geddes, Colin Hastings and Wendy Briner

How to lead *any* project effectively

~~~~~~~~~~~~~~~~

How to get the best out of your project team

~~~~~~~~~~~~~~~~

Plus a powerful Action Summary with questions aimed at enhancing performance

"If you want a book that will start you thinking about people, relationships and teams...try 'Project Leadership'."
Project Management Today

"...a thought-provoking book, interesting for its conceptual clarity and for the light it sheds on many of the problem areas affecting projects, and enjoyable for its easy, direct style."
The Training Officer

"...one of the best management books that I have read for a long time."
Sir Reginald Harland

A Gower Paperback

RIGHT EVERY TIME

Frank Price

How to think quality

~~~~~~~~~~~~~~~~

How to understand quality

~~~~~~~~~~~~~~~~

How to apply Deming's Principles and avoid the pitfalls

"For all managers interested in quality, this is probably the most interesting and comprehensible book they will find."
Management Week

"As a sequel to the highly successful 'Right First Time' this offering is also a winner and should be obligatory reading for anyone who desires advancement in the search for excellence."
Management

"One of the earliest practical exponents of quality control sets out its general principles, illustrated with instructive case studies."
Director

A Gower Paperback